Basically Queer

Studies in Criticality

Shirley R. Steinberg
General Editor

Vol. 485

The Counterpoints series is part of the Peter Lang Education list.
Every volume is peer reviewed and meets
the highest quality standards for content and production.

PETER LANG
New York • Bern • Frankfurt • Berlin
Brussels • Vienna • Oxford • Warsaw

Basically Queer

An Intergenerational Introduction to LGBTQA2S+ Lives

Edited by Claire Robson,
Kelsey Blair, and Jen Marchbank

PETER LANG
New York • Bern • Frankfurt • Berlin
Brussels • Vienna • Oxford • Warsaw

Library of Congress Cataloging-in-Publication Data
Names: Robson, Claire, editor. | Blair, Kelsey, editor. | Marchbank, Jen, editor.
Title: Basically queer: an intergenerational introduction to LGBTQA2S+ lives
   / [edited by] Claire Robson, Kelsey Blair, and Jen Marchbank.
Description: New York: Peter Lang, 2017.
Series: Counterpoints: Studies in Criticality, vol. 485 | ISSN 1058-1634
Includes bibliographical references and index.
Identifiers: LCCN 2017017423 | ISBN 978-1-4331-3346-6 (hardcover: alk. paper)
ISBN 978-1-4331-3345-9 (paperback: alk. paper) | ISBN 978-1-4331-4507-0 (ebook pdf)
ISBN 978-1-4331-4508-7 (epub) | ISBN 978-1-4331-4509-4 (mobi)
Subjects: LCSH: Sexual minorities. | Sexual minorities—Identity.
Sexual orientation. | Gender identity.
Classification: LCC HQ73 .B37 2017 | DDC 306.76—dc23
LC record available at https://lccn.loc.gov/2017017423
DOI 10.3726/b11747

Bibliographic information published by **Die Deutsche Nationalbibliothek**.
Die Deutsche Nationalbibliothek lists this publication in the "Deutsche
Nationalbibliografie"; detailed bibliographic data are available
on the Internet at http://dnb.d-nb.de/.

The paper in this book meets the guidelines for permanence and durability
of the Committee on Production Guidelines for Book Longevity
of the Council of Library Resources.

© 2017 Peter Lang Publishing, Inc., New York
29 Broadway, 18th floor, New York, NY 10006
www.peterlang.com

All rights reserved.
Reprint or reproduction, even partially, in all forms such as microfilm,
xerography, microfiche, microcard, and offset strictly prohibited.

Printed in the United States of America

To those who fought to make our LGBTQA2S+ lives possible, and to those who continue the work.

Table of Contents

Preface xiii
Acknowledgements xvii
Introduction 1

Section One: Why Does Language Matter? 5
Judy Fletcher and Bill Morrow, "Verbal Attacks" 7
Pat Hogan, Gayle Roberts, and Farren Gillaspie, "Why Does
 Language Matter?" 8
Basic Queer Vocabulary 18
Things We Get Called 20
Anna R. Westhaver, "Beware" 21
Pat Hogan, "A Jab Rap for All Who Don't Fit In" 23
Harris Taylor, "One for the Team" 25
Skylar Cogswell-Shears, "Was There Ever a Moment of Decision for
 You About Your Orientation/Gender I.D.?" 26
Skylar Cogswell-Shears, "I Am He" 27
Cyndia Cole, "Firm" 28
Jasmine Broeder, "I Am a Fucking Bisexual" 30

Pat Hogan, "Still a Lesbian After All These Years"................................. 32
Nancy Strider, "Plain Brown Wrapper"... 34

Section Two: Queer History... 39
Cyndia Cole, Val Innes, and Ellen Woodsworth, "Introduction to the
    History of the Queer Movement... 41
Christine Waymark, "Stonewalled"... 46
Bill Morrow and Judy Fletcher, "Homophobic Homo"......................... 49
Greta Hurst, "Love in Montreal".. 53
Ellen Woodsworth, "Standing Out and Standing Up as Lesbian Feminists"........ 56
Pat Hogan, "Before I Knew the Word".. 59

Section Three: What's It Like to Be Queer?.................................. 63
Claire Robson, "What's It Like to Be Queer?"..................................... 65
Candy Fine, "Misunderstood"... 68
Syd Oremek, "Young, Homeless, and Positive".................................... 69
Judy Fletcher, "My Walk in the Sunshine"... 71
Nancy Strider, "Last Dance".. 73
Chris Morrissey, "Life Insurance".. 77
Skylar Cogswell-Shears, "In-Between"... 78
Caroline Doerksen, "You Would Be Pretty If …".................................. 79
Judy Fletcher, "How Am I Different? Let Me Count the Ways".................. 81
Cyndia Cole, "Lost and Found".. 82
Caroline Doerksen, "First Queer Event"... 83
Val Innes, "First Time's Special".. 84
Harris Taylor, "Mercy"... 86

Section Four: Queers in Family.. 87
Val Innes, "Queers in Family"... 89
Skylar Cogswell-Shears, "You Aren't a Boy"...................................... 92
Harris Taylor, "For Sale: Used Family"... 94
Bridget Coll, "Adopted Grammas"... 95
Chris Morrissey, "The Last Goodbye"... 97
Robin Rennie, "The Drop-In".. 99
Val Innes, "Androgyny Is My Sanity".. 102
Chris Morrissey, "Class Ring".. 103

Judy Fletcher, "All Girls Can Have Curls" 106
Marsha Ablowitz, "Max Dexall" 109
Farren Gillaspie, "Faith" 115
Christine Waymark, "Not the Piece I Was Meant to Write" 119
GG, "The Way Forward—Notes for a Screenplay" 122
Paddy St. Loe, "Our Pam's Gone Funny" 127
Cyndia Cole, "Fighting for Life" 130

Section Five: Equal Rights or More Rights? 133
Chris Morrissey and Christine Waymark, "Equal Rights or More Rights?" 135
Syd Oremek, "The Queer Agenda" 140
Harris Taylor, "Gay Blue Jeans Day" 142
Christine Waymark, "Veiled" 144
What the Youth Had to Say About Rights 146
Chris Morrissey, "Who Says We Have All Our Rights?" 148
Paula Stromberg, "It's Not My 77th Birthday. We Got Married" 150
Cyndia Cole, "Just and Mighty" 152
Farren Gillaspie, "Love It, Leave It, or Change It" 154
Cyndia Cole, "Taking LGBTQA2S+ Rights to the World Stage:
    An Interview With Ellen Woodsworth" 156

Section Six: What Does It Mean to Be an Ally? 159
Val Innes, "What Does It Mean to Be an Ally?" 161
The Importance of Allies: From a Youth Perspective 164
Cyndia Cole, "An Ally in Queer Space" 166
Reba Broadhurst, "Boy Do People Ever Piss Me Off" 169
Gayle Roberts, "Dear Parent of a Gender-Variant Child" 171
Judy Fletcher, "Ham Sandwiches for No One" 173
Farren Gillaspie, "Cousin Maurice" 175
Marsha Ablowitz, "Jean, the Boy-Girl 1976" 177
Val Innes, "A Letter to School Teachers" 180
Val Innes, "Gay Pride in San Francisco" 183

Section Seven: Born or Made 185
Gwyneth Bowen and Nancy Strider, "If It Ain't Broke ..." 187
Gayle Roberts, "The Girl in the Pond" 193

Aleisha Ross, "Do I Have the Right to Write?" 196
Farren Gillaspie, "An Inner Yearning Yet to Be Named" 198
Skylar Cogswell-Shears, "Gender Is a Spectrum" 201
Gayle Roberts, "John Doe Android Instruction Manual" 202
Candy Fine, "As the Spotlight Shimmers" 205

Section Eight: Youth and Elders 207
Marsha Ablowitz and Farren Gillaspie, "About Youth and Elders" 209
Jake Marchbank, "What We Queer Youth Have Got from Working
 with Our Queer Elders" 212
Shawnee Gaffney, "Queer and in Care" 213
Val Innes, "In the Shadows of the Moment" 215
Chris Morrissey, "Widowhood" 216
Candy Fine, "Youth" 219
Stephen Hardy, "My New Moccasins" 220
Gwyneth Bowen, "Psalm 69 (and All the Other Numbers)" 222
Cyndia Cole, "Backflips" 223
Maggie Shore, "Shards and Scree" 225

Section Nine: Tips and Tricks for Living Queer 227
Claire Robson, "On Giving Advice" 229
Farren Gillaspie, "Start With a Smile" 231
Stephen Hardy, "Keep Healthy" 232
Nancy Strider, "Tips and Tricks for Asexuals (and Others Travelling Alone)" 235
Anna R. Westhaver, "A Practical Guide to Lesbian Identification
 in the 21st Century" 237
Queer 101: What Everyone Needs to Know, From the Youth 240
Queer 101: What Everyone Needs to Know, From the Elders 242

Final Thoughts 245
About the Authors 249
Recommended Reading 255
Index 259

List of Illustrations

"You Are the I in Pride," by Gwyneth Bowen	1
"Verbal Attacks," by Judy Fletcher and Bill Morrow	7
"Things We Get Called," by the Youth	20
"Reclaiming Queer," by Val Innes	20
"Plain Brown Wrapper," by Nancy Strider	34
"What It's Like to be Queer and Old," by Pat Hogan and Cyndia Cole	40
Sexual Orientation Laws in the World—Overview. International Lesbian, Gay, Bisexual, Trans, and Intersex Association	42
"Homophobic Homo," by Bill Morrow and Judy Fletcher	52
"Untitled," by Maggie Shore	64
"Max Dexall," by Marsha Ablowitz	114
"A Map of the Village," by GG	123
"Equal Rights?" by Chris Morrissey	134
"Allies," by Nancy Strider	160
"Born or Made," by Cyndia Cole	186
"Born AND Made," by Gayle Roberts	186
"Looking in the Mirror," by Candy Fine	205
"Untitled," by Gwyneth Bowen	228
"Hetero Lessons," by Bill Morrow and Cyndia Cole	228

Preface

Ever since I was a child, I knew I was "different." Of course, now I know I was in fact quite typical, by which I mean typical of many of the kinds of wonderful people sharing their stories in this book. In a sense, not much has changed for me since childhood—I remain, as old as I am now, a tomboy, and even with hair down to my shoulders, a person who is sometimes called on the street "sir"—as in "excuse me, sir," or in service areas, "how can I help you, sir?" When my niece got married last year, I wore a dress, the first time in a hundred years. And guess what? I really enjoyed it. My sisters were professionally made up, so fabulously that I didn't recognize them, and I found myself jealous that they hadn't invited me to be made over, too. I, and my partner, oddly and humorously felt left out. Apologizing, my sisters said they hadn't imagined I'd ever have dreamt of wearing lipstick and eye make-up, and didn't want to offend me by suggesting it. It's so odd: I fought most of my life to get them to respect that I wouldn't wear dresses, or heels, or make-up, and here I was wishing I could have been part of the girls' dress-up party. I must say that in the dress and touch of stuff I put on my lips and eyes for the occasion, I felt like a drag queen—and loved it. I wanted to strut about at the wedding, like an elegant woman. These days, I want to be whatever I choose, in that moment, to be. I want to be defined, and I don't want definition. Is this the wonderful paradox of the benefits of all the activism here in Canada of the last years?

Basically Queer is a nod to the decades-long work of the activists who have made this kind of story voicing possible. The pulling together of such a book may well still be a political act—a book that advocates change. But it is more than this. It is an act of generosity and kindness.

Basically Queer is a delightful collection of much needed, much appreciated information and stories in a variety of forms, about the variety of ways of expressing—I was about to say expressing gender, but it occurs to me as I write this preface, that it is about the variety of ways of expressing our deepest nature and the potential beauty of human life.

Stories typically have arcs, but some stories are still being written, not because there isn't an end to them, but because we, as queer folk, have refused the endings assigned to us by society at large, and we are still in the process of directing, unravelling, forming our narratives. These snippets of stories are powerful because they are like voices around a campfire in the night—sharing, revealing, confiding, imparting to each other a sense of belonging, of bonding and empathizing. The reader is also invited around the campfire: you can't help but relate, you hear the trajectory of life for older people who have lived with the pleasures of queerness and the burdens of society thereof, and you hear what it's like nowadays for young people, you see the unimagined gains made through decades of activism, and at the same time you hear very plainly the enduring and even deepening difficulties that young or emerging queer people face. The explanations and section introductions are like the elders stoking the fire, guiding and keeping the conversation flowing by providing the tools for us all to imagine and to help each other in creating for ourselves our own futures.

The most striking thing about *Basically Queer* is that it is a sharing, a willingness to communicate. The book is a community between covers, an alliance, and a bridge between difference and age groups. It is educational. Compassion lifts off the pages and has the potential to deal with and assuage the kinds of opposition that might come from outside. It is a wise book that speaks honestly and gently, through the power of storytelling rather than by theorizing or lecturing, and it speaks to allies, adversaries, friends, family and lovers who do not understand us yet whom we want or need to open lines of communication with. It speaks to educators and to those in power around us.

The paradox of keeping community is that while it has the power to safeguard us and allow us to be ourselves, community is made up of human beings—and every one of us is afflicted by attendant frailties, because we are humans. And so, accompanying this safeguarding is the possibility of policing and judgment. The stories in *Basically Queer* are an open hand, holding and soothing the discontent that runs within, under the umbrella of queerness, through communities within communities, where infighting for space is one of the most destructive results of increasingly scarce resources and ongoing social pressures. The book reminds us that while we insist on our own specificities, we ought not forget the many others to whom it would be wise and kind to be aware and to embrace. How long I have lived as a queer person, an activist, and still found within its covers stories and explanations that taught me something I hadn't thought about before, that opened my eyes?

In *Introduction to the History of the Queer Movement*, authors Cyndia Cole, Val Innes, and Ellen Woodsworth remind us powerfully of the gains the queer movement has made internationally and in particular in Canada, but they remind us too that "... the work is not done. ... Transgender legal rights are not fully adequate. Violence continues against queers, particularly against transgender people and lesbians. Few feel safe against the abuse of power by police. The lives of rural queers are more isolated and challenging than those in urban areas. Queer youth are at much higher risk for suicide and substance abuse. Lesbians struggle with empowerment as feminists within the queer movement. LGBTQA2S+ people, particularly lesbians and trans, face barriers due to low income. Strong anti-LGBTQA2S+ feeling, racism, homophobia, and heterosexism still persist. As queer people, we are acutely aware of both the tremendously positive changes and the urgent need for more." The stories that follow give flesh to these truths.

Story telling is powerful. Telling our own stories in our own words is most powerful. Words make us, and they break us. What these writers have done is take the word into their hands. I was struck by Pat Hogan's words, "Remember, when I was growing up in small town Connecticut we didn't use the word 'lesbian'; 'gay' wasn't a term we knew then either, for men or for women. There *was* no language, at least that I knew of." That wasn't all that long ago. And it says something grand that today GLB has been expanded to include a string of other initials and even figures. The writers in *Basically Queer* are not only using their voices to define themselves, but also they are giving us—*us* being like-minded as well as "other" folk—language with which to ask questions, with which to learn, with which to define and to assert a rightful, respected place in the larger community. When was the last time you corrected someone and explained, as in Harris Taylor's *One for the Team*, that a "faggot was a bundle of sticks"? I must remember this as a comeback, but only, of course, when the occasion can stand a little humour!

I have known, as I said at the beginning, that I was "different" since I was a little child. It has taken decades of me personally insisting on being allowed this difference to be comfortable in my skin, but I am sure that my most dire efforts would have been in vain had it not been for the larger movement of activism for the rights of queer people. It is with great pleasure and appreciation that I read stories from some of those older activists who had been there, out on the front lines, from the beginning. While their stories show the gains made, their presence in this book says, too, that the journey is long, the road winding and the end is, at times, little more than a faint, perhaps imagined, light in the distance. It is remarkable and moving that these people continue, as shown in the pages of this worthy book, to lend their power here. As Marsha Ablowitz writes in *Max Dexall*, "We haven't just found peace with who we are—we love who we are."

Shani Mootoo

Acknowledgements

The Quirk-e collective has been funded for several years by a Community and Neighbourhood Development grant from the City of Vancouver. We thank members of the council for their continued funding, without which this book would not have been possible.

We are more grateful than we can say for the support of Britannia Community Services Centre. We have met at Britannia's 55+ Centre for the past 10 years, and seniors' coordinator and programmer Anne Cowan has been our untiring ally and constant friend. She has helped us write grants, listened to our tales of woe, and joined our celebrations. Anne, you are a shining example of an engaged and enlightened administrator—we wish you could be cloned, but it would also make us jealous.

QMUNITY is the face of queer organization and activism in the province of British Columbia. We thank their staff and board for their help over the last years, and the assistance they continue to offer all BC's LGBTQA2S+ elders.

Quirk-e began as a project within the Arts & Health Project, founded and managed by the Vancouver Park Board. We were funded by and included within the community of practice of this project for more than five years. We would not have achieved nearly as much without that flying start. Our thanks go particularly to Park Board Arts and Culture Coordinator, the inspired and inspiring jil weaving, and to erstwhile Arts and Health coordinator, Margaret Naylor. These two hard-working women have been tireless in promoting community art in Vancouver's many community centres.

Youth for A Change began in March 2012 when a group of fairly marginalized youth (LGBTQA2S+, some roofless and poor) decided to make a difference in their lives and those of others. They began by educating themselves and offering workshops; now they range from artivism to political action. YfAC acknowledges the essential part played by Pacific Community Resources Society in providing various forms of support over the years, including providing a safe and accessible meeting space each week. YfAC would not function without the weekly (and more) facilitation by Sylvie Traphan whom we thank for her leadership, counsel, and cooking (Jen says thanks too for being her co-conspirator and wife!).

A big shout out to Cameron Duder for his meticulous work on formatting and indexing. He has been patient with our process, which has inevitably been slowed by our collective negotiations. If you can find your way around this text, it's because of Cam!

Many universities talk the talk about community engagement. Simon Fraser University has also walked the walk, as it has hosted our events, sponsored our intergenerational work, and provided funding for this book through a Rapid Response Grant. We particularly want to thank Dr. Elise Chenier (History), who has been a welcome visitor and a constant source of ideas and inspiration, and Dr. Willeen Keough (also History), who was an important ally during her time as Chair of Simon Fraser's Department of Gender, Sexuality, and Women's Studies.

Another ally, since Quirk-e's inception 11 years ago, has been novelist Wayson Choy. Although Wayson is one of Canada's best known, busiest, and most highly regarded writers, he has visited us often, been generous with his support, and provided us with constant encouragement.

Finally, we thank Shirley Steinberg, our series editor at Peter Lang. She bought into this project the moment she heard about it. We thank her for her work on this book and her faithful work to change the world. We thank acquisitions editor Sarah Bode and production editor Sophie Appel for seeing the book to completion.

Introduction

"You are the I in Pride," by Gwyneth Bowen

We have big hopes for our book, which offers an introduction (rather than a guide) to LGBTQA2S+ lives. We don't see it as a guide—because there's no one single way to be lesbian, gay, bisexual, transgender, asexual, or queer, and so the idea of being *guided* is often pretty unattractive to people who identify as queer. At some point, they'll have been told that it's not okay to be "that way," and so they should try to be something different from who they are and what they feel. We resist this kind of guidance. Instead, we want our book to open up ideas and debate rather than close them down, and to serve as a source of ideas and information to anyone who wants to know more about what it's like to be LGBTQ2SA+. We're hoping that our readers will include queer or questioning teens and adults as well as their friends, parents, relatives, and chosen family, their teachers and school guidance counsellors, their doctors, nurses, and therapists. Given that LGBTQA2S+ people make up around 10% of the population, this list probably includes almost everyone—even if you think you don't know anyone who identifies as queer in some way, chances are that you do. The person who hands you a coffee, or services your car, or teaches your kids, or does your hair might be queer, even if they're not out or visible. You're probably talking to someone queer every day, even if they're not open about it.

We're hoping that our book will answer questions about queer lives that sometimes the reader might have felt awkward about asking out loud. We understand that sometimes people find it hard to find the right words to open a conversation, and that they want to be respectful and avoid offence. We're also hoping that it will shed light on some current arguments and debates—about where LGBTQA2S+ folk fit in the world, what they want, what they are entitled to, and what their histories and lives have looked like in the past. We aimed to make the book fun and readable as well as informative, and we've tried not to be too preachy or academic. As a way to achieve this, we've included stories, graphics, and poetry in between the more expositional or explanatory sections. These will hopefully put flesh on the bones of the points made there, as they illustrate them with real life examples. Of course, these are our stories and our ideas—they are not universal and they are not *the* truth, but they are *our* truth, or at least, the closest we can get to it. We've organized the book into several sections that we hope cover the range of questions the reader might have: Why does language matter? What has been our history? What is it like to be queer? What is queer family and how might this look different from biological family? Do we want equal rights or more rights? Why are queer allies important? Are queer people born or made? How do old and young people navigate queer life differently? Are there any tips and tricks that might help the reader who is just out, or thinking about coming out?

Basically Queer is the result of a collaboration between two groups of activists from British Columbia, Canada. The two groups are known as Quirk-e (the Queer Imaging & Riting Kollective for Elders) and YfAC (Youth for A Change). We come together around a mission to make the world better for everyone, and specifically, to help LGBTQA2S+ folk to live openly and free from oppression. The elders in Quirk-e work to achieve this through the arts, as its members compose in many genres (written, digital, theatrical and visual) and show and perform the results in local venues. Youth for A Change is an advocacy group, and its members raise awareness of LGBTQA2S+ issues, protest injustice, visit organizations to offer education and training, and monitor local government policy. For instance, they make sure the rainbow flag flies at Surrey City Hall during Pride week and that the school board's policy is inclusive of LGBTQA2S+ folk. Most of the elders in Quirk-e live in Vancouver—a multicultural city on the west coast of Canada, just north of the US border. The members of YfAC live in Surrey—a large city just south of Vancouver, whose culturally diverse population includes many South Asian people. Both Vancouver and Surrey are places of contrast, from the wealthy to the poor, from yoga to street drugs, from mansions to basement rentals, and from gangs to robust community groups like ours.

Members of the two groups first met when a couple of the Quirk-es took a field trip out to Surrey to meet with YfAC. They'd heard about the youth's work and were curious to meet them. Instead of just chatting or eating pizza (though they did that too), they all decided to work on some writing together and ended up sharing the results in an informal impromptu performance. This was a good choice we think, and it's become essential to the way we collaborate. Lots of people believe that intergenerational work is necessary, but we understand that it doesn't just happen automatically and in a vacuum. In our view, people really get to know each other when they work together on meaningful tasks—projects that encourage them to solve problems, surmount challenges, and engage in talk that goes beyond the superficial. People tend to see queer youth as being "at risk" and elders of any type as "frail" or "vulnerable." It's true that queer teens are at greater risk for suicide and that elders are more prone to falls, isolation, and depression. Their bodies can be hurt more easily. However, people who are young and old are also creative, resilient, passionate, and wise; they are an excellent resource. So rather than having pity parties and telling our sad stories, we wanted to get out and change things. We wanted to *do*, rather than be *done for*.

Our first project was *Call & Response*. In sub-Saharan cultures, art is often a collective and collaborative process, as one person or group calls out, and others respond in dance or song or words. What we did is to have each group design writing prompts or calls for the other. Then each group sent off the resulting stories, poems, and artwork to the other group for feedback and critique. It was a way of asking some of those questions mentioned earlier—the ones you might not ask in a casual conversation—"Why do you have facial piercings?" "What's it like to be old?"—and it set the method for how the groups would work together. We turned our artwork and writing into a theatrical show that premiered in Surrey and Vancouver, and then kicked off Pride week in another BC city, New Westminster. We went on to get funded by the BC Council to Reduce Elder Abuse to design posters and digital videos about elder abuse in the LGBTQA2S+ community. Teams of youth and elders travelled across BC to show these materials when they were done. All across the province, they met with health providers and other interested people to discuss elder abuse in the LGBTQA2S+ community. The elder abuse project (more information is available at https://www.sfu.ca/lgbteol/lgbt-elder-abuse-2.html) has been showcased on national radio and television (CBC) and generated a large number of public events, as many organizations have wanted to learn more about this neglected topic.

This book you are reading is our third project, and as you can imagine, we are delighted that Peter Lang Press is publishing it worldwide. This is perhaps a good time to sneak in a big thank you to our editor, Shirley Steinberg. She truly "gets" the power of critical intergenerational work, and we are very grateful to her for making this book happen.

These projects have changed the world in ways we don't know about, as their ripples spread through our local community and beyond. They have also changed us. Youth and elders alike have learned to film and edit, design and compose, write and revise, act and speak out, plan and promote, and collaborate and negotiate. We've learned that even in the best of projects, there'll be disagreements, disappointments, and conflicts, but that these can be safely negotiated. The elders learned a lot from the youth—about how language, looks, and attitudes have evolved in queer teen culture and how young people are holding the line in passionate outspoken activism. The youth learned from the elders too—about the brave histories of those who fought, and continue to fight, for their rights and their voices, and about the humour, strength, and resilience of those who have survived the worst kinds of oppression. The most surprising thing we've learned perhaps is that youth and elders seem to us to be more alike than they are different. We share a passionate spirit of exploration, openness, and disruption. Our hope is that it infuses our work in this book, and that it will inspire you as you read it.

We invite you to use this book in any way that works for you—to read the sections in any order that is helpful and enjoyable. You might want to read the creative work first, for instance, before looking at the more expositional introductions. What matters is that you read it and use it to broaden and enrich your understanding of LGBTQA2S+ lives—a rainbow kaleidoscope of life experiences, warts and all, uncensored and as real and honest as we could be. Once you've read the book, pass it along to someone you suspect might like or need to read it. Chances are that you are probably right.

SECTION ONE

Why Does Language Matter?

Verbal Attacks

JUDY FLETCHER AND BILL MORROW

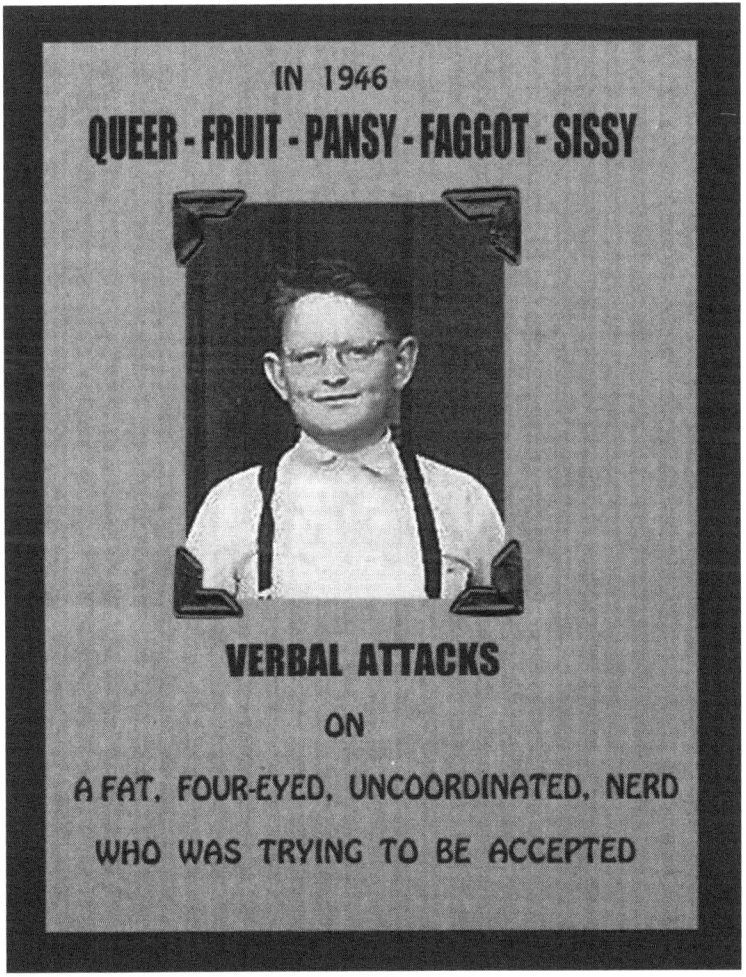

"Verbal Attacks," by Judy Fletcher and Bill Morrow

Why Does Language Matter?

PAT HOGAN, GAYLE ROBERTS, AND FARREN GILLASPIE

Language is used to transmit information, feelings, ideas, and values. Without words, we don't have oral communication. Though we do have the unspoken language of gestures, body language, and looks that can convey feelings, naming something makes it real, and communicable, and possible. Language can be hurtful and abusive; it has been used consistently against people in the queer community (as well as others), particularly during childhood and at school. This abuse and damage has led to repressed and troubled lives, even suicides. It continues to do so. That's why this section opens this book—language is how we make sense of the world; it's how we communicate our values and beliefs. This is why LGBTQA2S+ people pay close attention to the ways they are described and defined.

HOW CAN WE BE SURE THESE COMMENTS ARE MEANT TO HURT?

Sometimes it's obvious. When a belligerent, angry person stands outside (or inside) a gay bar and hurls insults randomly, it is for one reason alone—to attack the queer community. Hurtful remarks can also be much more subtle. As mentioned, we pick up hidden messages by the tone of a person's voice and/or body language. For instance, this occurs when someone uses a condescending tone to talk about something in the "gay" (using quote marks or hand signals) community, or mimicking an effeminate gay man with hand gestures and a swishy walk, rolling their eyes or changing the subject when someone brings up something about being LGBTQA2S+ or perhaps discussing a project they're involved with in the queer community. The list goes on and on. These condescending mannerisms are used as put-downs. You may have seen this yourself.

HOW DO WE AS A SOCIETY RESPOND TO HURTFUL/HATEFUL LANGUAGE WHICH IS AIMED AT OTHERS OR OURSELVES?

Safety is the first thing to be concerned with when protecting or defending someone being persecuted or degraded by another. Are you in a safe place to speak out? Are you alone, or, with others who you can count on to support you? Can you call 911 immediately, if necessary? If it doesn't feel safe for you to do this on your own, seek help—from the gay establishment (in the same room), from the police, or from someone in your presence you trust as an ally, such as a teacher or parent, if you feel like you can trust them. *Don't* ignore verbal abuse; it could turn into physical abuse. Then there are the everyday heteronormative assumptions that are so prevalent—that is, an assumption that everyone lives heterosexual lives. Do you assume that everyone's partner is the opposite gender, that is, female or male? That every boy wants a girlfriend—every girl wants a boyfriend or a husband?

SOME EXAMPLES OF HETERONORMATIVE PRIVILEGE

A lesbian couple living together get a call from some unsolicited business person who asks to speak to the "husband" or "head of household" when they hear a woman's voice at the end of the phone. Conversely, if they hear a deep voice, they refer to this person as "Mr." making the assumption of what a man or woman "should" sound like.

Other Examples of Heteronormative Assumptions

- Someone with short hair who dresses in overtly masculine clothes is a man.
- Queer people are accused of talking too much about their LGBTQA2S+ lives. "Why is this necessary?" our liberal straight friends ask. It doesn't dawn on them that they talk about their lives, their hetero families, and their pursuit of the opposite sex with ease. This conversation is always acceptable, is never questioned.

    What are some of the ways *you* can think of to educate people about hurtful language?

QUEER LANGUAGE

Queer language has developed and evolved from individual words which identify our individual sexual orientation—i.e., gay or lesbian—to now include all who identify as queer, whether it be gay, lesbian, trans, bi, cis, queer, gender fluid, etc.—something other than heterosexual. The terms and definitions now used in queer communities across the globe, such as many in the glossaries that follow this introduction, go beyond identifying sexual orientation. They allow us to identify ourselves, our gender, our orientation, our whole selves as we choose to. This includes one's choice of pronoun—for example, "he," "she," "them," "they," etc. The choice of pronoun is each individual's choice, no matter how uncomfortable it may be at first to hear and to use this "new" language. Queer people have the right, as all people do, to choose their own identity and not be defined by others.

Queer Language—Its History and Evolution

As the list of queer terminology developed and got longer, the "alphabet soup," such as LGBTGQQI2SA, came into our language. Is this a good thing? For some people, particularly young queers and academics, using the abundance of designated words to describe who we are is very important. Using these defining terms is the inclusive thing to do. For other folks, both queer and straight, it's way too many letters and words, too much to remember, too much to consider. Many people *do* want to say the "right" thing, but ... what's the right word(s), they wonder? "What is the right thing to call my friend?" "Isn't 'queer' a hateful word??" Here in this book we have used the term LGBTQA2S+, after considerable discussion. While LGBTQ is shorter and easier, we do have one author who identifies as asexual, and one who is two-spirit. In Canada and elsewhere, their identifications are all too often invisible, so we include them here in the term LGBTQA2S+ (the plus sign shows our openness to other people who identify as part of the rainbow spectrum of queer). Some of us hope that a shorter term might be found at some point. Many are using shorter terms such as "gender and sexual minority" (GSM), while some point out that specific identities (like asexuality or two-spiritedness are made invisible there). It's important to understand that this dilemma exists within as well as outside of the queer community. Clearly, not all queers think alike when it comes to language (or anything else for that matter)! Some women don't like the terms "lesbian," "queer," or "homosexual," and some do.

We live in a changing world, and it's definitely confusing as well as difficult to ask questions about what is acceptable language for fear of offending someone. However, it's also important to feel comfortable enough to ask. Most queer people will be glad to answer questions when they are asked in a non-judgmental way;

they will let you know what matters to them and how they like to be spoken about. Remember, everyone is an individual.

Another important aspect for everyone—queer and straight alike—to consider is that people whose first language is not English may be confused not only about the chosen identifying words queer people want to be known by, but also by their chosen pronouns which, for someone not fully knowledgeable in the English language, can be extremely confusing.

Occasionally, we either don't know what word to use or perhaps a word has not yet been invented to describe something with precision. That's why the words in the queer community change with time and new ones are invented. Language changes constantly precisely because it reflects our changing attitudes to life. Old words are sometimes dropped, and, for instance, different trans groups may use the same words but they might mean different things to the two groups. Or they might use different words.

In brief, it's difficult, if not impossible, to come to agreement on an acceptable way of talking about others and ourselves. Language evolves, and words will undoubtedly morph into other words in years to come. Individual identities change as our environment, culture, and communities impact us. "Become comfortable with ambiguity," says one political science professor.

Does Queer Identity Terminology Signify Our Sexuality or Our Whole Person?

Heterosexuality has dominated our language and our culture. Queer language is loaded; it has baggage. While queer identity has been described through our sexuality both from within and without the queer community, "queer" is about culture, camp, reclaiming words that have been used against us and making them ours, giving them power—for example, "dyke," "fag," "trans," "queer." The following glossary of terms is taken from *Supporting Transgender and Transsexual Students in K-12 Schools*, a book written by Carol Allan, Gayle Roberts, and Kris Wells. It is reproduced here with their permission.

GLOSSARY OF TERMS

The glossary of terms below may be helpful. As we noted, these terms do change over time but are accurate at the time of writing.

Ally—A person, regardless of his or her sexual orientation or gender identity, who supports and stands up for the human and civil rights of gender and sexual minority (GSM) people.

Asexual—A person whose interest in others does not include sexual feelings.

Bisexual—A person who is attracted physically, sexually, and emotionally to persons of the same and opposite sex.

Cisgender—A nontranssexual person whose gender identity, gender expression, and natal (birth) sex align with conventional (binary) expectations of male or female.

Closet—To be "in the closet" means hiding one's gender identity or sexual orientation from others in the workplace, at school, home, and/or with friends.

Coming Out—A process through which trans or queer individuals disclose to others their gender variance and/or sexual orientation.

Cross-dresser (CD)—Cross-dressers, who were historically often referred to as transvestites, are men or women who enjoy dressing as the opposite sex. Most cross-dressers do not identify as transsexual, nor do they wish to use hormones or have sex reassignment surgery. Cross-dressing also occurs in the gay and lesbian culture where gay men dress and perform as drag queens, and lesbians dress and perform as drag kings to deliberately exaggerate or parody gender stereotypes.

FTM or F2M—A person who is transitioning or has transitioned from female to male.

Gay-Straight Student Alliance (GSA)—A school-based gay-straight student alliance found in some junior and senior high schools across North America. Gender-variant students should be made to feel welcome and included as part of a school's GSA.

Gender and Sexual Minority (GSM)—See "Queer."

Gender Dysphoria—The emotional discomfort an individual experiences due to internalized conflicts arising from the incongruity between one's natal (birth) sex and one's sense of gender identity (a personal sense or feeling of maleness or femaleness).

Gender Expression—Gender expression is the manner in which individuals express their gender identity to others. A person's gender expression is often based on the binary model of gender, which is either stereotypically male or female. However, some individuals choose to express themselves in terms of a multiple model of gender, mixing both male and female expressions, since they do not see themselves as being either stereotypically male or female but possibly some combination of both or neither genders. Some individuals may receive aggressive reactions or violent responses from members of society who feel a woman is acting too masculine or a man is acting too feminine. The majority of homophobic and transphobic bullying is often based upon the enforcement of rigid sex role stereotypes, rather than a person's actual sexual orientation or gender identity.

Gender Identity—Gender identity is a person's internal sense or feeling of maleness or femaleness. Gender identity relates to how a person views oneself and gender expression relates to how they may present his or her sense of gender, usually along stereotypical binary lines, to the larger society. Gender identity and gender expression are often closely linked with the term "transgender/trans-identified." While sexual orientation and gender identity are separate and distinct categories, "many transgender people seek support and acceptance from the gay and lesbian community, where gender norms are often more inclusive" (Ryan & Futterman, 1998, p. 48).

Gender Queer—An umbrella word referring to gender identities other than male and female. Many youth prefer the fluidity of the term gender queer and reject the labels of transgender or transsexual as too limiting. For example, gender queer individuals may think of themselves as having both male and female gender identities, or as having neither male nor female gender identities, or many other possible gender identities not restricted to the traditional binary gender model.

Gender Reassignment Surgery (GRS)—Sometimes used instead of "sex reassignment surgery" or "gender affirmation surgery."

Gender Roles—The set of behaviours a person chooses to, or is expected, to express as a man or a woman. These are the behaviours that Western society most often calls "masculine" or "feminine." Gender roles can change with time and may be different from one culture to another. For example, many Indigenous communities have rich histories of multiple gender traditions.

Gender-Variant/Gender Nonconformity—Gender-linked behaviours which are different from those stereotypically expected of an individual's sex. Also used as a broad umbrella category for transgender, trans-identified, and transsexual identities.

Heterosexism—The assumption that everyone is heterosexual and that this sexual orientation is superior. Heterosexism is often expressed in more subtle forms than homophobia or transphobia. For example, allowing students to only bring opposite gendered partners to school dances or events is a form of heterosexism often exhibited in schools.

Heterosexual—A person who is physically, sexually, and emotionally attracted to someone of the opposite sex. Commonly referred to as "straight."

Homophobia—Fear and/or hatred of homosexuality, often exhibited by prejudice, discrimination, bullying, and/or acts of violence.

Homosexual—A person who is physically, sexually, and emotionally attracted to someone of the same sex. Commonly referred to as "gay" or "lesbian."

Hormone blockers—See transition.

Internalized transphobia—See transphobia.

Intersex—A general umbrella term used for a variety of conditions in which a person is born with reproductive or sexual anatomy that does not seem to fit the stereotypical definitions of female or male. Historically, the medical community labelled intersex persons as hermaphrodites and often surgically assigned them a sex in early infancy. Contemporary perspectives have sought to question and challenge the arbitrary practice of sex assignment surgery as a form of compulsory identity and/or genital mutilation.

LGBTQ/GLBTQ—Commonly used initialisms that are shorthand for lesbian, gay, bisexual, transgender, transsexual, two-spirit, queer, and questioning identities. "Queer" is often used as an umbrella category to refer to these identities as well as Gender and Sexual Minority (GSM).

MTF or M2F—Male to female. A person who is transitioning or has transitioned from male to female.

Natal Sex—The sex a person is assigned at birth, which is often equated to one's biological sex.

Pan Gender—Individuals who consider themselves to be other than male or female, a combination of the two, or a third gender. "Gender queer" is a similar term.

Queer—Historically, a negative term for homosexuality. More recently, LGBTQA2S+ communities have reclaimed the word and use it in a positive way to refer to themselves. Queer can also include anyone whose sexuality or gender identity is outside of heteronormative bounds. As mentioned earlier, a relatively new expression used instead of "queer" is "Gender and Sexual Minority" (GSM).

Questioning—A person who is unsure of his or her gender identity or sexual orientation.

Sex Reassignment Surgery (SRS)—Also referred to as gender reassignment surgery (GRS), or sex change operation, sex reconstruction surgery, genital reconstruction surgery, gender affirmation or confirmation surgery, and sex confirmation or affirmation surgery. Surgery that creates genitalia similar in appearance and function to that of an individual's target sex. Similar surgical techniques are used to recreate the genitalia of cisgender individuals who have experienced accidents or diseases.

Sexual Minority—An umbrella category for lesbian, gay, and bisexual identities.

Sexual Orientation—Sexual orientation generally refers to feelings of attraction, behaviour, intimacy, and identification with persons of the same or opposite gender. These deeply held intrinsic personal, social, and emotional thoughts and behaviours direct individuals toward intimacy with others.

Social Transition—See transition.

Target Sex—The sex that a transitioning person wishes to become. The sex opposite to that assigned at birth.

Tranny, Trannie—Sometimes used by nontranssexual people as a derogatory expression when referring to a transsexual individual. Also used as a reclaimed word by transsexual individuals when talking among themselves. When used this way, it is often understood as a positive expression.

Trans*—Term used to indicate the inclusion of all the different types of gender identities. For example, it includes transsexual, transgender, trans identified, transman, transgirl, gender queer, gender fluid, two-spirit, etc.

Transgender (TG), Trans-Identified, Trans, Trans*—These terms refer to a person whose gender identity, or outward appearance, or gender expression does not fit into conventional (binary) expectations of male or female. Also commonly used as an umbrella term referring to anyone who is gender variant. Transgender individuals normally identify with a gender that is different from the one they were assigned at birth. The term transgender and its abbreviations are used as an expansive and inclusive term to represent a wide range of gender identities and expressions. While "trans" and "trans*" have the same meaning, "trans*" is increasingly being used as a way to emphasize inclusiveness. The symbol "*" can be thought of as a "wild card" in much the same way as it would be used by a computer to produce a list of all words that begin with "trans."

Transition—The process of changing from one's natal (birth) sex to that of the opposite sex and living in that role. For adults, this process is often concurrent with the use of opposite sex male or female hormones. Later in their transition process, many (but not all) transsexual people elect to have gender affirmation surgery (sex re-assignment surgery [SRS] or gender re-assignment surgery [GRS]). If the person transitioning is a child or adolescent, the process is referred to as **social transitioning** and the medical procedure is usually different from that for an adult. **Social transition** refers to children or adolescents living full-time in the gender roles of the sex different from the ones they were assigned at birth. As part of this process, they may use hormone blockers to delay the onset of puberty and therefore undesirable secondary sex characteristics. The use of hormone blockers is considered to be fully reversible if the individual decides not to transition. Ceasing to take hormone blockers will cause puberty to resume as normal for the sex assigned at birth. At age 16, the individual may decide to proceed with hormone therapy and then later (age 18 years or older) may decide to have gender affirmation surgery.

Transman or Transboy—A person who is transitioning or has transitioned from female to male (FTM). Sometimes written as "trans man" or "trans boy."

Transphobia—Fear and/or hatred of transsexuality, often exhibited by prejudice, discrimination, bullying, and/or acts of violence. **Internalized transphobia** refers to the feelings of shame that a trans person may experience if he or she is unable or unwilling to accept his or her gender-variant identity.

Transsexual (TS)—An individual whose gender identity is not congruent with his or her natal sex. Many transsexual individuals frequently experience discomfort with the disparity between their physical body and sense of self (gender dysphoria) and, as a result, often begin transitioning with hormone therapy and may follow with surgery to make the body more closely align with his or her gender identity. All transsexual people are transgender but not all transgender people are transsexual.

Transvestite (TV)—See cross-dresser.

Transwoman or **Transgirl**—A person who is transitioning or has transitioned from male to female (MTF). Sometimes written as "trans woman" or "trans girl."

Two-Spirit—Some Indigenous people identify themselves as two-spirit rather than as lesbian, gay, bisexual, transgender, or transsexual men or women. Historically, in many Indigenous cultures, two-spirit persons were respected leaders and medicine people and were often accorded special status based on their unique abilities to understand both male and female perspectives.

* * *

The stories that follow expand and illustrate the points we have made about language. For instance, the glossary of terms provided by the youth authors looks somewhat different from the one above, offered by the elders. It's more direct, and it's funnier! The Wordle that follows, also by the youth, illustrates some of the derogatory terms that are all too familiar to almost anyone who identifies as queer in some way. Anna Westhaver's piece *Beware* shows what can happen in spaces that aren't queer-friendly and demonstrates the impact of homophobia over the long haul—a slow dripping like Chinese water torture, or what feminist writer Ann Cvetkovich called "insidious trauma." *A Jab Rap* by Pat Hogan is a comic reclaiming of some of the worst insults levelled at queer folk, and *One for the Team* is similarly upbeat, as it shows how language can be used for good as well as harm if you can think on your feet. Skylar Cogswell-Shears's two pieces, *Was There Ever a Moment of Decision* and *I Am He* provide excellent answers to anyone who questions the importance of exact and appropriate language where the transsexual experience is concerned. *Still a Lesbian* by elder Pat Hogan, *Firm*, by elder Cyndia Cole, and *I Am a Fucking Bisexual* by youth author Jasmine Broeder can all be read as defiant flags planted in the soil of language, as they stake a claim to a language space. They show how youth and elders alike have the right to define themselves exactly as they want and need to. We end the section with *Plain Brown Wrapper*, a piece by Nancy Strider about asexuality—an important and meaningful identification for many, yet one most people know very little about, even in the LGBTQ2S+ community.

Basic Queer Vocabulary

Brainstormed by the Youth

gay = sexual attraction to someone of the same gender

lesbian = a woman who is attracted to another woman

bisexual = a person who is attracted to both genders

pansexual = a person who is attracted to all genders; attraction is based on personality

asexual = someone who is not sexually attracted to anyone

demisexual = someone who is not sexually attracted to anyone unless they have a strong bond

scoliosexual = someone who is attracted to people who do not identify with the gender they were assigned to at birth

bicurious = someone who is curious about their attraction to people of the same sex

trisexual = someone who is willing to try anything once or twice

transgender = someone who does not identify with their gender assigned at birth

transsexual = someone who has gone or is going through sexual reassignment surgery

intersex = someone born with both genitals or indeterminable

two-spirit = Indigenous term for someone who has both male and female spirits

gender fluid = the individual's gender changes depending on their feelings that day

non gender binary = does not identify with a gender

gender queer = someone who identifies with all genders

gender = how someone identifies

sex = your genitals

gender expression = how you express your gender

Things We Get Called

Brainstormed by the Youth

"Things We Get Called," by the Youth.

"Reclaiming Queer," by Val Innes.

Beware

ANNA R. WESTHAVER

You are no longer in the safe haven of Commercial; the shorthaired women. The community has all vanished into its own urban continuum, and you are here in the naked reality of your own life. You are in the suburbs. You're walking down the street, past the group of boys that have been ominously loitering in your peripheral view for a while now. You have done this hundreds of times; only the faces change. In moments between this breath and the next there are an infinite number of possibilities; this, however, is one very familiar to you, a daily occurrence that never loses its effect.

You've somehow broken the silent mould at the wrong moment and have revealed your difference. Their eyes narrow, lips curling maliciously. You know what happens next because it is what always happens when you draw too much attention to yourself, despite your constant attempts at blending in. The moments between this moment and that prolong, as do the number of possibilities, each providing a possible eternity.

"Dyke!"

The word drips from their mouth in a single syllable of disgust; it shouldn't hurt, you know it shouldn't because it's just one word. It's a small drop in an ocean of things one can say to another so really what does it matter? A single drop ... then again, from what you've heard about things like Chinese water torture, it's sometimes the singularity of an event that does the most damage. Maybe, with enough repetitions of that single syllable you too will go mad—it sure as hell feels like it.

The thing though about water is that it is never truly pure; it's been on earth for millions of years and carries with it the history of all that it has seen. Within that single drop, that supposedly finite insult, lies a history whose multitudes are painful, yet still summed up in that single syllable.

You stop for a moment; that old rage builds up then subsides as the reality of your ability to retaliate comes into light, so instead you, as you always do, just pretend not to notice. Secretly, you wish more than anything that you could become invisible, because anonymity, as you now have realized, certainly has its benefits.

Breath streams in and the moment diffuses into the air, ending the continuity of that exalted moment. You pass by them and feel like you too could disappear into the air and into the pavement.

"Dyke!"

It shouldn't matter …

"Dyke!"

It's only one syllable …

"Dyke!"

The only thing about Chinese water torture is that it is the singularity …

"Dyke!"

… that causes the real damage

A Jab Rap for All Who Don't Fit In

PAT HOGAN

I call you Lezbo
you call me Dyke
but you're really Light in the Loafers
ready to take flight

Does the Grass Fairy
really seduce the Chi Chi Man?
Oh come on Muff Muncher,
you know Diesel Dykes don't give a damn!

Trolo, Putazo,
Puto, Flamer
names and more names,
what a blamer!

Pull My Finger, you Hooker, you,
Pervert, Poof, Girly Boy
Pansy, Princess,
My Little Toy

Did you know we Chicken Butchers
also Sing in the Choir?

Hallelujah Cupcake
I'm Den Mother on Fire!!

Femmes and Flaming Queens,
now there's a pair
one, oh so Swish
the other Au Contraire

We find ourselves, we play the game
a world alone, far from shame
free from shadows, free from fear
Our culture beckons
and it's oh so queer!

One for the Team

HARRIS TAYLOR

His name was Ray—a 10-year-old boy who attended the day camp where I worked as the sports instructor. He was disruptive and kept running away into the bush. That was dangerous because the camp was close to the airport. I rallied my group of kids to play football, and Ray disappeared. When I caught up with him, I asked him, "Ray. Why do you keep running away?"

"Because I'm just a little faggot."

"What does that mean?"

"I'm fat and stupid."

"Who told you that?"

"My father."

"Well, your father is misinformed. A faggot is a bundle of sticks, and you're not that. You're a boy, and you're a really fast runner. Running is the most important thing in football. All you have to do is pick up the ball and run with it."

We walked back to the field. The kids were running, throwing the ball. Ray picked up the ball and ran toward the goal. Then he stumbled and fell, splayed on the ground, helpless. His eyes filled with tears. All the kids froze in place.

I yelled: "Who's got the ball? Ray! Who? Ray! WhoRay for Ray!

All the kids started chanting. "WhoRay! WhoRay!"

"Just pick up the ball and run with it!" I yelled.

He picked up the ball and ran to the chant of his peers. "WhoRay! WhoRay! WhoRay!

Crossing the goal line with the ball in his hands, his face beamed, his chest swelled with pride. He threw the ball to the ground in triumph. Touchdown!

Hurray!

Was There Ever a Moment of Decision for You About Your Orientation/Gender I.D.?

SKYLAR COGSWELL-SHEARS

Yes, many times. First I came out as bisexual for about a year, then I found out what pansexual meant and came out as pansexual. Then I decided I don't really like girls very much, just mainly male identified people, so I came out as gay and genderqueer. Later I found out that I didn't really like being called a girl AT ALL so I came out as transgender, FTM, and gay. Recently I've been feeling more gender fluid though, and I recently came out as poly-sexual because I'll date male people and anyone under the nonbinary umbrella.

I Am He

SKYLAR COGSWELL-SHEARS

I am **he**. I am **him**. I am her worst nightmare. I am **he**. That is how I identify. **He** is how you would describe me to your friends. **He** is the pronoun you would use in a sentence about me. I am **he**. I am **him**. I destroyed *her*, sad but true. I am no longer *her*. *She* is no longer me. *She* has been dead for quite a while but she doesn't seem to realize that because *she* is what I hear most of the time. *She* is a word that hurts me because I am no longer *her*. And *she* is not how I identify. I am *him*. **I am.**

Firm

CYNDIA COLE

I am feeling my muscles in such a new way. I love the cuts becoming visible along my slender biceps and triceps. I ripped off the sleeves of this little blue t-shirt just to show them off.

It's the summer of 1977. Ginger, Frankie, Abby, and I are the only women who pump iron at Britannia Gym in Vancouver. I'm proud that I move the weights like a woman, without clanging them or grunting like guys do. When we finish, we cool off by swimming lengths in the pool, which is so fluid and easy for me. Then we luxuriate naked in the women's sauna, embodying comfort in the flesh. As I walk, I show off my thighs and calves in white shorts and Birkenstocks. In 1967, I was hemmed in by fishnet stockings, mini dresses, and cute little bras. One boyfriend praised me as "demure." Now I'm bursting into a confident stride, thrilled that my strength is coming out.

My stomach rumbles, in a hurry for the picnic after so much exertion. The day is gloriously warm as I walk through my unpretentious, immigrant neighbourhood. I pass the shops and eateries from everywhere along Commercial Drive. Then I turn onto Kitchener, noticing the older homes as I head toward shady Victoria Park. I walk right past one of the Italian espresso bars. This one lacks any sign or name. I'd love a hazelnut gelato, but my body doesn't need the constriction I'd feel warding off the penetrating stares. I won't make the mistake again of invading this space invisibly marked off for Sicilian Men only. I'm supposed to know, without any sign, that they don't want the likes of me or my money. They don't want anyone but Paisanos. On this territory, their evil eye is a weapon to protect them and their mafia money.

I'm half way down the block and in sight of the park when two young men exit the no name espresso bar. They strut and swagger as they overtake and pass me. Once I see their backs, one leans to the other and spits with guttural vehemence, "Faggot!"

I'm surprised my shoulders don't hunch. I don't brace or pull myself inward. They don't even look back. They're retreating, not approaching. It's midday, and I'm only a block from home. This is my turf. I stop myself from a guffaw. Do they actually think I'm a man? Or are they just so ignorant that they don't know the word?

I am a Lesbian. And, like the giant graffiti behind me says, "This is Amazonland."

I Am a Fucking Bisexual

JASMINE BROEDER

I stand behind a white wall of Ice and Lies
Behind a haze of stereotypes
Muffled by the words forced upon me by those who do not understand the meaning of
Bisexuality
Or its difference from
Pansexuality
Polyamory
Or polygamy
My words are strung along a fragile line of political correctness
Because god forbid I offend a stranger with a twitter account
And how dare I speak my opinion on that controversial topic that crazed ...
I don't know what
We hide behind a wall of ice and lies
Blending into the sceneries
Afraid that our personalities will not be good enough
Because we have placed humanity on a pedestal of never-ending greatness that makes it impossible for anyone to stand out
But the question is
Do I worry that I am drawing attention to myself?
Is it a worry that graces my mind?

That my personality draws me out from the crowds of people roaming amongst me
I stand behind a white wall of ice and lies trying to take a stance and make a difference
Trying to shout loud enough to be heard amongst the void of people standing between me and reality
Sanity
I break through this wall of ice and lies
Holding a sign above my head saying
I AM FUCKING BISEXUAL
Because this invisibility is driving me insane
But sometimes visibility can be just as mundane
These pretty words which utter from your mouth
Words from which your lips have formed each cure of ugly lies that lies between
A whirlwind of reality
Frozen in this white wall of ice and lies
Hiding in a fake persona perfected from years of role playing in a life that was never really mine
Spinning circles like socks in the dryer cycle
I want to stand out
Just enough to be able to make a change for those who do not wish to stand out
Like black paint on the white washed walls of society
I will not go away I am here to stay
So do not worry that I stand out
Because that is no longer on the spectrum of worries that run through mind
I am a bisexual activist with lesbian parents and DAMN RIGHT I can stand out if I wish to

Still a Lesbian After All These Years

PAT HOGAN

I cringed the first time I referred to myself as a lesbian out loud. It felt so, *weird*. The me I knew was lost forever. But that was a long time ago ... the 1970s, to be exact.

Remember, when I was growing up in small town Connecticut, we didn't use the word "lesbian"; "gay" wasn't a term we knew then either, for men or for women. There *was* no language, at least that I knew of. There were those words we heard used about weirdoes in Greenwich Village but really, they were a *lifetime* away from where I lived. They meant nothing to us.

Even though we knew about the gang of girls in our high school who had secret meetings, who reportedly had sex together—all friends of mine—there was no way to describe their lives. The Catholic Church made sure we lived with guilt for having sexual thoughts, or worse yet, *having* sex, but they were talking only about heterosexual sex, for God's sake. Sex between two females?? Not on your life!!

Sometimes we're led to our next destination; other times we just fall into it. I think my journey was a bit of both. I tripped upon the women's movement, feminism, and then ... lesbianism in the 1970s. I was alive, politically active, surrounded by in-your-face feminists and ... lesbian separatists. We were a decentralized radical arm of the women's movement. I thrived on the work we were doing to better the lives of women, to address domestic violence, job inequalities, sexism, rape, abortion rights. I knew all of that too well.

I Finally Got It: lesbians worked for, stood up, and spoke out for *all* women, and for children. But where were their straight, hetero feminist sisters when they needed support, needed them to march in unity with them on lesbian issues? Uh-uh. They weren't there. Lesbophobia. Luckily, everyone got smarter and wiser; more women of colour and working-class women took on the roles previously held by a small group of white, middle-class feminists. We can talk about it today without cringing. Right?

So, here we are today in the 21st century! What's it like to be an old dyke *and* call yourself queer nowadays?

Well, I don't think anything has changed for me. I'm still a lesbian, though I've adjusted to and accept the word "queer" as part of the lexicon of gay, lesbian, trans, gender fluid people. That includes me. The word "queer," like so many others once used derogatorily, has been reclaimed and now empowers our community.

But, I'm still a lesbian, still a feminist, and those years of building solidarity and community cannot be erased by words, or assumptions about how we must speak. I firmly believe there's ample reason and room in this world for lesbians to come together *on their own* to share their herstory and common bond, as should all people with diverse interests, similarities, and connections. We still will, and do, come together under the rainbow flag to fight for our collective lives. That's a given.

Look hard enough and you'll see the banners flying: Dykes on Bikes, Menopausal Old Bitches, BOLD, Old(er) Lesbians & Dykes and so much more …

We're here, we're queer, *and* … we're proud lesbians.

Language identifies us; let it not control us.

Plain Brown Wrapper

NANCY STRIDER

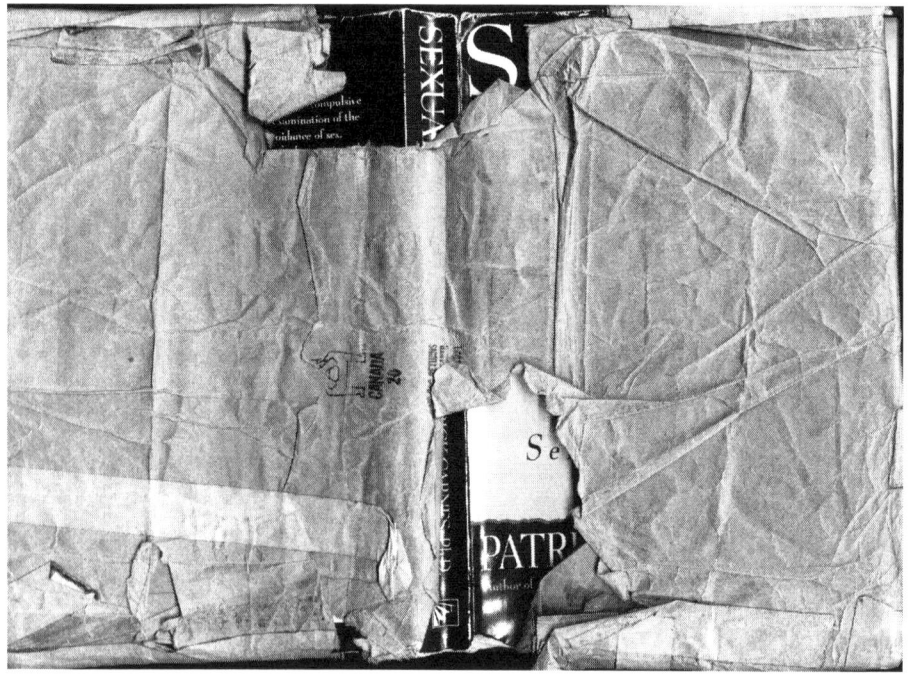

"Plain Brown Wrapper," by Nancy Strider.

You.

On the other side of the bus. I have noticed you, noticing me. Your body language is loud and clear. When I turn my attention to my reading, you turn your attention to my book. This could be an "I saw you" moment worthy of *The Georgia Straight*. Instead, I'll write you this letter.

Was it the tattered homemade paper-bag cover that caught your attention? The thin brown paper at the top of the spine has started to rip away, revealing the first word of the title: "Sexual." Are you trying to guess the rest of the title? Our glances just crossed, and you flushed a bit. Gotcha. Do you think that this book contains porn? What lurid sexy cover images would suit someone that looks like me? Or like us, since we could be mirrors of each other. We are both grey-haired ladies of a certain age. Couture by Value Village. We are wearing the same colours. Grey. Purple. Dark blue. Black.

Since we look so much alike, could I possibly trust you enough to share the title? Here it is: "Sexual Anorexia—Overcoming Sexual Self-Hatred," by Patrick Carnes. Not a racy book. But still, it implicates me. If I showed you the title page, would you feel a shock of recognition? Would you be surprised, and perhaps relieved, that this label exists? Back in 1997, the author of this book dissected the situation where fear of sex and one's own sexuality becomes an "extreme obsessive aversion." He sees the source of pain, at that level, to be the result of some kind of sexual trauma. He uses the eating disorders analogy to describe Sexual Anorexia as the inhibited Yin to the unbridled Yang of sexual addiction and offers this as a workbook to help those who want to unfreeze themselves.

A few years ago, I decided to give up on this book. But I still parked it in my "Do Not Recycle" box. Recently, I pulled it back out, with the intention of using it to make art about shame. First, I scanned the revealing cover, and then opened it to find some quotes that I could lampoon. Instead, I rediscovered the "Sexual Anorexia Inventory." You look like someone who might check some of those boxes. How many?

Seeing my own 20-year-old check marks in faded pencil triggered me. The list calls for a yes if a statement has ever applied, and I admit that I have carried intense family of origin sorrow. On top of that, I piled on the pain that I created for myself while growing up confused—thrashing around and making mistakes. But a few years ago, after receiving much help, I finally felt finished with examining my entrails. Even with professional counselling, I had found no memories or evidence that pointed towards sexual trauma having been inflicted upon me. That was the good news. The bad news was that I always came up empty as to why I was still not interested in sex. I've finally given up on trying to fix myself, letting go of as much of my self-inflicted suffering and judgment as I could. That was just a plain leap of faith, since I was still mystified about my lack of any desire for sexual desire. Now I'm finding clarity and context and have concluded that I wasn't broken in the first place.

But enough about me. What about you? After you caught my last glance, you suddenly got very interested in the bus ads. So I'll look away too and get interested in the other passengers on this bus. If you *were* feeling pain about lack of desire, and *did* want to feel your sexuality surge, you would have lots of company right here. Statistically, a lot of the other people on this bus right now—straight, queer, or those who have taken vow of celibacy—admit to sexual dysfunction in the private confessionals of surveys. I hear that "sexless marriage" is the most Googled phrase about sex and marriage. This compassionate book could help somebody who is motivated to try to change. Are you?

I tried. The first chapters, about self-nurturance, sensuality, and friendship were actually very useful for me. But as I read further, I felt a combination of resistance and deflation that kept me from finishing. I'd optimistically leave a bus transfer or receipt to hold my place and put the book away. After a few months, I'd try again from the beginning. This time, I noticed that the bookmarks pile up around the same spot. The stumbling block was always the section where the book moves onto assigning exercises on the theme of reactivating your sexual desire. I saw that, unless I tried harder, there was no point in going further. I just couldn't get interested in reaching for what I knew most people agreed was the brass ring.

When I read about how good desire felt and saw suggestions about how to kick-start my sexuality, I was only left feeling more confused. If I hadn't been sexually damaged, why did so many of the behaviours listed in the "traits" checklist still seem to apply to me? My check marks clearly showed that I wasn't feeling sexual desire. But, for me, they still didn't add up into the sexual anorexic's self-hatred and obsessive aversion described in the book. In fact, I secretly felt fine about my lack of interest in sex. What was wrong with me? Even after I closed the book, I thought for years that I must be a shallow person, stubbornly resistant to doing the work of getting healed. It was clearly my failing that I just didn't get it, *or want to get it*, about desire. Now I've opened the book again. I'm going to plough through, despite the boring bits, just to tell myself that I did. Perhaps there are other useful tips, now that I'm reading it through a different lens.

And no, this *is not* about my grey hair. When I told a friend about my lack of sexual energy, she observed: "What's the big deal with feeling no desire? It's an age thing. You just described me, many of my friends, and increasingly my husband." Sound familiar? But I explained to her that I had felt this way as a young person, too, though I skilfully faked otherwise. My disinterest has been consistent and enduring throughout my memories, even though I've only recently started admitting it. And if that sounds even more familiar, then you and I could indeed be kindred spirits.

Very thin people can look like they are starving themselves, when in reality they are just skinny. The good news for all of us on the extreme left of the "sex interest" bell curve is that, along with the sexual anorexics, there are those of us out here that are "asexual." This second label literally means "not sexual" and applies to people whose sexual identity does not include sexual desire. This alternate way of seeing oneself as "skinny" but not "starving" has emerged since this book about sexual anorexia was written in the mid-1990s. Increasingly, asexuality is emerging as another kind of queer sexual orientation, with all sorts of hyphenated variations of preferences around sex, romance, and gender.

So, by itself, asexuality is not necessarily a problem, but just another way of being in the world. However, I have a hunch that people who are asexual can also end up suffering from sexual anorexia. I myself feel like I dodged that bullet. Since I didn't respond "normally" to sexual advances, I was vulnerable to being shamed and pushed, which put me at risk for the sexual trauma and damage that could have triggered sexual self-hatred. That's why this book would be an important resource for asexuals, too, even if we pick and choose what is useful for feeling comfortable in our own skins.

What *is* about my grey hair is a sense of lost time. I regret some choices I've made, in the mistaken belief that they would make me healthier. Even though I've pretty well stopped beating myself up, I still feel some pain and fear associated with being outside the cozy "normal" bulge in the centre of that bell curve. And sometimes I tend to slip into isolation and outsider behaviour, rather than try to forge new ways of being together with other people. That's part of why I am trying to connect with you, now.

So all this hopeful news is leaving me smiling at you. But you just looked away, reached up, and rang the bell to get off the bus. As the air brakes sigh, I suddenly realize you still don't know the name of the book. There. I've quickly flashed you the title page, and I smile again. I wish this book was about asexuality—maybe I'll have to write that one—but at least it's a start.

You stand up, looking straight at me. From across the aisle, you say, "Leave me alone!" loudly enough for the driver to hear. The bus stops and you are gone, out the door. Escaping me, like I'm your evil twin.

Ouch. Oops. Maybe you *did* think this book was porn, and preferred it that way. Looks like I guessed wrong about you. Or maybe I'm right. Either way, I doubt that you were ready to see a book on the subject of sexual self-hatred being waved at you by a stranger in the middle of a bus ride. Sorry about that. Just trying to get the word out. Maybe your subliminal glimpse of that title might resonate for you, and would be a subject for you to research with Dr. Google. But for now, I've only got a few bus stops left, and want to get back to finishing the book, so I can pass it on. I have a friend who has asked to read it.

SECTION TWO

Queer History

What it's like to be queer and old

"What It's Like to be Queer and Old," by Pat Hogan and Cyndia Cole.

Introduction to the History of the Queer Movement

CYNDIA COLE, VAL INNES, AND ELLEN WOODSWORTH

Homosexuality and gender fluidity have been in existence as long as humans have been in existence. Lesbian, gay, bisexual, transgendered, queer, two-spirited (Indigenous)—LGBTQA2S+ history can be traced back to ancient civilizations in Africa, Asia, the Americas, and Europe. There is historical evidence showing social acceptance of queers in many major and minor ancient cultures despite the following centuries of persecution, shame, and secrecy.

Since the 1960s millions of LGBTQA2S+ people around the world have been fighting for rights with increasing support from allies. Some are gaining or have gained rights. However, many still live in fear and in the closet in countries that criminalize them. As of June, 2016, according to the International Lesbian, Gay, Bisexual, Trans and Intersex Association (ILGA), 73 countries and 13 entities criminalize LGBT people, with 10 of the countries having a death penalty, and another three countries outlawing LGBTI advocacy, while 76 countries and 85 entities provide LGBT protection with 47 countries recognizing same-sex unions (http://ilga.org/what-we-do/lesbian-gay-rights-maps/). Different groups have slightly different figures, but they cluster relatively closely to these figures.

The first international resolution specifically recognizing LGBT rights was passed by the United Nations Human Rights Council in 2011. A report from the Office of the United Nations High Commissioner for Human Rights (OHCHR) documented violations of LGBT rights such as hate crimes, criminalization, and discrimination. The UN Human Rights Commission then urged all countries to pass laws protecting LGBT rights. (https://en.wikipedia.org/wiki/LGBT_rights_by_country_or_territory). In 2016, the most recent United Nations report says

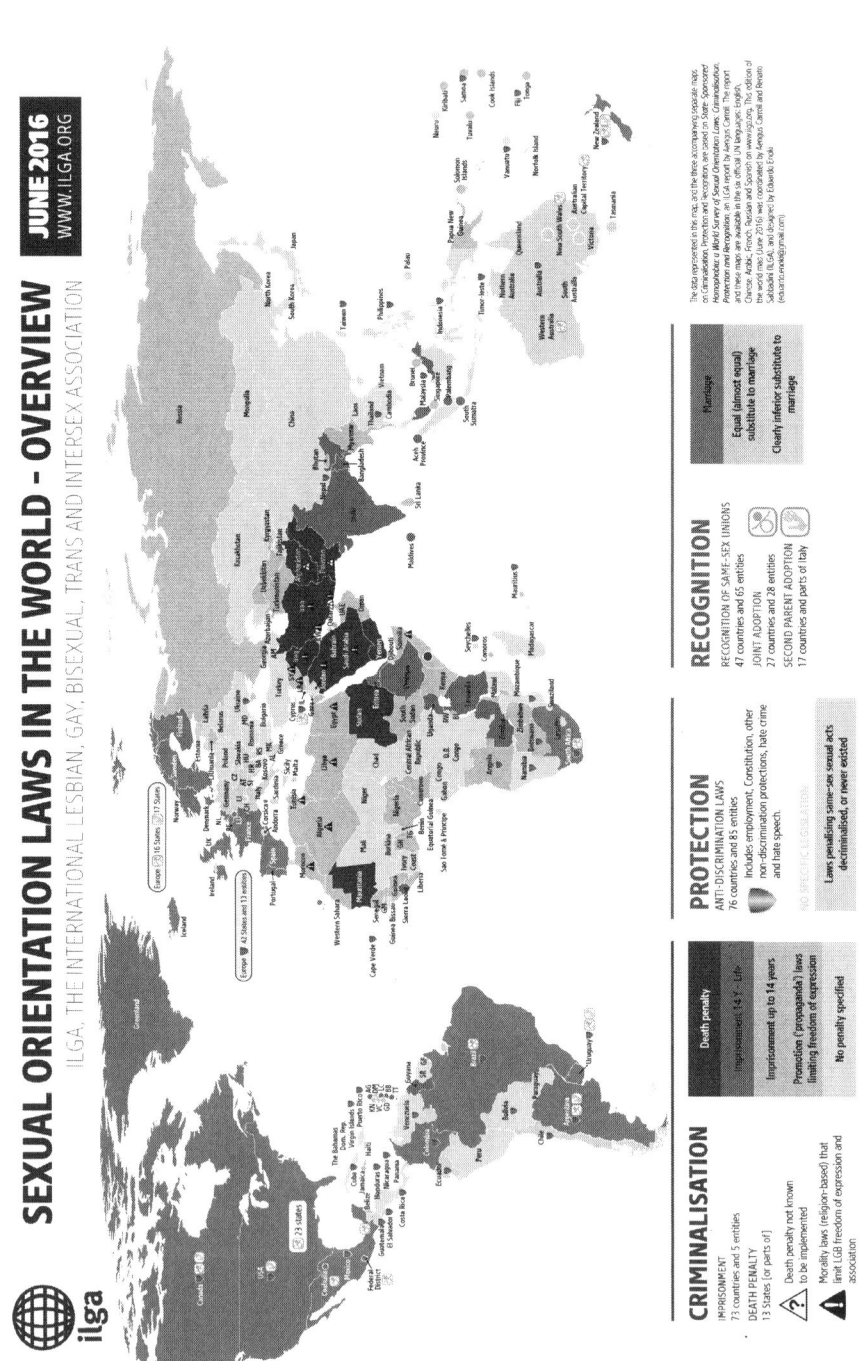

Sexual Orientation Laws in the World—Overview. Copyright 2016, International Lesbian, Gay, Bisexual, Trans and Intersex Association. http://ilga.org/downloads/03_ILGA_WorldMap_ENGLISH_Overview_May2016.pdf.

"that lesbians, gays, bisexuals, and transgender people are victims of 'pervasive violent abuse, harassment and discrimination' in all regions of the world and cites hundreds of hate-related killings." The report goes on to make "more than 20 recommendations including urging all countries to ban so-called 'conversion therapies' intended to 'cure' homosexual attraction as well as involuntary treatment, forced sterilisation, and forced genital and anal examinations." In addition, the report "calls for changing laws to remove offences relating to consensual same-sex conduct, investigating and prosecuting alleged hate crimes and prohibiting incitement of hatred and violence on grounds of sexual orientation and gender identity" (https://www.theguardian.com/world/2015/jun/02/lgbt-people-suffer-widespread-violent-abuse-discrimination-new-un-report?CMP=sharebtnfb).

Also in 2016, the UN New Urban Agenda for inclusive cities called for recognition of LGBTQ citizens, "but a group of countries including Russia, Iran, and Saudi Arabia successfully excluded LGBTQ rights" (https://www.theguardian.com/cities/2016/oct/19/un-new-urban-agenda–inclusive-cities-lgbtq-rights-habitat-3?CMP=share_btn_fb).

In North America, the position of homosexuals in the decades prior to the unleashing of the lesbian and gay liberation movement of the 1970s was grim. In the eyes of the government, police, medical profession, religious authorities, and media, homosexuals were criminals, perverts, and sinners with no rights. Many LGBTQA2S+ people dealt with a mental health system determined to "cure" them because homosexuality and gender fluidity were considered mental illnesses. LGBTQA2S+ people also suffered a long history of religious based bigotry and persecution. Individuals internalized homophobia. Yet despite this overwhelming hostility, in 1969 at the Stonewall Inn in New York City drag queens, gays and lesbians fought back against police persecution. This ignited the queer movement in North America.

The authors of this book are fortunate to be living in Canada, one of the countries where LGBTQA2S+ people have won civil rights and same-sex marriage. These rights were gained only during the last 46 years—within the lifetimes of the authors—and represent significant changes in Canadian law. The first steps came as changes to the Canadian Criminal Code in 1969. As justice minister and later as prime minister, Pierre Trudeau defended decriminalization saying, "there is no place for the state in the bedrooms of the nation," adding "what's done in private between adults doesn't concern the criminal code." In 1973, homosexuality was removed as a disease from the DSM (*Diagnostic and Statistical Manual of Mental Disorders*). In 1985, Section 15 of the Charter of Rights and Freedoms came into effect, mandating equality before the law and protection from discrimination on various grounds. Sexual orientation was confirmed as one of these grounds in 1995. By 1999, most legal benefits commonly associated with marriage had been extended to cohabiting same-sex couples, and by 2003 most Canadian provinces and territories had legalized same-sex marriage. In June 2005, the Civil Marriage Act extended this right to all Canadians.

All Canadian provinces have human rights laws that prohibit discrimination against all people, including trans people. As of 2016, Alberta is the only province where "gender identity" is explicitly listed as a ground in their human rights acts. To date, there is no explicit federal protection although Bill C-16, which is an act to amend the Canadian Human Rights Act and the Criminal Code of Canada to add gender identity and gender expression to the list of prohibited grounds of discrimination, is at the time of writing under review in the House of Commons having passed the first and second readings.

While it may read as if there has been a smooth progression from systemic oppression to legal rights, that's not accurate. The LGBTQA2S+ fight for acceptance and human rights has been met with persistent, loud, and sometimes violent resistance. LGBTQA2S+ individuals and organizations won these advances by speaking out, demonstrating, and pursuing cases to the highest courts. People took great risks and worked tirelessly to fund and support these legal battles. Combatting religious-based bigotry has played a huge role in our struggle for rights. Recently some faiths have begun to actively support queer rights. The United Church of Canada became the first church in Canada to ordain openly gay and lesbian ministers in 1988. We have also fought to educate ourselves and others about queer realities, building programs for schools and post-secondary departments of gender, sexuality and women's studies. The University of Victoria in British Columbia became the first in the world to establish a Chair in Transgender Studies. Over the decades, the LGBTQA2S+ fight has been influenced and strengthened by the global advance of human rights won by other social movements of women, African Americans, students, Indigenous peoples, people with HIV/AIDS and others working for justice, equality, self-determination, and peace. Most of the authors have been deeply involved in this fight for human rights. We do not want them to be taken for granted or reversed.

Without doubt, the situation for queers in Canada has improved tremendously. Laws and attitudes have advanced. However, we want to stress that the work is not done. Many of us in this movement think there are still fundamental changes that must occur to create a truly just and equitable society. Transgender legal rights are not fully adequate. Violence continues against queers, particularly against transgender people and lesbians. There is a lack of disaggregated data (that is, data broken down so that patterns, trends, and other important information are uncovered) to indicate exactly how much and to whom, but there is enough to indicate the problem of violence and hate crimes still exists. Few feel safe against the abuse of power by police. The lives of rural queers are more isolated and challenging than those in urban areas. Queer youth are at much higher risk for suicide and substance abuse. Lesbians struggle with empowerment as feminists within the queer movement. LGBTQA2S+ people, particularly lesbians and trans, face barriers due to low income. Strong anti-LGBTQ2S+ feeling, racism, homophobia, and heterosexism still persist. As queer people, we are acutely aware of both the tremendously positive changes and the urgent need for more. The situation in the United States at the time of writing, with queers facing a Trump/Pence presidency intent on removing their rights and protections, spells that out clearly.

While there are centuries of untold, and therefore missing, queer stories, queer literature has emerged in the last 40 years or so. In the stories and poems that follow, you will read some very personal intimate experiences of the pain and exhilaration as each of us has lived our own queer history. There are also rich resources available through the Internet for those who want to read more about our legacy. Queer history does not reside only in the past. It is still in the making.

The stories and art that follow are individual stories, but they serve to trace the history of North American queer lives as lived by some of the authors. Christine Waymark's account of her introduction to gay rights by way of the Stonewall protest demonstrate the way in which gay rights and women's rights have often intersected. Marsha Ablowitz's tender recollections of her Uncle Max, born in the early 1900s, demonstrate how pioneering queer community builders were often sidelined and ignored, even by close family members but served as important models to the activists that followed. It's followed by a piece of graphic memoir by Bill Morrow and Judy Fletcher, who show how family, church, and state conspired to condemn Bill's nascent sexuality in the 1940s. From a female perspective, Greta Hurst shares her story of coming out, demonstrating how internalized homophobia operates, for example, by accepting an empty room with a bare light bulb as a love nest. Ellen Woodsworth's first account of lesbians' struggle to establish their issues and struggles in the 1970s show how that was dogged by homophobia and ignorance even among those who might have been expected to embrace them—feminists who were themselves fighting for recognition and equality in the patriarchal culture of those times. We end with Cyndia Cole's memories of loss and courage during the AIDS epidemic—a dark period that deprived the community of many of its potential leaders, but at the same time forged important and enduring connections between those identifying as gay, straight, male, and female.

Stonewalled

CHRISTINE WAYMARK

From the radio I hear the news of riots in New York, gay men and drag queens in a place called Stonewall. They are rioting because of a police raid. I grit my teeth as I bend to pick up the kids' laundry for the day. Karen, thumb in mouth, is sleeping after her 6 a.m. feed. Four-year-old Stephen, already in the back garden, will be occupied enough with his trucks and the sand. Janet, soon to be three, and Kevin, five, have sheets of newsprint, crayons, and felt pens on the dining room table. They'll be okay together until I get the first load into the wringer washer.

All I can think is "Why aren't women rioting?"

My back and belly ache from the tubal ligation a few days before. Even with the diagnosis that another pregnancy could mean a wheelchair for the rest of my life, I've had to see four male doctors and get my husband's permission to get the surgery. Where are *my* rights? Who's protesting for me? It's *my* body and *my* life. I'm the one who carries and births the children. I'm 29 years old, mature enough to raise a family, but apparently my husband owns my womb.

I grab the basket of clothes and put it on my right hip, where I often carry a child. Flicking on the light, I hold the basement door open with my bum and continue down the steep wooden stairs and through the unfinished playroom to the laundry area at the back of the house. I keep my ears tuned to the sounds upstairs, ready to run. I know I'll have to carry the wet laundry back upstairs to hang it on the line that runs from the back porch to the end of the garden.

My rage terrifies me, so I bury it. Childhood taught me that my job was to help Mum make life easier for my dad and my brothers. I married at 20. It was the only legitimate way to leave home. I'm glad that my eldest is a boy. I won't, even unconsciously, expect him to be a parent. He'll be encouraged to drive and go to university. He won't be told to use his intelligence to raise clever sons.

Later that night, I check each child on my way to bed. Coming to the bedside of my eldest, I think about how Kevin prefers to draw, read, and practice piano than play outside with other children. His brother is impossible to confine. What does that make Kevin? The news of Stonewall is fresh in my mind. Could Kevin be gay? Will he grow up to be a drag queen? What could make a man want to dress like a woman? What could make a man love another man? If I can see it in Kevin, is it from birth?

My brother's friend is a drag queen, and Mum says it's because his mother let him dress up as a girl when he was little. She doesn't think her grandsons should have dolls or even stuffed animals. Mum tried to escape the poverty of a cotton mill town when she married Dad. When he couldn't get work in postwar England, she engineered our immigration to Canada. Mum uses her intelligence to run community organizations as well as her family of five children. She manages all the family finances, but has never earned any money of her own.

* * *

The office has a very large desk with a couple of framed pictures and a large framed blotting pad in front of the big black leather chair. The bank manager is prompt. "Good afternoon, Mrs. Partridge," he says, hand outstretched. I reach and shake it, wondering why I am here. This is the third time I've renewed our mortgage.

"We have your application for the mortgage renewal and I see that you are applying alone."

"Yes, my husband left in 1973, and the house is now legally mine."

"Would you have a brother or a father who would co-sign with you?"

I look at him, trying to get his meaning. "I've been making the payments, and the house is in my name."

"Mrs. Partridge, all banks in Canada have the same policy. A woman can't hold a mortgage or have any credit of any sort. Surely, you have a male relative who will sign for you?"

Where are my rights? I am raising the children alone and now I can't have a mortgage?

Why aren't women rioting?

* * *

This time, the office is a basement room in a United Church. I sit in the circle of four men and two women, all of us on metal folding chairs. This committee oversees me and other students who are candidates for ministry. I have been here several times and know the routine, so I'm quite relaxed.

"We hear you live with another woman. Does that mean you are a lesbian?" asks the new chairperson.

Mind racing, I think of my options. He isn't supposed to ask me this question, but not to answer would be evasion. Denial isn't possible for me. I have more rights as a woman, and now I take the next step.

"Yes," I reply.

Homophobic Homo

BILL MORROW AND JUDY FLETCHER

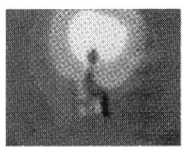

"Homophobic Homo," by Bill Morrow and Judy Fletcher.

Love in Montreal

GRETA HURST

It was June 1957, and I had just completed the retail course at Sir George Williams College. Lorrie was one of the salespeople in the sportswear boutique at Montreal's smallest department store, Ogilvy's. She was the youngest and friendliest of all the staff. Eight years older than me, she was unlike anyone I had ever met. She wore pants, a plain shirt, and no make-up to work—unusual for women in Montreal back then. The other saleswomen came to work wearing dressy clothes with scarves, earrings, and full makeup—as if they were going to a party afterwards.

She invited me home to dinner. She lived with her husband in a small house near the top of the hill in Westmount, a treed street in one of Montreal's upscale neighbourhoods. Nick greeted me at the door of an ordinary house; conventional furniture, sombre in colour, it seemed to reflect Nick's personality. Lorrie came out of the kitchen. She had prepared one of my favourite meals—roast lamb and eggplant.

As the three of us sat around the square dining room table, I thought Nick could have been Lorrie's brother; their personalities were so similar. They asked me lots of questions about my life and interests. Oh, I was full of myself! I told them about going every weekend to the country cabin in the Laurentians. I bragged about getting a B+ in my course. I didn't tell them about shovelling snowdrifts and freezing weather, nor that I failed 10th grade miserably. I didn't mention living in a rundown, working-class neighbourhood near the Main. I didn't tell them that until recently, I had been shy and introverted.

Montreal was the biggest, most cosmopolitan city in Canada. It was a fun-loving, jazz-crazy city with nightclubs that welcomed Afro-American musicians who were not able to perform in the United States. I tried to persuade them to come and see Oscar Peterson, who was playing at one of the clubs, but Nick said they never went out in the evening.

One evening Nick went off to a meeting. We were cleaning up after dinner when Lorrie suggested continuing our conversation about sex.

"Come sit on the sofa with me." She motioned me to sit beside her.

When I sat, she went on, "Have you ever kissed a woman? Would you like to try?"

Always game for anything new and possibly exciting, I moved towards her. She kissed me slowly. It was soft, tender, and long. "We have lots of time before he comes home," she said while her hands moved over my body. The hair on my arms stood up and blood raced through my body as she kissed my face and caressed my breasts. We became lovers.

Lorrie wanted to meet my mother—the dragon eater. The night before my mother and I were leaving on a trip, Lorrie turned up to help me pack. The next day she came to say goodbye, wearing a skirt and high-heeled shoes. My mother hated her on sight.

In that steely-eyed way of hers, she asked me, "Why did she come here?" I decided not to answer.

I called my mother on my morning break when I knew she'd be up. I didn't know why, but she did. She came straight to the point. "Either stop seeing Lorrie, or you have to leave home." My sister had betrayed me.

I moved in with Lorrie and Nick. My sister fed the firestorm by telling our mutual friends. Overnight, I was ostracized; I felt like a leper, a social outcast. Lorrie and I didn't know any gay people. As she didn't want her husband to know the truth, she rented an apartment where we'd have privacy—a love nest with only a mattress on the bedroom floor and a bare light bulb. That year passed in a blur. While Lorrie continued to work at Ogilvy's, I found another job. We didn't go out nor make any friends. I wanted Lorrie to divorce Nick. She did. But it didn't make any difference. Less than a year later, Lorrie showed me a ticket. She was returning to her family home in Europe.

"Why can't I come with you?" I despaired. She had asked her parents but they refused. I didn't hear from Lorrie again.

* * *

By January 1977, I was married, with three children under 10, and about to celebrate my 41st birthday. We had moved to Europe in 1973, going to north Germany for a year before moving to Brussels in June 1974. In Brussels, I joined an English-language feminist group, the Women's Organization for Equality. At the first meeting I attended, I stood at the back of the room, terrified. Listening to Lydia, WOE's matriarch, I realized I'd either have to leave the meeting immediately or change my life beyond recognition. I stayed, but it took me two years in consciousness-raising groups to fully understand the politics of being a wife and mother.

When our group hosted the March 1976 International Tribunal of Crimes Against Women, 2000 women attended. Speakers testified about the living conditions of women in their countries. Irish women told that birth control was illegal in Ireland. Abortion was still illegal everywhere, but marital rape was legal, not recognized as a crime. Lesbians from the United States reported being told not to discuss their issues in the National Organization for Women as heterosexual women would be upset—afraid people would think them lesbians. In most countries, lesbians didn't reveal their sexual identity to avoid rape by men trying to "re-educate" them. Women could be imprisoned and murdered for being lesbian. On day one, 200 lesbians from Berlin protested the fact that lesbian issues were to be discussed only on the last day. The agenda was quickly changed.

For me, the political became personal on a romantic level when I met Nicole, a member of our group. In January 1977, I came out as a lesbian. It was easily the most painful experience of my life. I left my children with their father and a babysitter. I moved into my own apartment. I wish I could have done it differently.

Standing Out and Standing Up as Lesbian Feminists

ELLEN WOODSWORTH

There were few images of what a lesbian looked like before the 1970s, though people might have discovered a couple of pictures of Radclyffe Hall from the early 20th century or a few lines of a poem by Sappho. Women who loved other women were hidden, didn't call themselves lesbians, tried not to look different, or hoped they were hidden in male or female roles. As lesbian feminists, we grew out of the gay movement, which emerged out of the hippy, student, women's, red, black, and anti-war movements. We were part of all of these movements, and we were also building our own, to change the world.

We wanted to be visible.

On the west coast, we wore hiking boots, jeans, and plaid jackets, anything that previously had been seen as male and made us feel comfortable and powerful. I remember designing an image that said "Lesbian Sisters, Proud and Strong Rise" with a semicircle arch of women using the symbol of Pluto which represents female and revolution. We put it on posters and wore it on our T-shirts.

Violence against all women and specifically lesbians was constant at that time. We had to be strong and work in groups.

We fought with the women who had survived by being butch and femme. We were fighting to free ourselves of all roles. We were sick of male power and privilege. We called ourselves lesbians at a time when most of our sisters called themselves gay. We didn't want to be invisible within the sexist gay movement.

When I came out in 1971, I was shocked and hurt to discover that my sisters in the women's movement, women I'd known for years, suddenly did not want to accept us as out lesbians. The Vancouver women's liberation newspaper, *The Pedestal*, refused lesbian content. They said that being a lesbian was an American cultural import. We needed our own paper.

I moved to Toronto in 1972 to work with another lesbian feminist to start that newspaper, which we called *The Other Woman*. We felt "other." As we fought our way into public life, we acted different, we looked different, and our energy was different. We were fighting to say it was okay to be a tomboy, to ride a motorcycle, and to wear boots. We were fighting for the right to hug, kiss, and make love with other women. We were fighting for our right to be out in the streets. We were rebelling against all the constraints that dictated what a woman had to look like, act like, and talk about. We had to push hard to create safe public spaces for ourselves. We had no legal rights and laws that imprisoned many of us in mental institutions. Our children were taken from us. We were treated as criminals, as crazies, as perverted. We were beaten up, raped and killed. We were shunned. We were women to be feared by other women and men. To be seen, to look like or act like or talk about lesbians meant we stood out.

Our only way forward was to flaunt our new lives. When we were in a group in a restaurant or on the street, we would act out by deliberately hugging and kissing each other. We had to protect that space, as men would often try to interfere by making hostile comments, coming on to us, or attacking us. Women would turn away from us. We asked the new women's centre at 31 Dupont St. if we could have a room in which to lay out our new national newspaper. After much discussion and hesitation, they agreed to let us use the top floor. We printed our first edition in late 1972. It contained articles on lesbians, the women's movement in Vietnam, poetry, photographs, graphics of women loving women and personal stories. We felt really proud that we had our own paper in which we could say what had never been said or shown before.

Feeling more and more sure of ourselves, we asked if we could set up a lesbian drop-in downstairs. Though we were somewhat accepted upstairs, it was made clear that the downstairs space was for heterosexual women. That fight went on for months, and it was very painful. Some of our biggest adversaries came out as lesbians months or years later, when it was safer. Finally we won and set up the first Canadian lesbian drop in the spring of 1973. Slowly lesbians started finding their way there.

We were part of other political activities. We supported the Artistic Woodwork strike, and some of us were arrested supporting the immigrant workers. We helped organize International Women's Day. We wrote about the terrible situation of Indigenous women. We wrote about women's unpaid work. More women were joining us, coming out, or supporting our work. With renewed confidence, we started planning the first Canadian national lesbian conference at a YWCA in 1974. We were told that women wouldn't come if we said it was a lesbian conference so we called it the National Gay Women's Conference. Some women came wearing paper bags on their heads, so they wouldn't be recognized.

We were feeling really powerful. Four of us started a lesbian feminist communal house, and my lover and I wrote "On a Queer Day We Can See Forever."

The more rights we won, the safer we felt; the more of us came out, the more we realized how terribly we were treated, both as women and as lesbians. "Lesbians were the rage of all women condensed to the point of explosion" as one article said.

We were like the tendril of a plant emerging from the crack in the sidewalk. We were nonconforming because there was no norm for us. We were awkward in ourselves, with each other and like any newborn, very sensitive. We were emerging from centuries of being forced to live hidden lives. We wanted acceptance, and if we couldn't get it, we would fight until we did. We were fighting our sisters in the women's movement who saw lesbians as a threat. We were fighting our brothers in the gay movement who were fighting for gay rights but not for women's rights. We were fighting our families, the laws, and people in the streets, landlords, and employers.

The world had never seen women loving women who demanded to be seen, heard, hired, housed and accepted publicly and equally with heterosexuals.

We were fighting for fresh air, space, and the right to walk proud. We were mad as hell. Was it worth it? Yes—though it was years of a very painful fight to get basic acceptance let alone human rights, and there is still a long way to go.

Before I Knew the Word

PAT HOGAN

Monday through Friday, I drive my red '53 Chevrolet convertible from home to Danville (pop. 800) where I work in the traffic department office at the factory, located right where the railroad tracks intersect Route 101 heading south to Rhode Island and north to Hartford. I fill out bills of lading and take notes for my boss in shorthand. It's not an interesting job; in fact, it's boring. But, I have to start someplace, and this was the best I could find after high school. $57 a week is not to be sneezed at.

Mr. Mercier, my boss, doesn't speak to me much anymore. This is not unusual here in the traffic department. The people who work on the floor have worked side by side for years, filling orders and packing boxes of sewing notions, which are shipped all around the world. They punch in at the time clock in the morning, punch out at night, often working in a dead silence that can, and does, continue for months, even years. No one knows anymore what caused these silences, why no one utters even a "good morning" to their coworkers standing across the packing table. It's just the way it is. Their lives go on, day in, day out. They do their work, take two coffee breaks—one in the morning, one in afternoon—either out on the platform where the freight is loaded onto trucks or in a dingy little bathroom downstairs. They have their lunch break, go home at night, return the next morning, and pick up their paycheques at the end of the month. It's life in The Quiet Corner.

Bob Wielder, the floor supervisor, isn't much help in easing the daily tensions. His rigid smile and body says it all. He too fears Mercier, and his job is at stake. At the top of the factory hierarchy is Mr. Posner himself. He shows up unannounced in our department on occasion, always wearing a pinstriped suit, white shirt, and tie. A tall and straight-backed man in his 50s, he peers around the department through thick, round-rim glasses, his thinning hair parted in the middle and slicked down on the sides. His darting eyes and his grunts as he examines the work put us on edge; if only he would smile once in awhile. But his face is waxen, expressionless. When he does speak, in his thick German accent, it's only to Bob or Mercier. On these visits, the usual tension in the traffic department expands and permeates the floor. It's agonizing.

When Mercier does speak to me, it's usually one liners like "What's the sluice, kid?"—his morning greeting (if he's in a good mood, that is) as he passes my desk on his way to his office, eyes averted, looking straight ahead.

One day stands out from all the rest. I get a call from Head Office. Someone wants to see me, I'm told. Head Office is at the opposite end of the building from the traffic department. Like most New England mills, the factory rambles on, spread out over several blocks. The clicking of my high heels echoes along the narrow passageway—a long wooden dusty floor with high stacks of packed cartons on either side.

I click past cartons waiting to be piled onto the trailer trucks that arrive each day at the traffic department's bay. Sewing notions are shipped to fashion designers around the world. "Sewing notions," I think, inconsequentially. "What a strange term. Why notions?"

I head down a flight of stairs, across another long passageway leading to the main building of the plant, up more stairs and into the waiting room. Am I getting fired, I wonder? I'm wearing one of my new Tycora sweater sets—a light blue short sleeve pullover with matching cardigan, and a reversible skirt (the rage) held together mid-calf with a big stylish safety pin. I look good.

Did Mercier get mad the last time I took time off? Or was I late for work one too many times? Am I getting a raise? Many questions whirl through my mind as I take a deep breath, push open the heavy metal door with glass window, and walk into the reception room leading to the head office.

The receptionist nods her head towards someone standing in the waiting area. "Visitor for you."

And there, standing in front of me, in dungarees, button-down shirt and sneakers is my friend Carol, looking cute as ever in her tomboyish, athletic way, hands on hips, head cocked to one side, grinning. Carol was my first dyke friend, even before I knew the word. She was the ringleader of a gang of girls who were having sex together in high school before they knew the word for what they were doing. The school dean, a woman, got in a flutter when she got wind of it. She crept into the girls' room when she knew they'd be in there, and crouched up on a toilet, feet up on the door, to listen. It was juicy, scandalous, unheard of in our high school!

The thing is, despite her escapade with the girls, Carol always had a boyfriend and married soon after high school. The way it went in those days for girls was this: you either went on to college after high school, got a job, or got married, or a combination of all three. Carol's wedding was a big event, and four of us from the old gang marched down the aisle in matching salmon coloured taffeta gowns and shoes. It was a typical Catholic wedding, church packed with family and friends from school; we knew everyone there. Everyone was counting on the reception after the church mass. A wedding reception meant music, food, dancing, drinking—a party! And a party it was! The bride and groom had the first dance together. We oohed and aahed. At the end of the day, we waved goodbye as they left for a honeymoon and their new home together a hundred miles away.

The marriage didn't last long—six months to be exact. Actually, it was annulled, and in the Catholic Church, that meant only one thing.

Today Carol doesn't waste words, just looks me straight in the eye and says, "Hey, Pat. I'm hitchhiking to California. Are you coming?"

Me, go to California? Hitchhiking? My jaw dropped.

I stammer. "Well, I … I have to think about it." Carol looks at me, somewhat scornfully, shrugs her shoulders, and leaves. She makes it to California, and we don't see each other for years.

Truth told, I was chicken—chicken to take off on a whim, chicken to ask my mother, chicken to do something out of the ordinary.

Three months later, I left my job at the factory. Mercier said nothing when I gave notice, but on my last day of work he came and offered me a gruff, "Good bye and good luck," and shook my hand.

I worked there for three years before heading for New York. The others were there for a lifetime.

SECTION THREE
What's It Like to Be Queer?

"Untitled," by Maggie Shore.

What's It Like to Be Queer?

CLAIRE ROBSON

How long is a piece of string? How many hours do you have?

What's it like to be "not queer," to be straight, or heterosexual? Is being straight just one thing? Can anyone describe it? Of course not!

Straightness is kind of invisible because being straight is the norm. It just is. Heterosexual people spend a lot of time thinking about who they're attracted to, but they usually don't think about their sexual or gender identities. They just go through their lives being all the other things they are: construction workers, video gamers, ballroom dancers, cooks, homeless, single dads … whatever. We're not saying that only queer people feel different. It's probably true that most people do. Difference is what makes the world interesting (for some) or unfriendly (for others). A white male company executive has different experiences of life from a refugee, or a young woman, or a child, or a farmer. There's social class, gender, age, ability and disability, education, race, ethnicity, and income, and these all strongly affect the ways we live in the world, the ways we see the world, and the ways that all those other people see us.

Though this book is about sexual and gender orientation—the ways in which queer people are positioned and the way we position ourselves—the authors are pretty different from each other too. Some of us are male, some female. Some are fairly old, and some are very old. Some are very young and some are in their early 20s. Some have nice homes. Some don't. Some are highly educated; some are not. Many have had careers of various kinds (prison workers, teachers, store clerks, and therapists); others are just starting out on their professional journeys or are still at school. What brought us all together is that we define ourselves as being queer artists of one kind or another. We are transgender, bisexual, gay, lesbian, asexual, two-spirited—queer in one way or another. We all do gender and sexuality differently from the majority.

So what's that like? What does it mean? How is it different? These are the big questions addressed in this section. Of course, in many ways this is an impossible task, but we'll still try because we know that some of you have picked this book up with those very questions in mind. Sure, we all put our pants on one leg at a time, but when you feel you were born a different gender from the one you were assigned at birth, when you have feelings for those of the same sex, suddenly, the world can become a different place. That can that feel pretty difficult, and even at the best of times, in the best of families and with the best of friends, it can still be confusing. A queer kid doesn't usually have queer parents, grandparents, other older relatives to look to for guidance and modelling—and that's generally how we learn how to be in the world—by looking at how other people operate. So, things like how we date, dress, and communicate, what we value, what we buy, what we say, even the jokes we make are influenced by what we hear at the dinner table or what we see on TV or social media. And the lives of queer folk are not often very visible in what we hear or see there.

Often, we feel that we're set apart as queer people. None of the stories we read or see are our stories. Sometimes this has got us into trouble—especially those of us who are older, because we remember the bad times—the times when being queer meant that we were shamed, locked up, given electric shocks, or fired from our jobs. We learned to feel ashamed or like we were weird or criminal or *less than* other people. That still happens. Some of the young authors in this book were kicked out of their homes to live on the streets, or bullied in schools. This kind of thing might be happening to you.

So, we're using this next section of our book to describe what it's like to be queer, at least from our perspective, which is pretty broad. We hope that a lot of people read our book—parents and teachers and counsellors, doctors and nurses and caregivers, police officers and social workers and bank tellers and shop keepers, and the people who phone other people up and make assumptions about their gender because of how they look or sound on the phone, or believe that because they are speaking to a woman, she must have a husband (or vice versa).

We're also writing this book for those of you who are wondering what it's like to be queer because you think that maybe you are queer. Perhaps, you're worried by that thought. Maybe, you're thinking that it might be a terrible thing. We want you to know that though it's not always easy to live queer, there's an upside, benefits, and causes for celebration. We have found those causes. We don't just accept our queerness. We enjoy it. We have fun. We dress up and go out dancing. We're out and we're proud. We haven't just found peace with who we are—we love who we are. We like being different and we believe that we have something to offer. Sure we want to be accepted, but we want more than that. We want the world to understand that our special perspective, our orientations, have made us creative, free spirited, inventive, insightful and committed to everyone's rights and freedom to be who they are.

We begin this section with a short but telling piece by youth contributor Candy Fine. We like it because in just three lines, it encapsulates a common feeling for LGBTQA2S+ people—that they want people to see below their appearance, to really *see* them, and that they want others to be really *seen* for who they are. We follow this with Syd Oremek's writing about living on the streets—an all too common experience for queer youth who are rejected by their families, and then by elder Judy Fletcher's contribution—a work of magic realism that captures a common experience for LGBTQA2S+ individuals, that of random homophobia as they walk in public spaces. *Last Dance* by Nancy Strider describes a somewhat overlooked perspective on queer life—that of the asexual person. This latest addition to the alphabet soup of queer identifications has rightly gained visibility in recent years, as many have stepped forward to claim space in the literature for those who simply don't experience sexual attraction. *Life Insurance* by elder Chris Morrissey, *In-Between* by youth author Skylar Cogswell-Shears and *You Would Be Pretty If* by youth member Caroline Doerksen describe the impact of everyday assumptions about gender and sexuality. Judy Fletcher's piece, *How Am I Different,* shows how these assumptions can accrue to undermine our sense of self and make us feel that we always live on the outside. *Lost and Found* by elder Cyndia Cole redresses the balance somewhat, as it offers a laundry list of the pros and cons of queer life. *First Queer Event* and *First Time's Special*, by Caroline Doerksen and elder Val Innes respectively, show how the positive impact and importance of entering queer positive space haven't really changed over time. For many LGBTQA2S+ individuals, entering such spaces has been a transformational experience—a realization that there is an accepting community of likeminded others. We end the section with Harris Taylor's poem *Mercy,* which is included as a testament to the enduring and redemptive power of love.

Misunderstood

CANDY FINE

The world of drag is misunderstood. I ask myself, why can't you see it's more than hair, makeup, and pretty clothes. It's a way to say "Hey! I'm here and I want you to hear me. I want you to see me." And I want to say to you, that you can be whoever you want to be.

Young, Homeless, and Positive

SYD OREMEK

It was a summer night on Granville Street, and the street youth and I were gathered in one of our usual sleeping cubbies. A woman came sprinting directly towards us; it was obvious from her facial expression that she was frightened. She placed herself in the middle of our group while she pointed to the street that she came from and began to tell her story of how a man had just tried to grab her. We pushed her to the back of our group, told her to stay there, while a few of the guys ran down the street trying to find the attacker. She stayed with our group until we had found a safe way for her to get home. The man was never found.

While living in the cubbies on Granville Street, it was very common for people to walk up to us and tell us that we were worthless, useless, and would never amount to anything. Some would come to tell us about how horrible their life is because that made them feel better that there was someone in a worse situation than theirs. While we slept, some would drop food, others, however, would spit on us, steal from us, and even attack us. Generally, most of these people were drunken clubsters. None of them ever thought that maybe we serve a bigger purpose.

Vancouver—British Columbia's biggest tourist location. We are known for many reasons, and one of those is our street punks. During the tourist seasons, many pictures are capturing our homeless youth. I personally have had my picture taken many times with tourists from all over the world. They sit and chat with me, just wanting to get to know us and what we do. We are known globally, and others are fascinated by us. Reasons? Unknown. Some people run to us for safety.

Why? Because we live those streets, know what is safe, and are always there. We are a permanent landmark on the city of Vancouver.

When you tell your local homeless person to get a job, stop and think: there's a lot more to getting a job than just handing in a resume. Here are some things that make it difficult: no one wants to hire a homeless person, generally the homeless don't have freshly pressed suits, and hygiene is more difficult when you don't have a shower at your disposal. What do you do with all your gear and what do you bring for lunch? Also quite a few homeless youth are either in school or have a job. The ones who have a job generally can't keep it long due to the lack of housing, and the ones in school have a difficult time finding someone to watch their gear or don't have bus fare.

And not all of us can put ourselves into the categories to get on welfare, youth agreements, independent living, and so on.

My Walk in the Sunshine

JUDY FLETCHER

I leave the Seniors' Centre at noon after my writing class and head out onto the street. Commercial Drive is a diverse neighbourhood lined with small shops, Italian coffee houses, food co-ops, and second-hand bookstores. I dodge pedestrians, off-leash dogs, hippie moms with their kids, and First Nation teens from Britannia High School. Eyes fixed on the sidewalk, I negotiate the crowds.

My stomach feels queasy, but I try not to look back. Every week, the walk to Broadway to catch my bus seems to get longer and longer. About six blocks from the Centre, I find that I am moving too fast. In my haste, I stepped into Charles Street, and I am almost hit by a car that is making a right turn onto the Drive. With an apologetic wave to the driver, I step backwards onto the sidewalk. Hearing a voice behind me, I assume that someone has commented on my "almost accident."

Without thinking, I instinctively turn toward the sound.

She was behind me the whole time! Apparently, when I stepped back, I closed the distance between us. She is middle-aged, neither tall nor short, neither big nor small, and she wears a housedress covered in pale yellow flowers. "Frumpy" is what my mother would have called her. She clutches a cloth shopping bag. She looks so very ordinary.

Then, she repeats what I had unconsciously turned toward: "Get away from me you dirty fucking dyke!"

She glares at me, her face contorted with rage. I look down at her half full shopping bag and think that this is the day that she will swing it at my head. My heart pounds so loudly that maybe the whole street can hear it too. I turn forward and force myself to put one foot in front of the other when I really want to break into a run and disappear down one of the alleys. My face burns with embarrassment, but I don't want to attract any more attention to myself and this woman. I imagine that she is still following at a safe distance. Block after block, I stare straight ahead.

Does she live around here? Is she just out shopping? Does she wait for me outside the Seniors' Centre every Wednesday? Why me? What have I, or any other queer person, ever done to her? It is the middle of the day, and there are hundreds of people around me, but I am shaking with fright over an encounter with this unremarkable woman.

I am not injured. Every day thousands of queer people endure verbal assaults or physical attacks. In some countries, this very day, a person is to be hanged just because they are gay, lesbian, or transgender.

Although I am not hurt, I don't feel like a rational human being anymore. Even surrounded by the noontime crowds, I feel very alone. I try to calm myself. After I board the Broadway bus, I take a quick scan of the people out on the sidewalk. I don't see her.

I avoid eye contact with the other passengers. You never know.

I just want to go home.

Last Dance

NANCY STRIDER

Did they just dim the lights? Where are the chaperones? This is a Frosh Dance for God's sake. They are supposed to be the guards.

STOP THIS THINKING. CHANGE THE CHANNEL. YOU'RE OUT HERE NOW. DANCING JUST LIKE EVERYBODY ELSE. NOBODY KNOWS ABOUT YOU. YET. THEY CAN'T TELL BY LOOKING AT YOU. SO COOL IT.

Oh my God. Here comes another dance. Let's hope this ends soon. I've survived this far. In fact, I've been dancing all night. That must be proof that I'm not walking around with "Frigid" branded on my forehead. Maybe now that I'm here, my loser days are over.

Hey, it's "Love Potion #9"! The Searchers are playing my song! Maybe, if I sing along in my head it will drown out the rest of my brain. Wonder if that gypsy ships to Toronto.

But maybe I'm not going to need a love potion anymore. Frosh week has been my dream so far. Free t-shirts, printed with the St. Mike's logo and our grad year. Games with teams already assigned. No captains arguing about which one has to take me. Everybody said we won the hunt because I found the boot. I couldn't believe it when Sylvia knocked on our door and asked Katie and me if we wanted to come and make toast in the kitchenette.

Huh. So the singer can't make it with the babes. Glad to hear that guys flop too. 1956 or 1968, it's all the same dance. But now we're in the stretch of this particular dance—the acid test of the New Me—and I haven't propped up the wall once, all night! This is the dance that counts. This sets the popularity ball rolling. Girls get picked here, or not. And I've been getting picked. I can't believe I'm still out here.

Still, the love potion in the song sounds like it's giving that loser quite a high. Where do I get some of that stuff? Does it improve your attention span too? Too late for me, now. What did this guy here say his name was? If I had thought, when he asked me to dance, that he wasn't going to walk away after the first song, as soon as the music stopped, I would have listened when he introduced himself. Problem is, I was the one who felt like walking away after the first song. Still am.

STOP RIGHT THERE. PUT A LID ON THAT "WALK AWAY" SHIT. JUST GET INTO IT.

Is there a manual for how to make this kind of a scene? I bet I'm the only one here that is this clueless. Everybody else was practicing for this at the high school dances.

THAT'S OVER. YOU'RE HERE NOW. HANG LOOSE.

This is my big chance. My shoes match my mini. I've got the right hair. I'm a thousand miles away from the in-crowd at St. Francis. All I have to do now is not screw it up.

Boy, everybody seems to be into this song. That couple next to us are still singing, waving their arms doing all the disgusted gestures and ... wait for it ...

I held my nose. I closed my eyes. I took a drink.

Yup. That's me. Hold my nose and just gulp. A-a-a-a-a-a-n-d ... here it comes ...

I didn't know if it was day or night.
I started kissing everything in sight.

There. Bingo. All it would take for me to bloom would be the right drug. Hmmm. Maybe we already *all* took a drink! This place is turning into a passion pit. Bet they spiked the punch with #9. If so, I've downed half a gallon! But looks like everybody else in this room is melting with desire—even the wallflowers. So what's with me? How come I don't feel anything? I drank that same punch!

Well, so much for that. Cop stomps on the bottle, and game over. Another song down, and they just announced the Last Dance. Yay! Almost there! Herb Alpert's dreamy "This Guy's In Love With You."

Oh my God. What's-His-Name here is singing along.

DON'T YOU DARE LAUGH! HALF THE ROOM IS SINGING ALONG. GET IN THE GROOVE. YOU SING TOO.

Pretend I am having a blast. Fake everybody out, or at least this guy right here. Act like I think he's a hunk.

HE IS A HUNK. OTHER GIRLS ARE WAITING THEIR CHANCE. GET WITH IT.

So, let me get this song straight. When the girl smiles at Herb, he has this soul-mate epiphany. So, pretend that this guy here is Herb and I'm a girl in a field of flowers, batting my eyelashes. Look up at him. Chin up. Smile! That was such a pathetic smile. Thank God we're both back to staring at our feet. It really would help if I remembered this guy's name. Next thing you know, I'm going to be calling him "Herb." What is it with me? Why can't I get it together?

CONCENTRATE.

Okay, so let's just look at this dance as a chance to do some research. Maybe I can learn something here. Do the Junior Scientist. Too bad I'm an Artsy. So first let's dissect this song. Herb is observing physical symptoms in himself that could either be intense passion or a heart attack. He's pressing Miss Eyelashes for direction about how he can demonstrate this love to her, since the word is out that she's got the hots for him. That's exactly my question, Herb. How *do* I show passion? Even though I don't think What's-His-Name here is particularly fine. It's not about him, anyway, so I might as well get with it, with him.

JUST GET TO WORK.

That couple next to us. Now *they* look like they know what they're doing. But what's with their pelvises? Wow. How do they get that close and still move their feet? Oh. It's not their feet that they're moving. Does she have a hickey? Already? Does it hurt? Did he just cop a feel? Are people allowed to do that? Where are the nuns?

THEY'RE PROBABLY THE ONES WHO TURNED OUT THE LIGHTS! CONCENTRATE.

Now Herb is begging. He's desperate. Yeah, right. You must be kidding. Like a guy really gets that bummed out. Like a girl could really get that hopped up. I just don't get it. What's the deal with the sex thing, anyway?

PACK THAT THOUGHT IN. RIGHT NOW. YOU ARE JUST A LATE BLOOMER. AND DON'T YOU DARE START AGAIN WITH THAT "NO BLOOMER" CRAP. EVERYBODY BLOOMS. NO EXCEPTIONS. YOU ONLY JUST ARRIVED HERE. YOU HAVE FOUR MORE YEARS TO FIGURE IT OUT. JUST TRY HARDER.

Okay. I'll try out some of those moves, next door there, on this guy here. His eyes are closed, communing with Herb. Okay, time to do that thing with the pelvis. Okay. Relax my backside. Lean into him. Okay.

Say you're in love, in love with this guy.
If not I'll just die.

Uh oh. Herb has stopped singing and What's-His-Name here has stopped dancing. Not good. He's leaning into *me* now. He's getting heavy. Big trumpet finale going on. Maybe if I keep swaying, he'll take the hint and start moving his feet again. Oops. Nope. Bad idea. Now he's stopped breathing. Whoa! Oh my God. What's that? Is that a "hard on"? Did I cause that? How do I make it go away? Gotta get out of this clinch. Get some air between that and me. That's it. Oops, his eyes just opened.

JUST DON'T MEET HIS EYES. LOOK AWAY—SPACE OUT.

I really *am* spacing out. I think I'm having an out-of-body experience. That, or a bad trip on the #9. Breathe. No, not like that! He's getting excited again. Not heavy. Just little, shallow breaths. There. Feel better? No …

That's it for the Tijuana Brass, and we're done at last. Someone finally gave us back the lights. Thank God. Couples around us are peeling apart. You can hear the Velcro. I need to untangle from this guy …

Did that last thing that I did with my pelvis mean he gets to walk me back to the dorm? Did I just commit to pizza? Do I have to say "yes" if he asks me out?

Two guys are waving at him from the door and doing the thumbs up. Shit. He just waved good-bye to them. Oh *yay*! Cavalry coming over the hill. There's the nun from St. Joe's here to take the Wallflowers back. She's my getaway.

SPEAK UP.

"There's Sister Saint Paul. I've got to go. Can't be late for curfew."

"Do you want to …? Can I walk you back? We could …"

"NO! Sorry … No."

WAY TO GO. NOT SOUNDING SORRY.

He's gesturing to his friends. They screech to a halt and wait. He's caught up with them, so now I'm the one that's been left behind. He's pointing at me and talking fast. They are all looking at me.

CONGRATULATIONS. YOU JUST BOMBED. HOW LONG DID YOUR AMNESTY FROM HIGH SCHOOL LAST, GIVE OR TAKE A SCAVENGER HUNT? A WEEK?

College wasn't far enough away, after all. Back there I totally earned being called "Brain" and "Dork." Then they nailed my true personality with "Frigid." Those names have just caught up with me. And now I've added, "Tease."

Life Insurance

CHRIS MORRISSEY

Quiet, slow, gentle morning
sounds of rain on the window
the ring of the phone bursts into the tranquillity—
insurance!
resurgence of fears
of sickness, of death, of preparedness.
There is no escape.
Yet today the table turns.
I resent your question.
No, I do not have a husband.
I am a lesbian and I have a partner.
Today it is about life!

In-Between

SKYLAR COGSWELL-SHEARS

Walking down the street, I fear that I will not be accepted for who I am and who I want to be. I am not quite male, but yet I am not quite a female. I am somewhere in-between. It's difficult being in-between because the simplest things tend to become the most difficult tasks, like using the washroom. I have to stand in the hallway thinking which washroom will be the safest to go into, or picking clothes and people thinking that I am buying them for my partner.

You Would Be Pretty If ...

CAROLINE DOERKSEN

You didn't have your head shaved
You didn't have so many piercings
You didn't wear such dark lipstick
You dressed normally
You didn't have tattoos
You didn't wear so much eye makeup
You had naturally coloured hair

You're a feminist?
So you're a lesbian?
Do you shave?
So you hate all men. Which man hurt you?

You're a lesbian.
Can we have a threesome?
Do you like all girls? Can I watch? That's hot.
Which man hurt you?

It's probably just a phase.
You just haven't met the right guy yet.
Do you have daddy issues?

But you're too pretty to be a lesbian.
If you're going to date a butch woman, why not date a man?
Are you into kinky stuff?
If you're going to use a dildo, why not have sex with the real thing?
Who's the man in the relationship?
Who pays for dinner?
How do you have sex?
Do you scissor?
It's not real sex.
You just need a good fuck.

How Am I Different?

Let Me Count the Ways

JUDY FLETCHER

I have always felt like a stranger in a strange land; my body disowned, my mind a battlefield.

I am a girl more comfortable in boy's clothes. I would rather play with a Meccano set than with a Barbie doll.

I am a Christian in the gay community and a queer among the disaffected.

I have been to psychiatric purgatory and back and have the label-covered satchel to prove it.

I have recently discovered that I am mad as hell but I don't want anyone else to know about it.

I only feel safe when I am invisible, but I continue to resent it when people don't see me.

I am a child of the '60s who never experienced the '60s, the '70s, or the '80s, for that matter.

When the pain becomes unbearable, I will turn to self-injury. When overwhelmed by loneliness, I will go and hide.

As long as I can remember I have lived in space, the space between people and the space between my ears.

So how am I different? I am different in countless ways, but in just as many ways, I am a survivor.

Lost and Found

CYNDIA COLE

Lost:
my country of origin

Found:
my place of peace

Lost:
my inhibition

Found:
myself dancing

Lost:
my temper

Found:
my limits

Lost:
my treasured friends

Found:
my way forward

Lost:
my constant self-critique

Found:
my listening ear

Lost:
my flirtatious nature

Found:
my lasting love

Lost:
my sylphlike body

Found:
my solid ground

Lost:
my job

Found:
my mission

Lost:
my fat salary

Found:
my creativity

Lost:
my reputation

Found:
my unshakeable faith

First Queer Event

CAROLINE DOERKSEN

The first queer event/group that I went to was in Vancouver when I was in grade 10. I remember that the day before the parade, I told my parents that I was a lesbian. At the time, I thought that having a long-term girlfriend meant that I was a lesbian. I've now realized that I am queer rather than lesbian, but those two memories are very important and significant for me. I remember my stepmom telling me that I had to be careful because there would be a lot of media downtown and "what if your grandparents saw?" I don't think she meant for it to be insulting. I went to Pride with my gay best friend Mitch. I wore a tank top that said "Gay!" all over it, fish net tights, knee high boots, and tiny black shorts. I had half of my head shaved, glitter everywhere and full thick false lashes. I remember that a group of gay men told me that I looked like Madonna.

This was a most joyous day! I felt very liberated, and I miss that feeling. As I reflect back on that time now, as an activist, it's difficult to feel the joy I once did as a young lesbian.

When I attend Pride now, I don't look at it the same way. I am aware of issues of consumption, capital, and the patriarchy.

First Time's Special

VAL INNES

She'd done her homework, as much as she could. She'd done the reading, furtively buying books whenever and wherever she could find them. She'd made the phone call, talked to the gay and lesbian phone line helper, Jennie, and now she was ready. Wasn't she? Well, anyway, here she was. She should fit in pretty well, Jennie said. She had on faded jeans with rolled up cuffs over her boots and a red and black plaid shirt over her T-shirt.

She looked around. Yep. Looked like a dance hall. A bit gritty—old, wooden floor, tables and chairs, dingy green paint on the walls with some ancient nature pictures hanging a bit askew. Sounded like a dance hall. Lots of loud music, talk, and laughter. Felt like a dance hall. Had that vibe to it. But, wow, something different, though. ... Look at all the *women*!

Women dancing together, laughing with each other, hands in the air to *Sisters Are Doin' it for Themselves*, bodies touching, clinging, breaking off to swirl back, hands on hips, flirting, teasing, breasts touching. One couple was doing a great jive to the music, and a whole group was dancing together around them. And at the tables, more women, sitting talking, drinking, smoking—a group near her arguing loudly almost over the music, and over there, a couple of women making out—kissing! And against the bar and the walls, women watching the action, like she was. Some drinking, some just quietly talking, some just propping the wall up, watching. Women everywhere, all over the place.

And here was one woman moving towards *her*!

Mary watched as she came near—tall, attractive, with a tan set off by her white shirt and black jeans, a silver chain around her neck, silver rings on her fingers, short blonde hair swept back and intense blue eyes seeking hers.

"Hi there. I'm Terry. You're new here, aren't you?"

"Yes, I am. New to everything here."

"Ahh … first time?"

"Yes."

"Well, then. Come and dance with me! First time's special. I'd like that. To be special."

Mary paused. Looked at her. Looked at the women dancing. Felt a tingle right down to her toes. And said, "Let's dance!"

Mercy

HARRIS TAYLOR

I found mercy in a stranger's bed
as I lay alone in sweet, dim light
clutching my emptiness to me
like a vampire clutches night.

My own red blood must nourish me
tears of my veins sustain my will
to walk in hopeless daylight, to speak
to careless offerings—my hapless soul to fill.

I've laid my head on nameless ground before,
called it home and slept deep into the earth.
a certain peace I called it—
a certain measure of my nameless worth.

Now I lay me down to sleep with Mercy—
holy woman's face—
and I sleep quiet as a prayer,
resolute inside her velvet grace.

SECTION FOUR

Queers in Family

Queers in Family

VAL INNES

Family is seldom uncomplicated when you're queer, although today's families in general can be very different from the ones in which we queer elders grew up. Many are not that much different though, and being a queer kid in a potentially homophobic home in any era or area can be an experience varying from forced dishonesty to being kicked out the door. Those of us who were lucky were accepted when we eventually came out; many didn't emerge from that particular closet until after one or both parents died, and some just never did come out.

Today, how your family will react varies enormously depending on where you are and what laws you live under, what your parents believe (which may depend on what religion they embrace, if any), the culture they belong to, whether or not your parents are straight or queer, and finally, on whether there are other queers in your family. In Canada, same-sex marriage is legal and queer rights are protected, so in most urban areas, it's easier for your family to accept you—indeed, your parents may be queer themselves. In rural areas, however, the picture may be entirely different, as it was for most of the authors growing up in the 1940s, 1950s, 1960s, and 1970s in North America—and for many queer people today who live in countries that do not have legal protection for gender and sexual minorities.

Family is important to most of us; we're a social species, so regardless of how accepting our families of origin were or were not, most of us started to add onto family and build family in some interesting ways. Those of us who were rejected by our original families looked for love, comfort, acceptance, and support from other people in the queer community: from friends who, in sharing similar challenges and similar social lives, became family, the people you share with, march with, support and turn to in need, the people you spend holiday feasts with, the people you celebrate with, the people whose shoulders you cry on and whose tears you dry.

And now, as time has passed and laws and attitudes evolved, queer biological families have emerged. There's sometimes a genetic factor involved in whether we're queer or not, so, not surprisingly, queer kids can have queer siblings, and queer daughters and sons can have queer daughters and sons too. Families then start to look different from the "normal" nuclear family of the 1950s. They might be two lesbians with a couple of kids who have a queer grandmother or grandfather or two among the straight ones, or the transgender man with the lesbian spouse now adjusting, or the two gay guys fathering or adopting, again with straight or queer grandparents. And for many of us, our ex-partners have morphed into honorary "brothers" or "sisters," whose new partners, often enough, may join the extended family.

Family is so much more broadly defined today than it has been. At the end of the day, family is what you make it be, along with what society lets it be. We're lucky in that respect in urban Canada, but we created our families well before it was legal, and we fought for them together, supporting each other, squabbling along the way, of course.

But then that's family for you.

The stories that follow chart experiences of family for some of our authors—both positive and negative—as they describe both biological and queerly constructed families. We begin with Skylar's poignant account of growing up trans—a rejection that is all too common for youth who identify differently. It's followed by a similarly bleak account by an elder author—Harris Taylor's bitterly amusing attempt to unload her family to the highest bidder. We follow these with two contrasting stories of acceptance—Bridget Coll's account of becoming an "adopted gramma" and her partner Chris Morrissey's account of how new family can be created through coming together through political action (even though their sexual orientation remains an uneasy secret). Robin Rennie's story *The Drop In* will ring true for many LGBTQA2S+ people, in that it traces a common process of "coming out" and finding likeminded people or a queer "tribe." The poem *Androgyny*, and the two stories that follow (*Class Ring* and *All Girls Can Have Curls*) describe the discomfort and sense of dislocation that many older queer people felt as they grew up—the need to hide their true identities from biological family members, the feeling of not fitting in despite their best efforts to conform, and their sense that they are, ultimately, a disappointment to their parents. *Max Dexall*, by Marsha Ablowitz, describes another (and often underreported) phenomenon in queer life—the presence of a family member who serves as a kind of icebreaker, traveling through the frigid waters of homophobia flaunting a proud rainbow flag of encouragement to those who follow. *Uncle Max* is a testament to the courage of many early pioneers of queer community. It's followed by a story of reconciliation and redemption, as Farren Gillaspie finds his lost daughter, *Faith,* and a counter story of loss, as Christine Waymark mourns the disappearance of her partner Robin into the awful abyss of Alzheimer's. *Not the Piece I was Meant to Write* is a sad story, so we follow it with GG's more upbeat account of what queer family can look like. Though names have been changed and identities concealed, *The Way Forward* is a true account of family life and genealogy as it has been reconceptualized in the 21st century. We conclude with *Fighting for Life* by Cyndia Cole. Our book would not be complete without work about the AIDS epidemic that took many lives as it also formed enduring bonds between gay men and lesbians in the 1980s and 1990s.

It must be noted here that both Christine Morrissey and Christine Waymark lost their partners, Bridget Coll and Robin Rennie, both members of Quirk-e, to forms of dementia in recent years. We include Bridget and Robin's work posthumously in honour of their lives and their many contributions to the queer community. We also include the work of another late group member, born comedian Paddy St. Loe, whose story *Our Pam's Gone Funny* touches upon another often untold queer family narrative—the business of *not* coming out to our families.

You Aren't a Boy

SKYLAR COGSWELL-SHEARS

"You aren't a boy! You're a girl!"
 I shake my head watching him. "No!"
 "Yes, you're a fucking girl. You have boobs, curves, and a high voice! You're a girl!"
 "No I'm not!"
 "No matter what you do to change your body, you will never be a boy."
 "Yes I will."
 "You will always be she, girl, daughter, princess."
 "I am the fucking king. I am he. I am a boy and I am your son."
 "You will never be my son, she, her, girl, daughter, princess."
 "No it's not true!!! I am a boy!"
 "You're too feminine."
 "I'm gay!"
 "No you're not. Girls can't be gay if they like boys."
 "I am a boy! Why can't you see that?"
 "You were born a girl, and you will live as a girl."
 "Why can't you understand that it's making me depressed?"
 "You're just looking for attention."
 "No, I'm not. Stop! Oh god. Please make it stop. Why can't he understand?"
 "Who will give me grandchildren?"
 "I'll adopt!"
 "That's not the same!"

"It is though!"

"You will never be my son. I never wanted a son, and I'm not going to get one."

"You will always have a son."

"No I will always have a daughter!"

Days have passed by.

Maybe if I killed myself he would understand.

On the news there was a sad story of a 12-year-old transgender boy who committed suicide after his dad judged him till no end. Where is this dad now?

He's crying over that little boy's tombstone. He's saying he's sorry. He's realizing that he loved his son.

The tombstone had the wrong name. Instead of "Seth" it said "Sarah."

That little boy looked down and hated his father for doing that to him.

For Sale

Used Family

HARRIS TAYLOR

- Six Members minus Seller
- Christian, Sexist, Racist, Homophobic
- Twisted but not Bent
- Damaged but completely compostable
- House-trained and like Dogs
- Comes with collection of Art and Guns
- 64 years old but very well preserved in Alcohol

WARNING: Could be flammable

This Special Family will be yours for the low once-in-a-lifetime price of $19.99.

CASH ONLY

Must see to believe!   Requires advanced sense of humour.

SALE IS FINAL

No Refunds or Returns.
Must pick up with own Backhoe!
Comes with Complimentary Survival Kit.

Adopted Grammas

BRIDGET COLL

I am not a parent, but I am a grandparent.

I never thought I would be called Gramma Bridget until I discovered a hairdresser on Commercial Drive. I discovered to my delight that she is a lesbian (this was the first time that I had met a lesbian who was pregnant).

On one of my visits, she told me that she was leaving the hairdressing salon because she did not want the child she was carrying to be affected by the chemicals that were being used there. She invited my partner, Chris, and me to her home and said that if we wished, she would continue to be our hairdresser. A few months later, she invited us to a baby shower, where, to our surprise, she announced that we were to be the Grammas.

On December 18, I came home from work and listened to our phone messages. One said, "Colleen was born at twelve minutes after six this morning."

I said to Chris, "I think we should go and see this child since we are the Grammas." We saw this tiny child, held her, and fell in love with her.

We brought her the classic Pooh Bear, the first of many gifts. We were regular visitors at Colleen's home. We accompanied Colleen to Santa Claus Parades, to St. Patrick's Day Parade and went to her school concerts. In her first preschool concert, she was *A Little Duck in New York City*. She got a standing ovation for that and was happy with her performance. Needless to say, her Grammas were very proud of her, as were her mothers.

When our hairdresser and her partner moved to Bowen Island, we were frequent visitors to our granddaughter's new home. When Colleen was able to talk, she would see us and call out, "Here come the Grammas." When her moms went out together, we babysat and watched every stage of her development. We played with her, and one day we got really excited when she smiled at us, and then even more so when she called us Gramma.

It was a new learning experience to have a child in our lives, and we had a lot to learn. I needed lessons on how to hold, give bottles, and change diapers. After several trials and errors, I became an expert—especially on how to change diapers. In the beginning, I was puzzled about putting diapers on the right way. However, I did learn ever so slowly.

As every Christmas approached, Chris and I tried to figure out how to buy a present for her. In the end, we went to Toys R Us and followed women around the store who were accompanied by children the same age as Colleen. We watched to see what toys they played with or begged their mothers to buy. Then we would buy that toy.

Colleen opened up our lives to a whole new experience of nature. She liked to walk around the garden, even in the rain, dressed in a yellow raincoat with Wellingtons to match. She would walk in front of us and every so often, she would bend over, look down, and say, "Hi slug."

On her last birthday, Colleen called us and said, "I am now officially nine years old."

What a joy to have such a child in our lives and to be called Grammas!

As I wrote earlier, a child in our lives is a new experience. Now Colleen comes to visit us. She looks around and sees her photos in every room in our house. She looks at us and says, "I know you love me."

We are adopted.

The Last Goodbye

CHRIS MORRISSEY

The Santiago airport stretches across the fields on the outskirts of the city, like an apron surrounding the girth of a large woman. Craggy, snow-capped Andes Mountains dominate the skyline in the distance. Cerro Navia, the hill we have seen every day of our lives for the past eight and a half years, rises like a woman's breast in the foreground.

Inside the building, there are the usual counters, glass, and lights. This airport is simply a smaller version of those of New York, Toronto, London. The luggage carts are full of suitcases, full of clothing and gifts, as most prepare to fly north for Christmas to visit those who have been in exile, chosen or imposed. Fortunately, there is air conditioning, which helps the travellers cope with the heavier clothing picked for travel to the north, despite the hot summer weather out of doors. People chatter away to each other in Spanish. There are laughter and hugs. There is an air of anticipation and excitement.

Bridget and I stand apart from the others. We are surrounded by Kety and her children, Lenia, Astrid, Ruben, and Vladi. Vicki holds the hands of Checho and Rene, while Claudia, her daughter, stands alone. Five-year-old Salvador clings to me, and I to him. He is my godson, and we have been with him through homelessness, illness, and abandonment by his father. I cherish him, the child I do not have, will never have. These have become our family.

My thoughts and voice startle me. "We should have hired a bus so all the others could have come too." I know that there are already too many people here, more than I can bear. We are a sombre bunch, looking more like a family waiting for the funeral procession to begin.

Someone tells a story. "Remember when Maria came to the airport with food for Raymundo when he was going home?" We all laugh. The lunch was the same that we all packed for a day at the beach or when we climbed San Cristobal for the feast of *La Virgin*. Hardboiled eggs, chicken legs, bread, a bottle of Chilean wine from the Botellaria down the street. Maria had never travelled on a plane and did not know that Raymundo would be given food.

Someone says, "I have a cousin in Canada. She was exiled after the coup. She lives in Ontario. Will you go and visit her?" I explain how big Canada is and that Ontario is as far from Vancouver as Arica is from Punta Arenas. We are making small talk. We all know it.

"Will you come back?" Kety asks. "When Clara left she said she would be back but she never has."

We promise to return. It makes it easier for all of us.

We have journeyed together, though you do not know about our journey. We have learned, laughed, and cried. We have stood side by side in the streets in protest, huddled in doorways to avoid arrest, stood soaking wet at the back of a church awaiting the negotiations that would allow us to leave. We have joined you in hunger strikes, demanded an end to torture, and visited your political prisoners. We have celebrated, singing your folk songs, drinking your wine, waving your flag in the streets. We have bought bread daily at the kiosk, shopped weekly at the street market, watered, and swept our streets.

After fifteen years, you have overthrown the dictator Pinochet, and his forces. You begin anew, rebuilding your lives. I have learnt from you about oppression, about finding a voice, about taking back one's freedom. Now I must strike out and take a new path, leaving the safety and security of my 29-year convent home.

Sadness overwhelms me. I hate to be leaving you. I especially hate not sharing my truth with you. I long to have you celebrate with me as I have with you. But I dare not break my silence. I cannot tell you who I am, that I too am stepping out from under what has become an oppressive rule of life.

As the plane lifts off, I see the flag flying high over the tower. I hold Bridget's hand tightly. Tears stream down my cheeks. It will be years before I truly know my freedom, but the journey has begun. Together the two of us take those first steps. We take them together—worlds apart.

When we step off the plane in Boston, Paula and her partner will be there to meets us. It will be the first time that Bridget and I will appear in public as a couple.

The Drop-In

ROBIN RENNIE

After leaving my marriage, I enrolled in a three-month residential growth intensive on a small island in Georgia Strait. Surrounded by ocean and islands and touched by the winds of the strait, I got much of what I needed to turn my life around. Soon I came out as bisexual, and some of the women were clearly intrigued, as were most of the men. We had very little privacy; in fact, that was an intentional aspect of the program. We lived together, ate together, and most days we met in the round workshop building with our leaders, exposing our worst and our best selves in the group. Few secrets survived the three-month program, but I held on to my bisexuality. In that sexually open early 1970s environment, I had almost convinced myself that it was true.

After the program, I was on my own for the first time in eight years. I sought out others from the program; five of us found a house to share in Kitsilano. One man self-identified as a transvestite and was enthusiastically supported by the two other men and woman. I remained silent, confused, although I was awed at his audacity. When he dressed as a woman for Halloween, I noticed how radiant he looked. He later transitioned to become a much happier woman than she had been as a man. I nevertheless continued my own fiction of bisexuality, which must have been transparent to the others, as they were all acquainted with the woman for whom I pined. I did not pine quietly.

I put a carefully worded ad in the Georgia Strait and waited nervously for a response. Weeks later, she called as my housemates and I were eating dinner. She said that she was answering my ad—could we get together? Innocent. Friendly.

But her accent was unfamiliar, and in my sheltered life I had experienced few accents beside my own. I had put the ad out of my mind, and now I was freaking. I could sense my curious housemates listening politely: how could I face them? I was mortified, and any chance of a positive encounter was burnt away by my shame. I choked out from my closed throat. "I-I-I've decided not to go." I hung up and sat back down at my place at the table, not looking at my housemates. Eventually someone went back to a previous topic, or maybe introduced another one. I excused myself as soon as I thought I could walk. To my relief, none of them ever asked me about it.

I'm not sure how I found out about the lesbian drop-in. It took several weeks to build myself up to go. I dressed with care, even though I hadn't a clue what to wear. Not wanting to appear too eager, I decided to walk in late. I had never experienced a drop-in and thought perhaps people came and went. Of course all eyes were on me as I entered the store. I was welcomed, and another chair was brought out. As I sat, these women, these *lesbians*, continued their conversation, giving me time to get used to being there. I listened as well as I could. Under the circumstances, my dissociation was not unusual, but it made it hard to relate. I had high hopes for this meeting, and naively I thought these lesbians would be more like me than they seemed to be. I had always felt so different from everyone else. As I peeked out from the place of my highly unrealistic hopes, I was dismayed to find these women were just like everybody else. Except, of course, they were all lesbians.

I thought, "Maybe being lesbian is the only thing we have in common." It didn't dawn on me, then, that getting to know them might help. After all the buildup to this moment, in my fear and alienation, it became obvious I had a whole other hill to climb in strange new territory where old rules did not apply. I had so much riding on this evening, and I felt shaken. I had so much to learn. The women were different from me only on the surface, most a bit younger, and several from somewhat different backgrounds. I was shy and had to work hard at making social connections. Of course, I made none that evening. I did know before the evening was over that there was no artifice there, and no judgment. I also knew that these women were essential for my evolution as a lesbian.

The others all knew each other. When I arrived, one young woman was well into describing an argument with her lover, which had upset and angered her. Her lover often attended the drop-in, but because of the quarrel, she had stayed away. I noticed the group in general was not focused on the angst and hazards of identification as lesbian; instead, they were discussing the complications of lesbian relationships. As I had only flirted hopefully at the edges of lesbian relationship myself, I thought the complications of being lesbian had to do with pursuing a reluctant love object. This was the first time I heard women speaking of their relationships with each other as if it was just a fact of life. I began to relax. I went to the pub with them after some meetings and learned about Queenie's.

At Queenie's, a wide set of stairs off a downtown alley led directly to a second floor with one huge room painted black. Boldly, I went on my own mid-week, which I thought would be safer than Friday or Saturday night. I was right. The dim lights illuminated fake palm trees and sparse groupings of women, talking and drinking. I ordered a drink, maybe two, and rather than sit where I could be seen, I sat behind a palm tree and just watched and breathed it all in. This was the only lesbian bar in town in 1974. I went again and again, alone, and sat, absorbing the atmosphere of women with women. I continued to thaw.

Despite my early feelings of alienation, I went to the drop-in every week. While I never became close with any of the women, I found my feet, and my association with them gained me access to other venues. I went to Queenie's irregularly and eventually made contact. I crept my way up the hill until it became less steep, and then levelled out. Along the way, I discovered that my desire to meet myself in another woman was rooted in my old bugbear of fear, wrongly thinking that finding myself out there would prove to be a safe and easy thing. I shed fear and gained identity. I found, amongst the burgeoning and diverse community of lesbians of that time, that there was acceptance and room for me.

I still have problems deciding what to wear.

Androgyny Is My Sanity

VAL INNES

I wear
    a tie
        and earrings

not all your efforts
mother
to put me in a dress
made a lady of me

I am a woman
who makes her own way

strangely
you would have liked that

Class Ring

CHRIS MORRISSEY

Another day at school.

I was always the last one to be picked for a team. As if my immigrant accent wasn't enough, I was always a little fatter than the other girls, and I couldn't hit a baseball to save my life. There'd been no Halloween trick or treating back in England and no big birthday parties or Friday night trips to the movies with classmates. I learned to adapt, climbing out the window to go to the movies and seldom arriving home at the time I was told. I learned by listening in.

Today, it had been all about boys.

Amy had begun the conversation at recess. "Who do you have a crush on?" It wasn't directed at anyone in particular.

Leslie was first, "I think Archie's cute, and besides he's Father Green's golden haired boy. Maybe, if Father Green knows, I'll get better marks!" They all laughed, and I held my breath. No way was I going to say how I really felt!

Just the weekend before, Leslie had asked me to go for a drive with her. She was the only girl in the class with a driver's licence. She got to drive her father's Chevy Impala with power steering. I loved watching her hands as she turned the steering wheel. So effortless. So intriguing. We'd gone back to class and said nothing.

When school was over, there was no choice but to drag my way home. I was trudging down the alley when I heard the sirens. As I got a little closer, I saw the smoke rising. It was coming from the roof of our house.

After the firefighters left, we all went in.

I saw black everywhere. Walls, counters—every surface was covered in soot. My dad pointed helplessly at his most precious possession, a hand carved crucifix that had travelled with us from England. The smell! I could hardly breathe.

I got out as fast as I could. Heart beating. Would I ever go home again?

Dad sprang into action. He ran to a neighbour's house and called his boss.

I had met Bob Shields a few times—a short man, even when he stood up straight. His clothes always looked new to me: pastel-coloured Brooks Brothers shirts with button down collars, beige trousers, always well pressed. My dad bought his clothes from the Simpson Sears catalogue. His trousers were baggy and shiny, and he only wore a jacket and tie when we went to mass on Sundays. He worked hard, but I guess he didn't earn a whole lot. Mr. Shields drove a shiny black Buick Electra 225 Riviera four-door sedan. We had a second-hand '52 Chevy.

Before the firemen left, Dad gathered us all together. He told us that we would be staying in a motel for a couple of days, and after that we'd move to Mr. Shields' house. Mr. Shields would move in with Bobbie, his new girlfriend.

The fruits of sin.

Although my dad had tried to keep his boss's divorce hush-hush, I'd overhead him talking to Mom, "Imagine! At his age! I mean I know they're not Catholic—but living with another woman? I ask you!"

Every summer, Mr. Shields let us stay at his cabin on Bednesti Lake for exactly one week. It was the highlight of my summer. We had never been to his regular house, but I just knew it would be special.

We pulled up in front of an expansive lawn with bushes and a winding path up to a two story white house with black shutters. *I knew it!* I thought. I had always wanted to live in a house on Patricia Boulevard instead of on the last street in the city. Dad gave me the key while he got a couple of bags from the trunk, and Mom got my brothers out of the back seat. I headed straight to the French doors at the back. They opened onto a wonderful garden: more grass, a bed of red and pink roses, fragrant, multicoloured sweet peas that climbed the white fence surrounding the garden.

I never wanted to go home again!

I had Bobby's bedroom. The sun streamed through the large window that overlooked the back garden. The single bed, up against one wall, was covered with a brilliantly white bedspread. On one wall, there was a poster of guys playing soccer, on another wall, a poster celebrating a Porsche that had won a race in Mexico. I remembered my dingy little room and its single poster of Cary Grant and Debra Kerr in *An Affair to Remember*. When my friends came over, they always thought that it was there because of Cary Grant.

As I looked around my eyes were drawn to the dresser, and I noticed a framed picture of a woman in her 40s. Standing next to the picture, there was a hockey trophy and a ring. It was a class ring of 1957, gold with a large blue stone. I looked into the stone and knew it held the answer. It wouldn't change the past. It might change my future.

I picked up the ring and slipped it on my finger. It was too big, but I knew that all I needed to do was to wind tape around the back. The next day, as soon as I was out of the house, I slipped the ring on my finger.

Before going through the door of the school, I took the ring off and carefully put it into my pencil case. All morning, I kept touching it. I hoped it wouldn't spontaneously combust. Why didn't my school uniform have a pocket? Glancing around, I moved the ring to my lunch box. Would I have the nerve to put it on at lunch?

When lunch was over, I put the ring on my finger and hid my hand behind my back.

"What are you hiding?" Amy asked. Tentatively, I brought my hand out and showed them the ring.

"Where did you get that?"

"Whose is it?"

They were all talking at once.

"Well," I stammered, "I was keeping it secret, but you guys are always talking about boys, and I could never join in. So now here. It's my boyfriend's high school ring. He's away in Toronto at University."

My hands were shaking. Would I get away with it?

Would I be able to get away with the real secret?

All Girls Can Have Curls

JUDY FLETCHER

A few months into my first year of high school, my mother decides that I need a new look, one that will get the attention of the boys. The transformation begins. She wraps elastic bands round each of the braids that I have worn since I was six, and then she cuts them off. She lays them in a box lined with pink tissue paper. Mom may have seen this touching ritual in a movie or on TV. Almost immediately, the box is misplaced, and the braids are never seen again.

The Toni television and magazine ads feature a pair of perky teens in matching sweater sets—no Clearasil for these squeaky clean sisters. They are blondes with soft waves of curls, framing their delicate features and glowing complexions. My mousy brown hair is pulled away from my flat Irish face, which is always covered in freckles and occasionally visited by outbreaks of acne. Toni Home Permanents are marketed to women who can't afford beauty salon prices. Not only can we not afford such luxuries, we live so far out of town that there isn't a salon for miles.

For the next five years, every two months, my mother cuts a few inches off my straggly hair, thus preparing me for the pathetic ritual to come. Each time she hopes the day will end with me, the little tomboy, looking like one of the sweet cheerful Toni Twins or the Toni Twin's second cousin on their father's side. The whole family hope so too.

Shorn like a sacrificial lamb, I wrap myself in a plastic cape to protect my favourite blue jeans and my brother Tommy's cast-off T-shirt. The misery begins with a thorough review of the ten-page instruction booklet. I study this as if my life depends on it. Somewhere in it, I want to find the key to avoiding another hair disaster. My mother, her grey hair too thin to hold a curl, is also wrapped in plastic and wears huge yellow rubber gloves.

She lays out the equipment as I recite from the instruction book.

The most difficult part of home perms is also the most important. Learning how to section and block your hair so that each part has a uniform thickness can be a little tricky, so take your time and practice to avoid an uneven look.

"Yes, yes, I know how to do it," she barks at me.

She begins by combing a few hairs in to a single layer, folds an end paper around it and wraps it around a plastic rod. She snaps it shut against my scalp.

"Ouch, Mom, it says: don't pull the hair too tight, or you'll damage it."

On and on it goes for what seems like hours. Some of the curlers refuse to stay where they're put. They pop open, expelling the hair and soggy tissue and bringing forth a stream of unusually colourful language from my mother. Eventually, the successes outnumber the malicious pop-opens and we finish off using cut-up newspaper as replacement for the mound of tissue pulp on the kitchen floor.

We have stopped talking some time ago.

I dare not tell her that the different coloured rods are different sizes, and they should follow the pattern in the booklet. Even though my head is covered with these plastic sticks, my mother jams in a few more of the small ones for good measure. My eyes are watering. Our plastic capes are in tatters, and we're both soaked.

According to the booklet, the solution will break down and retrain my hair.

I think of my braids, tidy in their little coffin, whereabouts unknown. I pray that the chemical dousing will work some miracle on what is left of my hair.

Once all of your hair is rolled up, thoroughly saturate every curl with the perm solution. Use all of the solution. Perm processing times are extremely important, so don't get distracted. Never, ever, leave the solution on longer than specified in the instructions. You won't get more curls. You'll get frizz, or worse, your hair could break off or dissolve into a gummy mess.

My mother applies the solution, starting at the back. Within seconds, the stinging liquid runs into my ears and down inside Tommy's T-shirt. I try desperately to keep it out of my eyes with a wadded up facecloth.

After it's done, I wrap myself in a dry towel. We set a kitchen timer and watch the clock. And silently we both pray. I steal a look to see if my mother has her rosary beads in hand. I wonder if there are special prayers for curly hair.

The timer rings and my mother pours gallons of water over me to remove the perm solution. I am wet from head to toe, but we are headed into the home stretch.

Apply the neutralizer. This solution begins the process of re-forming the broken proteins in your hair.

I don't see how this awful smelling stuff can repair anything. It produces enough ammonia to euthanize an elephant, if an elephant were to be so foolish as to want kinky hair to go to the school dance in hopes of attracting a mate.

A family of skunks sits on the porch staring in our window.

My mother uses both hands to unlock hundreds of curlers and hurls them towards the sink. Some of them actually land there. Most of the end papers land on the floor.

There is nothing more to do.

Consummatum est.

We march slowly towards the bathroom mirror.

Forlornly staring back at us is a Little Orphan Annie look-alike, only sadder, much sadder.

Silently we clean up the kitchen.

I wonder if this is a good time to tell her that I don't like boys anyways.

Max Dexall

MARSHA ABLOWITZ

When I was nine, a man with dark wavy hair and an accent came for dinner. He brought expensive chocolates and planted a soft wet kiss on my cheek.

Mom said, "This is Uncle Max Dexall."

I wiped my cheek with my sleeve.

"Call me Cousin Max," he told me years later when I visited for tea. "Uncle sounds too old." He flashed a smile and pulled up his pant leg to show off his thin ankle and smooth calf. "You should see me in my emerald heels and matching evening gown. No one has legs as beautiful as mine." Later, friends told me about his fabulous dress collection, and I regretted being too shy to ask him to take me upstairs to unlock his mahogany wardrobe.

Max was born in 1907 in Antepol, the Gorodno district of Belarus on the Polish Russian border. His grandfather was a poor Jewish farmer who painted and decorated churches to make a little extra money. After Max's death, my elderly cousin Melvin showed me a family photo of Max with his mother and four siblings standing barefoot outside a log house on a rutted dirt street. Melvin said the house had a dirt floor.

Around 1915, the Russian Czar sent Cossacks to brutalize the Jewish *Schtetl* in Belarus and evict them from their property. Max was a young teenager when they murdered his father. He escaped to Canada, and later, thanks to money sent by my great-grandmother Sara Goldberg, his family joined him. They were very poor but managed to start a boarding house in Vancouver. Max earned money through odd jobs—selling newspapers on the street and helping in relatives' shoe stores. He worked hard and managed to save a thousand dollars, which he used to open his own shoe store in the 400 block of Main Street. This was in 1928. Within a few years, a large bank wanted his desirable corner location, so the bank officials agreed to move his store, which ended up at 10th and Granville.

Max Dexall's Shoe Store was known throughout the city. Max displayed the latest styles. He was effusive with his European accent and manners; he knew all his customers by name, and when a new mother came to buy her baby's first pair of shoes, Max would kiss the little one on the forehead and give her the baby shoes for free. "I love to pay for the baby's first shoes. And this way the customers are happy, and they always come back," said Max.

Cousin Melvin told me, "In the early days here in Vancouver, Max organized surprise parties for the whole family almost every month. But we didn't all like him. He was sort of effeminate, and when he didn't get married, the parties stopped. Our family didn't get along so well. Max must have felt badly that he was not invited to family weddings, bar mitzvahs or Seders."

My dad came home once from helping decorate the windows at Max's shoe store. I heard him laughing nervously and complaining to my mom.

"Well. Did anyone do anything to you?" asked my mom.

"No," said my dad. "But I was nervous down there with Max and all those fairies."

I got very excited but also confused. "Dad, Dad, did you really see a fairy? Is Uncle Max really a fairy?"

"Not that kind of fairy, a different kind. You know, a homo."

"Don't use that word, Myron," said my mother.

"Well, what should I call them, then?" asked my dad.

"I don't know," said Mom.

Years later Max took me and my partner to a fancy ocean view restaurant. He delicately cut his lettuce with the silver cutlery, winked at the waiter, and in a sexy whisper explained how he stayed involved with the Jewish Community after his family rejected him.

"Marsha, I went to the *Shara Tzedeck* every *Shabbas* to pray, and I cruised in the men's section of the synagogue. There were lots of gay Jewish men there, so sexy in their silk *tallisos*. Most of them married to hide. This was the 1950s, before Gay Liberation."

Cute lively young men came to work at Max's shoe store. He was their boss, their mentor, maybe their lover. Vancouver's drag queens came to try on high heels. Max ordered extra-large sizes in the latest styles.

"I told those queens how lovely and how feminine they looked. Marsha, you can only imagine them, six-foot beefy hunks wobbling round the store trying to walk in their high heels. None of those queens had legs as beautiful as mine. You should have seen me in my emerald gown."

Max loved to tell the romantic story of how he first met George Hill.

"One day during WWII, I was working in the store. Suddenly a tall, handsome air force man walked in. I shooed the other sales boys away and rushed to serve him myself—I always fell for men in uniform."

As soon as George left the air force, Max offered him a job at the store and personally trained him. They fell in love. For 40 years, they ran the shoe store and attended concerts and the opera. They happily redecorated their home on 38th near Granville. As a young woman, I'd wander through their manicured garden with bright red and golden tulips and ornate metal garden furniture. In the art-cluttered house, I stepped gingerly on the Persian carpets. I stared at the oil paintings, the statues, and the rooms filled with gleaming antique wooden furniture. Max and George even hired a young gay artist to hand paint the kitchen wallpaper with columns of coloured birds and flowering vines. Off the entry hall was a red walled Chinese den with large porcelain lion dogs and gilt flowered vases. The living room was crowded with rose crystal and dozens of Royal Doulton figurines. There was a needlepoint ladies' screen near the fireplace.

"This is to protect the ladies' pancake makeup from melting in the heat of the fire," whispered Max.

"My mother told me to never clean a dirty house," Max said. "She told me to always clean a clean house, so I put on my frilly housewife's apron and get out my red feather duster."

While Max enjoyed being the housewife in his fancy aprons, George complained about all of Max's *chatchkas*.

"They just collect dust," he said. George was the man of the house. He did the home repairs, took the car in for servicing, and did all of the heavy gardening. "Well Max might pick the odd flower," said George. One of their neighbours was a homophobic doctor who never spoke to them but threw garbage and rotten fish over the fence into their spotless yard.

"What do you do George?" I asked.

"Nothing, there's no point!"

"But you must do something."

"Well. Very rarely, I throw it back."

In 1978, they sold the business and travelled the world, bought antiques, and enjoyed entertaining in their home and garden. George attended his Anglican Church and Max his Orthodox synagogue. In the 1980s, they helped organize the first GLBT Jewish group in Vancouver. They had some lively parties and talked about celebrating a gay Passover together, even starting a gay synagogue like the one in San Francisco. Then the young man who spearheaded the gay Jewish group was jailed for embezzling at his job. Max and George visited him in prison.

"I always dreamed of praying in a gay *minyan*, but thank G-d we never invested any money with him for that group," Max told me afterwards.

I took my little nephew, Adam, to visit Max and George in the 1980s, and they fussed over the youngster, kissing him, giving him money, feeding him ice cream, and telling him stories. Adam was wide-eyed as George did magic tricks.

When I took one of my lesbian partners to meet Max, he planted a soft wet kiss on my cheek, then on hers and said, "We are so delighted to have another gay in the family. Isn't Marsha beautiful?"

"I think so," she said.

Over the years, I would bring various partners to meet Max and George. Graciously they invited us out to lunches and to dinners. One evening, they took us to the Gay Men's Chorus production of HMS Pinafore. At intermission, a dyke in a suit ran up and hugged Max.

"Max! Max! Remember when you gave my baby his first pair of shoes?"

"This always happens, wherever we go. Even in Squamish," George told us.

I started bringing all my gay Jewish friends to visit Max, and he soon became everyone's gay uncle, helping a new generation of young gay men with work, recommendations, and encouragement.

Max tracked down his own nephew, Cousin Bruce—a professor in New York. Bruce had finally come out, and, like Max so many years earlier, Bruce had been rejected by his family. He immediately replied to his Uncle Max, thanking him for the emotional support, and Max and George flew east to visit him.

"Bruce is just beautiful," said Max.

"He is so smart, and he writes books," said George.

Bruce published an essay he wrote about meeting his gay uncle, and Max showed it to everyone. Then Bruce became sick with AIDS.

Max phoned me and invited me to come for a visit. When I arrived, Max and George told me the sad news.

"We hadn't heard from Bruce for a long time. We kept phoning him and wondered why he didn't answer," said George.

"Finally he called back. We talked to him on the phone. Bruce was crying, and we were crying," said Max. "He told us he was dying."

"We have been praying for him," said George.

"We wanted to fly out and see him one last time, but he said no," said Max.

When Bruce died, Max recited *Kaddish*, the prayer for the dead. The *Kaddish* prayer glorifies God and is recited at home and in the synagogue daily. Traditionally, this prayer is recited by children for their deceased parents, and by parents who have lost a child.

"I have been saying *Kaddish* for Bruce for a long time," Max told me.

Max died of heart failure in 1991. I told my little nephew that we wouldn't be visiting Uncle Max and George anymore.

"Well, at least George is still alive," he replied. At the Orthodox cemetery, we threw dirt down onto Max's coffin and said the *Kaddish* for him the way he had said it for Bruce.

After the funeral, we went to his and George's beautifully decorated home for the reception. It was a sunny day, and through the lacy curtains, there were views of the red tulips in the garden. Everyone was talking and eating. After all the straight relatives and friends left, George and a group of old gay men leaned back on the embroidered couches in the antique-filled living room telling stories about Max. We were sipping tea from fine china cups and whiskey from crystal shot glasses. I was sitting on a tiny chair next to the ladies screen. George served fancy sandwiches and little pastries. One of the men sitting near me said he had been a high school teacher at Lord Byng. I told him I was a student there. He was a tall thin man, slightly stooped, with an English accent.

"Oh we had some great parties," he said. The other old men laughed.

"Remember when the police stopped our car and we were all in drag?"

"Remember the boys at the shoe store?"

"Remember the first Pride Parades?"

"Remember his emerald gown?"

"Max Dexall," by Marsha Ablowitz.

Faith

FARREN GILLASPIE

Motivational speakers like to say that our inner world is reflected in our outer world. Well, that seemed the case in 1989. The Exxon Valdes crashing and spreading toxic sludge over our pristine coastlines in March mirrored the crash of my own toxic relationship, and as the tanks rolled through the streets to Tiananmen Square wiping out protestors en route, I'd packed up my objections and moved out of the West End to North Vancouver. By the time the Berlin Wall came down in November, I was coming into a newness of my own.

But let's begin with my Exxon Valdes, David. Physically, he was an incredibly beautiful man. He modelled part-time while studying in an aesthetics program. We were both adult children of alcoholics. I was the eldest and overresponsible. David was the youngest and irresponsible. We broke up and made up five times in five years. I remember wondering what crisis he would present next as he walked out for the final time. At this point, I felt I would be okay spending the rest of my life without a partner. And with that out of the way came the almost instinctual urge to have a child. It was a need to give back, to mentor, to just guide another young being along life's road and to know that I was responsible for that. Through my work, I had a lot of contacts with social workers, and so I started trying to foster a child. Over the next few weeks, I received several profiles of troubled young teens.

Then the call came. It wasn't the social worker; it was my younger brother, Russell. We always had an unusual but caring relationship, the redneck, and the fag.

"Ha ha you sucker! Mr. Perfect! Mom and Dad's golden boy! I thought there was more in your closet than you were telling us. Well bro, we all have to pay the piper some time. Looks like it's your time."

"What are you babbling about, Russell? Are you high?"

"No. But I have a letter here that sounds pretty interesting. Yeah. From some 17-year-old girl looking for her daddy. Says her Mom's name is Simone. Ring a bell Bro? Wasn't Simone that pretty little French girl you dated before you told us you were gay? You are gay aren't you? Did you and Simone actually do the nasty?"

"God, Russell! There's no hope for you. One of us must be adopted. I dated Simone, yes. The rest is our business."

"Well, not any more Bro. All of the Gillaspies got this letter."

"Is there a phone number on that letter?"

"Sure is. Want it? Are you thinking of changing teams, Bro?"

"Just give me the damn number."

I called right away. It rang several times before a woman answered. It had been 17 years, but the voice hadn't changed. "Simone! It's Farren."

"You got a letter? I'm sorry. I told her not to try, that it wasn't fair to you, but she has her own ideas.

"Simone. She says I'm her dad."

"Well, you are, Farren. Remember when we decided to go our separate ways, and I came back to see you at the farm one last time? It was a special weekend, wasn't it?"

"I remember it feeling like goodbye, Simone."

"Well, it was. But after I got back to Ottawa, guess what? I knew you and I wouldn't work, but I wanted a kid, and Diane said she'd help me. Knowing it was yours was special. I really wanted you to be the father of my first."

I sank deeper into my old leather Lazyboy as I listened, stunned.

"I did something very wrong though. Not only did I not tell you, but I told Faith that you hadn't wanted anything to do with us. I thought that would put a stop to her questions, but I was wrong. It just made her sad. I didn't really see it at first. Then just after her 16th birthday, her boyfriend committed suicide. I was worried, Farren. She was crying and asking what was wrong with her, so I told her the truth. I told her not to try to reach you because I didn't think it was fair, and I guess I knew I should have told you from the beginning. I was so foolish and independent then. I'm so sorry you had to find out this way."

"Simone, I have to ask. Are you absolutely sure?"

"You'll know when you see her. She's a Gillaspie."

"Simone, a whole lot happened after that weekend. I forced myself to realize that I was actually gay. Well, at first I eased into it by convincing myself I was bisexual. I have been out as gay now for a long time."

"I'm not surprised. You weren't like most of your friends," she hesitated. "In a good way. Are you happy?"

"Actually, not that happy right now. I've had a couple of really crappy relationships. The last was the worst. We broke up so many times I saw more of the back of his head than the front. But it's done. And now this. It all seems so surreal. If I fly back, can I meet her?"

"Of course!"

"It will take a couple of weeks to get covered at work. I'll call you as soon as I get a date."

I was still walking around in a daze the night the phone rang. When I answered, it was David. "What now?" I thought. "How can you better your last crisis?"

"I need to see you Farren."

"Sorry David. That's not a good idea."

"I have some news I need to share with you."

"David, is your Mom okay?"

"She's fine. It's about us."

"David, please, there is no us anymore. Just say what you have to say."

"Farren. I have AIDS. Not just the antibodies. I have it all." He started crying.

I have always been able to think quickly on my feet and respond intelligently. This time I sat down in a blur. What kind of joke was this? The Universe gives me a child I never knew I had, and now, it takes my life. I took a deep breath.

"David, we went to the AIDS awareness seminars together. We agreed we would always have safe sex when we weren't together."

"Sorry Farren." He started sobbing and hung up.

That phone call was the last I ever heard from him. I heard from friends that, true to our former patterns, he accelerated his party agenda and passed away a year later in Toronto, where he'd moved to be near his brother.

Meanwhile, I raided all of my cupboards, throwing out anything that remotely resembled junk food, white sugar, jams, processed foods, the works. I fasted, changed my vitamin regime, and rejoined the gym. My mania was interrupted by a friend who pointed out the obvious, so I went and got tested, so that I would know where I stood with this virus.

A very supportive nurse at the clinic did the test for me. I tearfully told her my story about Faith. How I had wanted a child so badly. Someone I could nurture and love. Now, I would die on her like her boyfriend, or worse, she would have to look after me until I died.

When I returned for the results, she came around from her desk. She was smiling, but I thought, *this is bad*.

"You are negative," she said as she gave me a hug. "You seem really healthy, so I'm sure the antibodies would have shown up already, but we will have to test you again to be really sure."

The second test was negative as well.

The good news came just before I headed back to Ontario. I could have flown without being in the plane.

When I entered Simone's home, Faith was standing behind her. At 17, she could have been my sister's twin at that age. "Well Faith. It's been 17 years and five thousand miles."

We hugged. This tall slender, vulnerable girl in my arms was actually part of me. Unbelievable. I choked and silently gave thanks.

Faith came to stay with me that summer. My gayness was of no consequence to her.

"I tried to have sex with my girlfriend once, Dad. Sorry, but it was pretty gross."

Father and daughter went shopping. I think she must have worn heels when she first learned to walk. She was never out of them. To pacify me, she actually tried on a few skirts, but tight skinny jeans were her comfort zone. She was a teaser, much like myself. A couple of times when we got to the checkout, she would give a treacherous smile and in her sexiest voice say, "Thank-you Daddy. You are so good to me!" The cashier would grin, and I'd turn red. I would threaten that if she did that again I'd walk out. Of course she did, and of course I didn't.

She insisted on going to the clubs to see where I went dancing. "Heels were made for dancing, Dad."

"You can't drink, Faith."

"But I can dance, Dad."

She hardly left the dance floor. When drag queens weren't exclaiming over her long legs or her heels, handsome young men were hitting on her.

"I thought this was a gay bar Dad. Why are these guys hitting on me?"

"Guess it's a different time Faith. Young people don't seem to care about labels anymore."

"So some of them might be straight?"

"Yes. Or bi, or questioning."

She headed back to the dance floor. Not long after she came back towards me followed by yet another handsome young man.

"Jared. This is the man I have been looking for all of my life."

His well-defined chest sank.

"My Dad."

Not the Piece I Was Meant to Write

CHRISTINE WAYMARK

As I look at the straining zippers on the big blue suitcase, I remember the first time I saw her pack. She'd started with a list, crossing off each item as she put it in its niche.

"I want to be able to manage my luggage by myself. And leave space for treasures I find," she said. Later I learned that stones and driftwood were often part of her trove.

She rolled her socks and tucked them into an inside pocket. "Mum and Dad gave me this suitcase set for my graduation."

"Which one?" I asked, watching her wrap a small flashlight in a handkerchief.

"Oh, my MA. Mum got them at Eaton's with her employee discount."

She'd put her toothbrush and toothpaste and brush and comb into separate drawstring bags and tied each bag carefully before tucking it into its pocket. In the lid pocket, she put underwear and PJs, folded flat so they didn't squash the t-shirts. Slacks and shorts went in the main compartment.

"I haven't seen a Seagram's bag since we used them as purses in High School," I laughed. "I got one from my uncle since dad didn't buy much whisky."

"My parents had plenty," she'd said, putting her sandals in one and slippers in another. With a snap she closed the case, locked it and fastened a leather strap around it.

"Done."

* * *

Today, I've written her a list.

I hand it to her.

"What's this for?"

"It's just some suggestions. See, I've done one for my packing. Eve will help you tomorrow, after she does the laundry. Remember she did that last time and you said she was really good?"

"Yeah! She folds things really flat."

"Wanna go over the list?"

"Later maybe. I'm tired. I just carried the suitcases upstairs."

On Friday, Eve and Robin pack together and put the suitcase on the couch in the living room. On Sunday, I notice that it looks much fuller. In the outside pocket, I find a National Geographic, three books, her electric toothbrush wrapped in a scarf, an umbrella, and a box of Purdy's chocolates.

I open the case. Two more books are stuffed down the sides of the clothes and two are on top of a jacket. I notice her toiletries bag is too stuffed to close. Gently lifting a few things, I see that at least the neatly packed clothes that Eve helped her with are still there.

Oh shit! Will she remember what is there? Will she be anxious if I take things out? The new things aren't labelled, as requested by the respite centre.

I am so tired. I try to think it through.

Then I take a deep breath, and, with great difficulty, I zip the case.

* * *

Sunlight bounces from the kitchen counter tops and brick red floor tiles. Bright yellow walls hold the sunbeams. We designed everything for two women who are less than 5'1." The shelves in the upper cupboards are adjustable, and under the counter are shallow drawers for kitchen tools plus deep drawers holding all the other big stuff a cook accumulates. I cook, and Robin cleans up. She's taught me about organizing drawers and cupboards.

When I check the messages on the phone, I hear her familiar voice: "Where are you, and when are you coming back?" By the ninth, she is sounding sad. "I think I might have left a few other messages. But when are you coming home?"

The last message is from Robin's niece. "Hi Christine. Maria here. Just wanted to let you know we took Anna to see Robin yesterday and had a great time. Robin held Anna and even carried her around to meet some of her new friends at the centre. We sent you some pictures."

I start to assemble things to make a pie for Robin's homecoming. Flour, salt, shortening … whoops! Where's the bowl?

I open the drawer with the Tupperware containers. Nope. I look in the pan drawer. Nope. Nope. Nope.

Okay! I'll get the measuring cups and spoons. Oh damn! Can't find them either, but I do find the phone charger I've been trying to find for weeks. Tears flow as I go through the drawers returning vagrant items to their places.

The aroma of apricot cherry pie fills the kitchen.

Tomorrow she'll be home.

And I'll still be missing her.

The Way Forward—Notes for a Screenplay

GG

Characters in order of appearance:
Charlie
Anna
Jacob — Charlie's brother
Todd — Jacob's partner
Tyler — donor dad and friend of all the above
GG, the narrator — Anna's mother
Nan — GG's partner
Opa — Anna's father
Popo — Opa's wife
Gramma — Charlie's mother
Grampa — Charlie's father
Farmor — Tyler's mother
Farfar — Tyler's father
Finn — Charlie and Anna's baby daughter
Gabrielle — former partner of Anna
Frankie — Gabrielle's wife
Ayla — Finn's half-sister, Tyler's bio-daughter
Naomi — Ayla's mother
The over-enthusiastic bocce player will remain anonymous
Lola — the French maid

All names have been changed to protect the narrator from the shackles of strict veracity. We are a real family, but if you don't take to us, you can pretend we are fictional. If you think you recognize us ... hello!

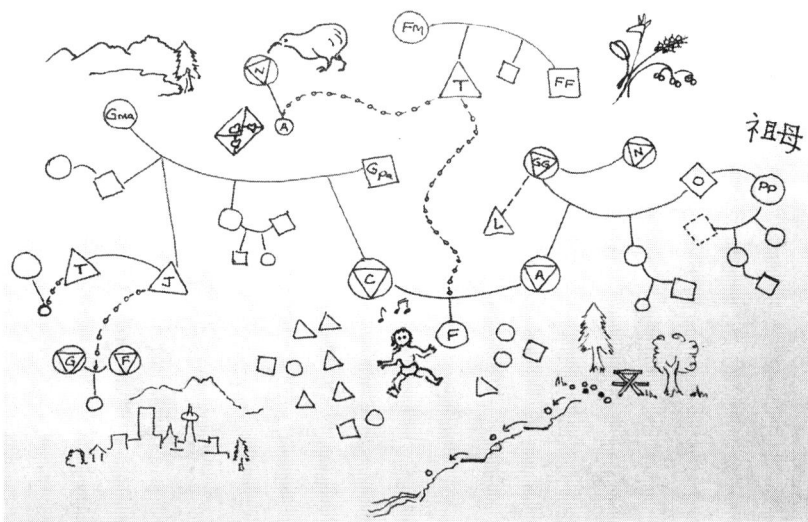

"A Map of the Village," by GG.

Scene 1

Even before she thought of herself as a lesbian and began to organize her life plans around that idea, Charlie used to be pretty sure she didn't have marriage or kids in her future. (These days, she laughs at her younger self, except perhaps occasionally as she does a load of diapers at midnight.) Her ideas shift when she meets—online, of course—Anna, who is pretty sure she does want all that wife-and-kids thing, if available. Three years on, their wedding, organized around the priorities of sustainability, their own enjoyment, fun, and games for the guests and amazing local organic catering, happens in Jacob and Todd's east side backyard. The summer evening stretches into a party under strings of appropriate fairy lights that make the scene magical, as the six parents-of-the-couple congratulate each other and gradually take themselves off, leaving the space for the mixed gay, lesbian, straight, whatever, young crowd to celebrate. Before I leave, though, I make a point of meeting Tyler. Tyler is a long-time gay friend of Charlie's, and his parents are also here from two provinces away. They are excited about meeting the new wives, who, they hope, will be bringing up their grandchild. Quaintly, Anna and Charlie have waited till after the wedding to work on this next project: Tyler has been recruited to donate sperm.

Scene 2

I am privileged to know the approximate date of the optimistic meeting of reproductive materials. I go to the funkiest flower shop on the east side and pick out a small selection of stalks bearing flowers and seed pods that most resemble generative body parts, eggs, and tadpoles. Hoping I won't be thought of as completely creepy, but deeply excited, I sneak in darkness to Anna and Charlie's basement apartment door and leave the flowers in an Avalon organic milk bottle, with no message. This is my way of praying.

Scene 3

At different family gatherings during Anna's pregnancy, the older generation discuss grandparent names. Anna's birth parents each have a new partner, resulting in three grandmothers and one grandfather. Charlie's straight parents have already have earned the titles Gramma and Grampa. Tyler's parents are eager to have a role in the baby's life too. Five grannies and three grandpas?? How to minimize the confusion for the little one? We pick grandparent names for ourselves based on our ethnicity, nostalgia for our own grandparents, and whimsy. I am to be GG for Granny Gael. The moms-to-be are very happy to have a readymade village eager to embrace their child—a village that includes also Charlie's sibs, their partners, and the raft of gay wannabe uncles who, with Charlie and Anna, Jacob, Todd and Tyler, form an exuberant social circle. I am mainly delighted that this topsy-turvy extended family is so amicable and relaxed together.

Scene 4

Finn is born at the hospital where Anna works. Well-wishing coworkers pop their heads in at intervals to check on the progress and to welcome the dark-haired, alert little pixie person who is my first granddaughter. Where *did* she get those incredible eyelashes? (Later, Tyler claims them as his.) Charlie and Anna, exhausted, glowing, are allowed home with Finn the same day because the midwife and the staff know they can cope.

Scene 5

The tendrils of family spread further. Jacob and Charlie have always been close; as the two queer sibs in a family of four, for sure, but it goes beyond that; they plan to work together in the near future. Now Jacob agrees to be a sperm donor for Gabrielle, a friend of Anna and Charlie's, who was actually Anna's partner for a few years. I bump into Gabrielle, rotund, and her partner Frankie at the Folk Festival and share their excitement about the pregnancy, and at the way this family keeps on burgeoning.

Scene 6

Nan and I host Anna, Charlie, and Finn at our January rental house in a dusty little Mexican town. Finn loves the beach—we all love the beach—and Finn gets buried up to the chest in sand for the first time. Over meals, Nan and Finn sit and grin adoringly at each other.

Scene 7

A visit is planned from another branch of the evolving family. Finn, now 18 months, gets a letter—her first!

"Dear Finn, I hope you love seeing your big sister for the first time and I JUST can't wait to meet you. I hope I am going to love you so much that I can't say how much I love you. I say goodnight to your photo beside my bed everynight. If I had to wait any longer to meet you I would just burst into one little bubble. Lots and lots of love from your sister, Ayla."

Ayla, six, and her mom Naomi live in New Zealand now; Ayla is the result of Tyler's first burst of generosity involving bodily fluids. He has visited them already, and now it's their turn to fly around the world to consolidate the new family links. Amazingly, the meeting of the half-sisters is every bit as joyful as Ayla is hoping, and the adults bask in the radiance throughout a spring weekend.

Infused through all scenes:

> Yes, it is real life. Of course, doting GG sees everything through the proverbial rose-tinted, etc. So in order that you believe my story I will say that, also of course, Charlie and Anna work very hard and are often sleep deprived, and money can feel very tight. Sometimes it takes lots of extra laundry hours for Anna to get the ammonia smell out of the cloth diapers, and Charlie's commute is a bitch. Finn's development has given rise to some medical worries, and she has had many appointments with various specialists, and tests involving needles, restraints etc. Fortunately, you couldn't find a more courageous and sunny tiny two-year-old anywhere, but it's an ongoing concern that the moms also handle amazingly well. We are all convinced she will be fine.

Scene 8

Tipperary Park is pretty hilly. This does not deter the several gay uncles and a couple of straight ones from playing bocce at Finn's second birthday party. Fuelled only by tea from delicate china cups, they play with gusto, so that while Finn rips wrapping paper off a huge pile of gifts, one of the guys is seen running after a blue bocce ball from Charlie and Anna's new set; it trundles relatively slowly out of the park but gathers speed down steep Fourth Street all the way to Columbia, crossing five intersections on the way. The pursuing uncle gives up, rejoins the party, and the ball is found later by a search party, way down near the river. The rest of the family and friends, maybe twenty of us, catch up on the news as we sit around in the mellow September sun enjoying canapés and tea and lemonade prepared by Anna and Charlie the evening before. Done with bocce, the uncles pass Finn around and chat with her, indulging her penchant for plunging her tiny hands into their beards. Is that why children are supposed to need a father, I ponder? Really, it seems clear to me that something like this crazy, unwieldy, tight-knit, devoted village is all that a child could wish for, upon any passing star.

Lola the French maid? I admit she is a fiction. There is no Lola. Although I expect sometimes Anna and Charlie could fantasize about such a being …

Our Pam's Gone Funny

PADDY ST. LOE

"Our Pam's gone funny," said my sister-in-law in the midst of a family get together.

"Funny like how?" I inquired.

"Well, she dumped useless Larry last year, and she seems to have taken up with this Erica woman."

"You mean she's become a lesbian?"

"Oh, I didn't say that," replied Gillian hastily. "Oh, I don't really know. We're all just going along with it. She insists that if Erica isn't invited to things, she won't come. Everyone's polite, but nobody's asking, if you know what I mean."

I did know what she meant. I hadn't been home for years and found I was now part of the older generation. My parents and most of my aunts and uncles were gone. The ones that remained weren't thinking too clearly. I had been quite an out lesbian at home in Canada for some eight years. It had been my hope that my generation of cousins in Britain would be more accepting, and that I could reveal myself to a more enlightened bunch. Not so apparently. There was Cousin Pam living her life out loud, and no one was prepared to talk about it. I was definitely going to have to have a visit. Perhaps she was the one I could come out to first; she'd be able to tell me how the wind was blowing queer-wise.

I found a seat beside Pam and Erica and did the how-do-you-dos while clutching a glass of plonk and plate of nibblies. "I don't think I've met you before," I said to Erica.

"No you wouldn't have. We've only known each other a year."

"I'd love to have a proper visit with you before I go back to Canada," I said. Hum ... I'd said *you*—that could mean Pam or *you both*. That wasn't too clear.

Fortunately it didn't matter. "We'd love to have you! How about Saturday lunch?"

I turned up clutching a loaf of "good bread," as instructed. I had decided to jump straight in and announce my lesbianism. If I was way off course I could always get up and leave. They beat me to it. "You do know you've entered a den of iniquity and will surely go to hell if you hang out with us?" announced Pam.

I chickened out. "What do you mean?" I said faintly.

"You've been home the better part of a week and visited with the relatives—surely someone's mentioned us?"

"Well, only Gillie. She said you'd dumped Larry and 'gone funny.'"

"That about sums it up. None of them want to know. At gatherings they're all polite, but visits and invitations have just about dried up."

"What would happen if you just announced it—I'm taking it that you are lesbian—at the next family do?"

"We talked about it and decided that it would spoil whatever event was going on."

"They'd have to take a position then though, one way or the other," Erica said.

"Personally I don't give a damn, yet I've come to like the ones I do know."

"And really," Pam added, "Do we care that much? So what if the family splits over it? Maybe it's better they all stay in blissful wilful ignorance than have to face up to something threatening."

"Typically British," was my take on it.

"You seem fine with us," queried Pam.

"It takes one to know one," I said.

I told them I'd had every intention of coming out on this visit and had hoped for a more liberal acceptance. They both wondered where I'd got that idea. I had to admit it was from the British comedies I watched on TV at home in Canada. I was told that there was a UK law that said if you portray community on screen, then it must represent all sections of the community. So if I saw gays, it wasn't necessarily because they were an important part of the plot. They cited *Coronation Street* as their example.

I left and we vowed to keep in touch.

So what was I to do now? Come out to one person? The logical choice would be Gillie. She had been my friend, and I had married her brother. She accepted our divorce—had got divorced herself. But how could I tell her I had divorced her brother, a decent and funny man, and left him with no one because I'd realized I was a lesbian? I hadn't told her brother that. The reason I'd given for wanting a divorce was that I wished to leave our small town now that the girls were launched. He, on the other hand, was content to settle down even further.

If I was thinking to tell Gillie, expecting that she in turn would inform the family as and when, then she wasn't really the one to do it. I had to all intents and purposes abandoned her brother for another life. And, for her to be told later by some other member of the family, when I'd been staying in her house, wasn't really on. Pam and Erica would no more out me than I would out them. The family was constrained in their presence but basically would be fine until someone actually came out with the word "lesbians"! If I came out maybe I'd precipitate that very thing, and Pam and Erica weren't prepared to flaunt it. They had decided to go along as they were. I'd be long gone back to Canada, and they might well be left with a family divided in their acceptance of them.

So I ended up returning home to my other life, despite my earnest intentions about coming out. I still think of this from time to time. Revise all the what ifs. Was there also a measure of lacking the courage to actually do the coming out bit? Was I afraid to face people's reaction?

I'll never know now, but I wonder.

Fighting for Life

CYNDIA COLE

Andrew has a life-threatening disease. The disease can spread from one person to another and in 1987 people are frightened of it. He doesn't want them to know. He must take care not to expose others and he does. He appears healthy. His disease is invisible. He confides in me late at night sitting in his car. I respond with tears, a feeling of deep appreciation for him, and a resolve to fight for his life.

Life is normal. Five months go by. The secret stays inside. Then Andrew tells me the virus is reducing his body's defences to a dangerously low level. The fundamental darkness is eating his life. Again I urge him to fight, to fight. I say he is not alone, to remember he is not alone, that against all odds he can win.

The next morning I nearly faint two times struggling to walk to the bathroom. The weak point in my back has given way. The pain is intense. My chiropractor says I am in shock, emotional shock. It is my own fear and cowardice I am facing. I must challenge myself to walk. I must find confidence for Andrew.

My friend Gregory died of this disease three years ago. I remember each visit with him in hospital—his simple joy in sharing with me cheese and crackers, sherry, and chocolates. That particular day, for a change, he could eat. With his death, Gregory taught me to appreciate life as though this is my last moment, to enjoy being alive and not to take it for granted. It's a gift I promised to treasure. Can I share it with Andrew?

Two more months pass. Andrew tells me that his former lover James died instantly today after being hit by a truck. James had been ailing and one week before the doctors confirmed he had AIDS. Andrew is certain that James put himself in front of that truck.

Andrew holds a good-bye party for James, whom I never met. I peer intently at the paintings James made and at the photographs others took of him. I am uncomfortable with the people I don't know. James was handsome and vital, brilliant, talented.

My alternating sympathy, fear, and toughness with Andrew are replaced with respect. To live even one more day is a courageous choice. To keep going for 24 hours is a victory. To do anything other than give up is indeed to fight.

At this time, my client is an older lady who is dear to me as I am to her. We simply enjoy each other's company. As I peel carrots and onions, Mrs. Scott is distraught over Rock Hudson's five million dollar mansion that no one will touch. "Why not?" I ask. "Because of how he died," she says incredulously.

"You can't get it from the furniture," I say flatly.

She says nothing.

A month later, Mrs. Scott is despondent again. Liberace's death is imminent. "I don't know why it should get to me so much," she moans.

I do, I say to myself. You love him—with his flashy clothes, soft voice, and candelabra music. You love him, and now you feel that's wrong.

Many more months pass. Because of his job, Andrew is often out of town. I can see he is getting skinny but otherwise seems well.

Outside today in the sunshine of New Year's Day, Andrew is feverish, wild looking, and hoarse. He is giving away pamphlets called *The Art of Living*. I am irritated when he gives me a clinging hug in view of a crowd.

Soon after, Andrew is at home with pneumonia. I avoid going there, both to spare myself and so as not to tax him. Tonight, however, I am needed for he can't be left alone. I drop what I'm in the midst of and go.

Andrew's father is cradling him and speaking softly. This completely new and touching intimacy is broken by my arrival. Dad goes out to wash the dishes before leaving, while I take in my old friend. Physically, he is a wispy shadow of himself, barely able to converse because of the oxygen mask. Yet in his eyes, Andrew is more intensely alive, a will, more than ever, a force to be reckoned with.

This is our last time together, and though I don't know that or don't want to know that, I am compelled to be totally honest. I express my thanks for the ways his life has improved mine. I enumerate them briefly. He is surprised. "You are so full of appreciation," are Andrew's last words to me.

The next day, Andrew is in hospital. I go to visit but he is too weak to see me. I support the others there who love him and come home at midnight unable to sleep. Two of us stay up writing a song for him, or for us, called *Never Give Up*.

At the memorial service, there are 200 people. Their eyes are wet and throats are tight but the air is light. The people with and without AIDS are warm to each other. Suddenly life is precious to us, more precious than all the treasures of the universe.

SECTION FIVE

Equal Rights or More Rights?

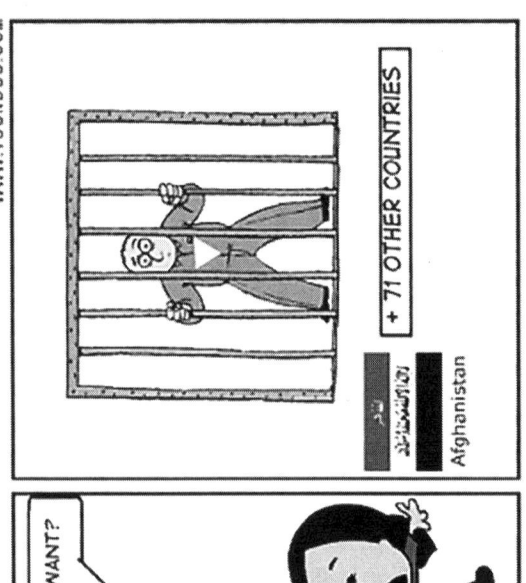

"Equal Rights?" by Chris Morrissey.

Equal Rights or More Rights?

CHRIS MORRISSEY AND CHRISTINE WAYMARK

The Quirk-e group recently worked together with Youth for A Change to hold a public performance of our work. The youth group presented a piece called *The Gay Agenda*. We include this as the first piece in this section, because it speaks to a perennial issue. Older LGBTQA2S+ adults were constantly accused of having a "queer agenda" as we came out. We were accused of asking for more rights. We made many court challenges that resulted in changes to many laws in Canada. Did they result in more rights for LGBTQA2S+ people or equal rights?

KEEPING YOUR JOB—LGBTQA2S+ HUMAN RIGHTS IN CANADA

In Canada, we take for granted going to work every day and, provided we do a good job, keeping our job. We all need to support ourselves financially and to have the ability to pay for shelter, food, and clothing. However, gays and lesbians have not always been allowed these basic rights.

In 1990, Delwin Vriend, a teacher at Kings College in Alberta, was asked by the president of the College to disclose his sexual orientation. He was asked to resign when he said he was gay. He refused and was fired. Delwin had begun as a part time employee. After his promotion to full time, he had positive evaluations and was given a raise. Clearly, the only reason he was fired was his sexual orientation. Many of us, out of fear of losing employment, kept our sexual orientation secret. Some of us were outed, like Delwin. Many of us lost our jobs rather than deny who we loved. Our heterosexual parents, siblings, friends had the right to be open about their sexual orientation without fear of losing their employment. It took several challenges in Canadian courts before gays and lesbians gained the same right.

In 1992, the Ontario Court of Appeal ruled on the omission of sexual orientation, stating that it is a discriminatory practice, directly or indirectly, to refuse to employ or continue to employ any individual, or, in the course of employment, to differentiate adversely in relation to an employee.

In 1993, in Haig v. Canada, the Ontario Court of Appeal found the omission of sexual orientation as a prohibited ground of discrimination under the Canadian Human Rights Act (CHRA) violated section 15 of the Charter. The Court ordered that sexual orientation be "read in" to the Act. This decision protects LGBTQA2S+ individuals from discrimination in employment.

Article 7 of the Canadian Human Rights Act says that it is a discriminatory practice, directly or indirectly:

(a) to refuse to employ or continue to employ any individual, or
(b) in the course of employment, to differentiate adversely in relation to an employee, on a prohibited ground of discrimination.

Human Rights in Canada as a Couple—Benefits as We Age

When a person turns 65, they can apply for the Old Age Security benefit. If that person lives with someone in a coupled relationship, and the other adult is between 60 and 65, and together they have a limited income, the second older adult can apply for a "spousal benefit," so together the couple gets more money.

This was true only for heterosexual couples until 2000. Jack Egan and Jim Nesbit had lived together for almost 50 years. When Jack turned 65, he applied for his OAS. When Jim turned 60, they applied for his "spousal benefit" which was denied because they were a same-sex couple. They went to court in 1995. The Supreme Court judgment said that Jim and Jack were being discriminated against. It also said that it was reasonable to do so. It wasn't until 2000, that the Federal Government passed a law called the Modernization of Benefits and Obligations Act recognizing that same-sex couples are entitled to the same benefits as opposite sex couples.

What we achieved from these challenges is rights equal to rights of those who are heterosexual.

More Rights for All

Queer or Straight: Sponsoring a Partner Takes a New Turn. Sharon, a heterosexual Canadian, was in a common-law relationship with Bill, a US citizen. She wanted to sponsor him to become a Canadian resident, so they could live together. The only way to do that was to legally marry. However, in 1990, it wasn't possible for Canadian Chris Morrissey to sponsor her lesbian partner for permanent residency because they weren't married, since marriage was defined as a relationship between a man and a woman. In 1992, Morrissey cofounded LEGIT, a Lesbian and Gay Immigration Task Force, which lobbied the government successfully so that the definition of "spouse" in the Immigration Act of 2002 was changed to include same or opposite sex common-law partners. That also allowed heterosexual common-law partners to maintain their chosen relationship. By 2003, those of us who wished to be legally married could be.

Life's Beginnings. The birth of Della Wolfe in B.C. in 2013 brought about another necessary change. Her mothers wanted each of them and the genetic father to be on the birth certificate. Canada, like many other countries, allowed only two people on the birth certificate. Their challenge was successful, and Della and her sibling have two mothers and a father on their certificates. Our challenge made it possible for heterosexual couples and a surrogate mother to be legally named on birth certificates. Further change came in February of 2015, when Great Britain, at the vanguard of mitochondrial science, became the first country to respond to the technology of in-vitro fertilization (IVF) by allowing three parents (using genetic material from a third person in the IVF process) on a child's birth certificate (https://academic.oup.com/bmb/article/ 115/1/173/260760/ Social-and-ethical-issues-in-mitochondrial).

Canada Still has Room to Grow (2016). While Canada has made strides in extending rights to sexual and gender minorities, most of these were achieved through individuals and groups bringing challenges to the courts. There continue to be areas in Canada where LGBTQA2S+ individuals are not protected. For example, in contrast to Malta, which is rated the best GSM country in Europe, Canada does not yet outlaw nonconsensual medical interventions to modify sex anatomy of a child, including that of intersex people.

When a child is born, parents are issued a birth certificate that provides name, place and date of birth, father and mother's names, and your sex. Sex is defined exclusively by the baby's genitalia.

When Alex was born, his gender marker was F. As he grew up, he knew that he was a male, making his marker M. He had to apply to BC Vital Statistics to change his birth certificate. Transsexual persons still have to go through this process, an additional burden for transsexual people.

These are some other areas where change is needed to bring about greater equality:

- Gender identity and gender expression are still absent in Canadian human rights legislation. Challenges are brought and won using "sex" as the

discriminatory ground. While there is no explicit federal protection of gender identity and expression, at time of writing, Bill C-16 a bill to remedy this lack is under review in the House of Commons.
- Gender markers on passports leave gender variant people at best in uncomfortable circumstances and at worst in danger for their lives when travelling.
- In Saskatchewan, owners who reside in one unit of a duplex may discriminate on the basis of sex and sexual orientation with respect to the tenants of the other unit.
- The Yukon Human Rights Act defines sexual orientation in a way that excludes minors from protection.
- In Canada, all benefits are either individual or couple based. Bisexual people are forced to either identify as single or choose how they identify themselves as in a heterosexual or same-sex relationship, thus keeping their identity as a bisexual person invisible.

Criminals—In Canada and Around the World. In 1965, George Klippert was the last person to be tried, convicted, and imprisoned because of his sexual orientation in Canada. (In 2016, the Canadian Government proposed giving him a pardon, posthumously). In 1969, Pierre Trudeau, as Minister of Justice, removed homosexuality from the Criminal Code. In contrast, there are currently 73 countries and five entities in various parts of the world where people are still arrested and convicted and 10 in which they may be killed only because of their sexual orientation or gender identity (http://ilga.org/what-we-do/lesbian-gay-rights-maps/). Akiki, a Convention Refugee in Canada, shared a video that he had on his phone. It showed a friend of his being brutally beaten with sticks by a number of villagers. He died. Another refugee claimant had a photo of a friend who had been killed as a result of his being thrown from a tall building. There are many images on the Internet of people being arrested, hanged, and beheaded for their sexual orientation or gender identity.

The Universal Declaration of Human Rights (UDHR) is a milestone document in the history of human rights. Drafted by representatives with different legal and cultural backgrounds from all regions of the world, the Declaration was proclaimed by the United Nations General Assembly in Paris on 10 December 1948. General Assembly Resolution 217A is a common standard of achievement for all peoples and all nations. It sets out, for the first time, fundamental human rights to be universally protected. The first three articles are very explicit:

> Article 1. All human beings are born free and equal in dignity and rights. They are endowed with reason and conscience and should act towards one another in a spirit of brotherhood.

> Article 2. Everyone is entitled to all the rights and freedoms set forth in this Declaration, without distinction of any kind, such as race, colour, sex, language, religion, political or

other opinion, national or social origin, property, birth, or other status. Furthermore, no distinction shall be made on the basis of the political, jurisdictional, or international status of the country or territory to which a person belongs, whether it be independent, trust, non-self-governing or under any other limitation of sovereignty.

Article 3. Everyone has the right to life, liberty, and security of person.

CONCLUSION

The Universal Declaration of Human Rights makes it clear that all people have the same basic rights. However, 73 countries and five entities still criminalize members of our community and several routinely kill them for their orientation. We continue to work for equal rights that have clearly been declared as basic to all human beings. We continue to work towards the goal of acceptance of our right to live and love in the way that is natural to us. In 2016, the most recent United Nations report, acknowledging "that lesbians, gays, bisexuals, and transgender people are victims of 'pervasive violent abuse, harassment and discrimination' in all regions of the world and cit[ing] hundreds of hate-related killings," calls for "changing laws to remove offences relating to consensual same-sex conduct, investigating and prosecuting alleged hate crimes and prohibiting incitement of hatred and violence on grounds of sexual orientation and gender identity" (https://www.theguardian.com/world/2015/jun/02/lgbt-people-suffer-widespread-violent-abuse-discrimination-new-un-report?CMP=share_btn_fb).

Rights have changed, and they will continue to do so; this next section of writing traces some of those changes through the personal experiences of our writers. We begin with *The Queer Agenda* by Syd Oremek, which responds to the idea that queer people who advocate for themselves have a "queer agenda." We follow this with *Gay Blue Jeans Day* by Harris Taylor, which recounts a story of antigay violence on a small university campus in Canada in the 1980s. We follow this with *Youth Rights,* written by our chorus of youth, which examines how queer young people are learning about queer rights. Next up, *Just and Mighty* by Cyndia Cole and *Love It, Leave It or Change It* by Farren Gillaspie shift the tone to take a more optimistic look at how queer rights have changed over time. We conclude this section with an interview between Cyndia Cole and Ellen Woodsworth, who has been working for women's and LGBTQA2S+ rights since 1964 and was the first openly lesbian city councillor in Canada; the interview looks both backwards at Ellen's life's work and forward toward new projects and areas for continued work.

The Queer Agenda

SYD OREMEK

I am here to corrupt your kids, destroy your marriage, and end all peace and order as you know it. Hello, my name is the queer agenda. I am the thing that middle-aged white man fears. I am the whisper in the night, "equality." I am the rock of liberation thrown into the glass wall of corruption and mistreatment. For a long time now, I have been gathering Intel on what you, the ordinary people, hold dear to heart. You cherish your ignorance; if you pretend it is not there, then it simply has no other choice than to disappear, correct? WRONG! That is where I, the queer agenda, shall invade and plant the bomb that will explode your mind. My warriors call it "being open minded." *maniacal laugh* Yes! We shall invade your mind and with us bring all the rainbows and sparkles that we can dare carry, and we shall march to the top of you brain and plant our rainbow flags deep in your mind, and claim this land, "IN THE NAME OF ALL THINGS EQUAL AND FREE!"

"Come"

(Everyone steps forward)

My army of homosexuals will then stand back and watch as the ordinary suburban household crumbles and with it everything good and sane.

(Everyone walks up behind them).

It will begin with the men trading in their beers at the local pub for a pomegranate martini at the clubs; their dirty old blue jeans and lumberjack shirt to be exchanged for bright blue denim cut-offs and a V-neck shirt. The women will begin cutting off all their hair, stop shaving, and wear pants. And as the men slowly stop doing their hard "dirty" work and instead apply for jobs as secretaries, the women will bear-to-arms a hammer and tool belt with which they will construct the rainbow houses of the future. Gay Pride parades would be happening on all streets everyday as people decorate themselves with "Born this way" t-shirts and place rainbow pride flags in front of every house.

All marriages would fail, causing mass divorce in the world. Babies would stop being born because the men would refuse to touch the women and the women would refuse to even be in the same room as a man. There would be riots because of the escalating number of new-found gays who would want to get married and the government would finally have to start listening to the demands of their country. Everything heterosexual would cease to exist and the world would crumble into a rainbow black hole of total gay-dom.

And that would be it. The extinction of the heterosexual race. Ladies and gentlemen, women and men, badass bitches, and sissy boys:

Choral: I am the queer agenda, and you have just heard my roar.

Gay Blue Jeans Day

HARRIS TAYLOR

In 1982, at the University of Guelph in Southern Ontario, Gay Blue Jeans Day yielded a fabric display that I could never have imagined. Flowered dress pants made of gingham, plaid outfits not seen since the Bay City Rollers, skirts of black, red, green that I wouldn't be caught dead in. But, there they were, all students decked out in anything BUT blue jeans.

At Canada's number one agricultural school, the University of Guelph, Aggies ruled. University professors, the Monks of Monsanto, inculcated the minds of their students with the belief that success in agriculture could be achieved only by the genetic modification of plants and animals in concert with the heavy application of chemicals DDT, PCBs, and Agent Orange. These chemicals were responsible for the near extinction of many species in the 1960s and 1970s. But, it didn't matter. The whole point of agriculture was to make money.

The elimination of unwanted species became the biological imperative of Agro-business and the principle of "elimination" was evident in the social values of right wing Christians who widely broadcast their homophobic beliefs. These Christian farm boys hated queers just like their hard-working Aryan brothers did in the Nazi regime. They believed they had a right and a moral obligation to eliminate the unwanted species called "queer," the right to beat the hell out of nonconforming students who cared not to wear the uniform of heterosexual gender compliance.

Those of us in the know knew enough to guard the secret of our lust and love. We met for dances at the old school house at night, at a countryside location that required a car, a password, and a travel group to gain entry. That's where I met Bev at my first gay gathering. She was big, butch and bitchin' as she pulled me close on the dance floor. I remember thinking, "Don't get me wrong Bev, but if a man grabbed me like that, I'd throw him flat on his ass." Bev was not my type, but apparently, she was part of "my community."

The community grapevine conveyed information that was important to note, like the fact that, after we parted that night, Bev stopped at a red light on her way home, was dragged from her car by a bunch of men, beaten black, and left for dead one block from the police station. Covered in blood and dragging herself to the cop shop, Bev was turned away when she tried to report the assault. Cops said, "You're drunk" before they slammed the door in her face. She flagged a cab to the hospital where the doctor had her jaw wired shut because it was shattered in so many places. She spent six weeks in hospital, sucking juice from a straw and receiving syringes stocked with painkillers that promised to cure her. But, nothing could make her the woman that society demanded. Nothing could comfort her. Not visitations from queer friends, not the flowers that I brought, not the promise of spring in a town that delivered such brutality.

Shocked, angry, and defiant, the Queer community rallied, in private to strategize about taking action. It seemed like an ember of political passion flickering under darkening skies. Darker, darker, darker. Quiet. Then the tornado touched down in downtown. Many big trees were lost, reduced to matchsticks, roots ripped up revealing triangular holes in Riverside Park. Springing to action, some secret city worker planted those triangles with pink petunias and Riverside Park became a site of queer resistance, a reminder that we're here, and we're queer.

More than Monsanto makes a crop worthy of harvest.

Veiled

CHRISTINE WAYMARK

The new church is on the opposite corner from where our old one stood. It's a large white building with big oak doors. In 1961, "new" for the United Church of Canada means straight lines and blonde wood. The windows are tall and narrow, with stained glass in an angular design. Inside, a plain silver cross hangs by a chain from a narrow steeple set into a circle of skylights. The electric organ and the choir stall face the pulpit rather than the congregation. The only colour is the blue carpet down the central aisle.

I'm 20 and the first bride to go down this aisle. We wait next to the sanctuary door. Mother confiscated my glasses, so I see a blur. Under my homemade gown, I wear a borrowed crinoline, which keeps me from standing close to anyone. On my thigh is the blue garter mum wore on her wedding day.

My veil is a circle of net with a deep lace edging. I wear it folded into two and gathered into the headdress mum thought might make me look taller.

I don't like it.

Five bridesmaids line up behind me in the English tradition. Made from the same pattern, the long dresses are the newest fashion of flocked nylon over taffeta. The maid of honour wears lavender, followed by two friends in pink and two small flower girls proud in blue. Mum made matching headdresses and fingerless gloves for them all.

I long for the old church. The mahogany pews shone with the buffing of many generations. It was easy to sing out favourite hymns to the music from the gold pipes behind the tiered choir loft. The carved oak pulpit cradled an ancient leather Bible. The deep maroon carpet matched the gowns of the choir. One Sunday, looking down from my place in the teen choir, I'd noticed bobbing and sliding on the pew. As Jean dropped down to the floor, the minister stopped his sermon. "We'll wait until young Jean is back with us," he said gently. Red-faced, she emerged with her shoe in hand. Many of us laughed along with her friend, Robin.

They are here today at my wedding. Jean, a tall slender athletic teen, will walk this same aisle in five years to marry my brother. Curly haired Robin, who has a big smile and a beautiful voice, will take a different route.

It's time.

Mum bustles up and drapes half of the veil over my face, kissing me on the cheek as she does it. Now what I see is even blurrier. The mother of the bride marches down the aisle. I take Dad's arm to go into the sanctuary. As the organist strikes the first chords of "Here Comes the Bride," Dad says quietly, "It's not too late to go the other way."

"Keep walking," I hiss, and we turn for the long walk past the decorated pews, filled with family and friends, to the altar where the men wait. I am about to become Mrs. Reginald Partridge.

I try to look around, but I can't make out who I'm looking at and feel a little queasy as I try. So I look straight into the blur in front of me. The music seeps into my consciousness, and with the words "big, fat, and wide" ringing in my mind, I remember that I asked not to have this music. I dismiss the thought that no one ever listens to me.

I walk with purpose towards the man I have chosen. I know his face well, and my brain fills in what my eyes can't see. I love his dark, curly hair and blue eyes that show his Celtic ancestry. We talk politics and religion. He is artistic and loves jazz. He is gentle and loving with my four-year-old sister, missing his own teenage sister who still lives in England.

Reverend Kennedy begins the well-known words. "We are gathered together …"

I am getting married.

We promise to love, honour, and cherish, until death do us part. I'm modern enough that I don't promise to obey. Reg lifts my veil, placing it gently over my headdress and hair. My eyes have grown more accustomed to seeing, and as we turn to face the congregation, I look at my church full of family and friends and feel the warmth of their support.

I tuck my arm into Reg's, and we stride forward into what I believe will be the rest of my life.

What the Youth Had to Say About Rights

Social justice 12 was the only place I first learnt about a lot to do with the community. With backstories and present stories about the community, I had always been very open minded, but this was the first event that opened my mind further and got me hooked as an honorary queer. (Reba)

WHAT RIGHTS WOULD YOU LIKE TO HAVE WHEN YOU ARE AN ELDER?

The right to renew vows. The right to live in an assisted living with my partner in the same home. Access to hormones and financial aid for transsexuals if finances are tight. (Kaleb)

I hope that the LGBTQA+QIA2S+ community receives respect; as a queer woman I do not have any particular interest in receiving acceptance from a heterosexual community that thinks the right to get married is important and necessary for some of our community. I also think this can be diluting as the fight doesn't end with marriage (which has many benefits but is also linked to capital gain), the right to live with partners in an LGBTQA+Q+ care home, and health care. (Caroline)

The right to request care takers who are aware of queer issues. Doctors who have knowledge and experience working with queer people. That if I or my partner end up in critical care, my partner will be granted the right to decide what to do if I am unable to consent or respond. My partner can live with me in a care home. To be able to go out to queer events. The right to use whichever washroom I want. (Shawnee)

In a utopic society there would no longer be any homophobia; all the seniors prior to entering the care home would have to pass a screening to make sure they weren't homophobic. All clinicians and care home providers would be educated on LGBTQA+Q acronyms, language, and history. It would be as relevant and important as all other forms of training they receive. Partners would have the ability to be referred to by the status they wanted (i.e., girlfriend, husband, partner, and wife) and not as "my friend" because it makes someone else uncomfortable. (Aleisha)

LGBTQA2S+ care home, medical clinics for LGBTQA2S+ seniors, equal marriage, access to same insurance and banks and services, to be able to sign off with my partner (will, power of attorney, end of life papers) and to be allowed to live with my partner in a care home. (Shilpa)

LGBTQA+ care home, LGBTQA+ friendly care workers, LBGT friendly doctors, and the right to love who I want. (Reba)

LGBTQA+Q elder home, allowed to room with my partner, right to be a part of my partner's medical stuff, right to wear whatever I want to, right to wear makeup if I choose to. (Candy)

Who Says We Have All Our Rights?

CHRIS MORRISSEY

The room is stark. Chairs are piled up and lined along an indeterminate beige wall. A few folded grey tables rest along another. Only a skylight serves to light the room, though it's not much use under the greyness of Vancouver skies. An empty bookcase stands in one corner. The outlets are without covers.

An older woman with short white hair unlocks the door and enters. Her white t-shirt is emblazoned with a rainbow of maple leaves. She takes off her olive green backpack and puts it on a chair. She looks around at the tables and chairs, sighing. She arranges a table and a couple of chairs, pulls out her laptop, and waits. She comes here once a month and waits like this. Though there is no clock on the wall, she hears one ticking. Perhaps this will be one of those days that nobody comes. She wonders if she can maybe leave early.

A staffer comes to the door. "Chris, Julie had a call an hour or so ago. There's someone coming who wants to talk to you." Chris sits down again, takes out her laptop, and begins looking at emails. As they download, she sees the headers: "Help!" "Urgent Asylum Seeker!" "Needs Sponsorship!" So many requests. So many desperate people. She begins typing a reply to the first, using the usual template. "Before anyone can help you, you must leave your country …"

She hears voices and looks up, "Here you are," Julie says to the man standing next to her. Chris stands up and moves towards the door.

"Welcome. I'm Chris. Come on in."

He appears to be somewhere in his late 20s or early 30s. He holds a bag close to his chest, his arms locked around it. He sits and looks down at the floor.

"So how can I help?"

"I don't know. Someone told me I should come here. I've been in Canada for several years and I'm afraid I'll have to go home. I can't go home. I've been to see several lawyers but they haven't been able to help me."

"So why don't you tell me a bit about yourself. What's your name? Remember my name is Chris."

"Mohammad."

"Great. Thanks. First of all, can you tell me what your status is in Canada? Are you a student? A visitor? Perhaps your visa has expired? Don't worry. We are here to help you as best we can. We don't work for the government or any other official agency. Can you tell me what country you are from and how you got to Canada?"

"I'm from Malaysia. I came as a student five years ago. My father found out I'm gay and has cut me off. He told me I have to come back. I just can't go back!"

"So how can we help?"

"I don't know. I've been to see several lawyers. Paid them lots of money. I've made several applications and each time I've been denied. I just don't know what to do now."

"Did any of them suggest you make a refugee claim?"

"It never came up."

"Were you out to them?"

"Yes, I think so."

"OK. I'm really shocked that not even one of them suggested a refugee claim. Are you open to making a refugee claim?"

"Anything that will help me stay. I just can't go back. They'll pressure me to get married. I just want to live a normal life. I want a relationship with someone." He looks at the floor again, "Maybe I could even have children."

"Just so you know, in Canada all those things are possible. It is possible for two people of the same gender to be in a relationship, get married, and have children. Now, back to how to stay here. Rainbow Refugee has been supporting LGBTQA2S+ folks making refugee claims for the last 15 years. Most have been successful. Coming from Malaysia, you have a very good possibility of being successful. We can start you off in the right direction. Let me get you a sheet from the other room."

Chris returns to the room, a piece of paper in her hand.

As she reenters the room, Mohammad is standing up, tears in his eyes. Chris approaches him, paper in hand. He throws his arms around her.

It's Not My 77th Birthday. We Got Married

PAULA STROMBERG

Same-sex marriage became legal on July 8, 2003, in British Columbia, the second region in Canada and North America to pass such a law. Just a few months later, my sailor friend Butters, a then 77-year-old lesbian who lives on the Gulf Islands, left an unforgettable message on my answering machine. Don't imagine that being 77 years old renders Butters feeble. She teaches chainsaw graffiti and has lived her achievement-filled life in fierce resistance to ageism and sexism. Woe betide those who dare ask her age, question her May–December relationship, or treat older lesbians as invisible. And if you are her friend, you dare not phone her on her birthday. Butters shouts at misguided well-wishers, "Don't call me on my birthday. It's depressing. Who wants to be reminded you're one step closer to that?" Knowing her birthday had just passed, I was surprised to see Butters' message blinking on my answering machine …

Oh, too bad. It's your voice mail. We're calling with some news. We just sailed home and want you to know we got married Monday. We didn't want a fuss. Just four of us were there. We went to a nice justice of the peace—female—with our friends Sara and Betty on Saturna Island. Eighteen years living together, and now we're married. No family, nobody knew. When our island friends act shocked at our news, we tell 'em we couldn't invite a soul on Pender for fear we'd leave somebody out …

But you know, the real reason we kept quiet that we were getting married was 'cause we didn't want to discuss it. Not everybody, even in our own lesbian community, agrees with this marriage business. But I don't want to hear all those opinions.

I don't care. … And you know, some of my older friends are embarrassed to hear the word "gay." When we were young, you'd never admit openly or say so-and-so was your "lover." It just wasn't done. Even if there was a funeral, it was just "Oh, my friend died." The word "lesbian" was shameful. We covered it up. I was like that 'til I got with Louise 18 years ago. She made me change, and believe me, I had a lot of changing to do—being 59 with a 29-year-old lover. Louise. Oh boy, when we fell in love, we were the scandal of the inlet. Lots of my friends wouldn't talk to me, taking up with a hippie artist half my age. And a proud lesbian at that. So beautiful, she turned heads everywhere we went. Ha! I liked makin' people jealous.

"Now society's changed. Getting married is my right. You might not understand now, but back then, we felt dirty. That's hard to shake. So now the law changed, you bet I got married!"

Just and Mighty

CYNDIA COLE

Maria tells her story to this room of amazing women. From the corners of Canada, tender as 19 and wise as 80, all 65 of us are bonded after three days of talking, chanting, eating, meeting, three days in the fresh air and fallen leaves of October, 2015 in rural Caledon, Ontario at the Buddhist SGI Centre for Culture and Education. We've dedicated these three days to fulfilling Coordinator Kate's prediction, "We come here as strangers and leave as friends."

I've known all along Maria could shake the world with her story, and now I feel the quaking. Her secret sorrow sheltered in the cave is about to become her banner as it salutes us from the summit. She's so tiny, but she holds us spellbound in the big conference room. Earlier, we'd been raucous with singing, dancing, jokes, and skits. Yet, now we are silent, raptly attentive. We hang on her struggle for the words that really say it.

"I was competing internationally on the Mexican rock climbing team and living two lives. When I slipped up in keeping my lesbian life hidden, I was off the team. Just like that. I lost my footing. I lost everything that I loved. I lost my passion. I lost the dream that gave my life meaning."

She speaks in a tongue she has wrestled to befriend for six years. Only one other woman here speaks Spanish and, like most, she is straight. Maria has to stretch for English words but takes it on with grit and joy, just like she took on climbing rock faces in Mexico, Ecuador, and California. She wants us to grasp not just the facts of the matter, but the heart breaking and heart healing of it.

"After the crash," Maria says, "I read that homosexuals had rights in Canada. I left with nothing and came to Vancouver with no money, no job, no friends, no English, no clue. And now I have all these things. I can lead students up the Squamish Chief. My first handhold was making one friend. Through her I made many others. They became my ropes. I won Protected Refugee Status as a lesbian from Mexico even though we are supposed to have legal protection there. I had to find witnesses to swear our lives are in danger there, but they can't witness because their lives are in danger there too. I chanted Nam-myoho-renge-kyo and never let go until I found witnesses in Canada. I am a Canadian citizen now. Finally, after six years, I can risk a visit to my family in Mexico next month. I can return safely to my fantastico new life here. And soon I will find someone who loves me just like I love her."

I ride the wave of exhilaration sweeping the room as we stand for the ovation. We are standing with her now. She has lifted us up. She will never go it all alone again. My efforts to honour and empower her have returned to me one hundredfold. Her victory is our victory. We are awestruck, drinking in the expansive view we have gained. We have climbed up to Eagle Peak, the place of enlightenment, brought along by mi amiga, Maria, Just and Mighty.

Love It, Leave It, or Change It

FARREN GILLASPIE

Love it, leave it, or change it. This has been my mantra for maintaining my sanity. Life is too short to be wallowing for too long.

After five years of a slow burnout in a mental health job in Calgary, I found myself in Vancouver. There was a zero vacancy rate and supposedly no jobs to be had, but in my second week in town, I found a nice two bedroom on the top floor of a three-story walk up. Good, I thought, I can just rest and get myself together before working again. Fear set in the first month, and I sent out two resumes. I was offered one of the jobs the following week. It was a small organization supporting folks with disabilities. No problem, I thought. I'll just work for a year until I find a real job.

Little did I know.

I quickly found out that the core group of board members at my work place were devout Christians.

I can do this, I thought.

I was single, and I didn't offer any unrequested information about my personal life. I had made myself a promise that I would not lie. I firmly believed that if someone asked a question, they must be ready for the answer. Fortunately, no one asked. The parents I was working with had fought long and hard for equal rights for their disabled children. I believed in equal rights for everyone, so we were close. A few years later, I found out my assistant was HIV positive. I was concerned there would be an uproar from the families. I requested at a coordinator's meeting that we have an in-service training to inform staff about HIV, precautions, etc.

The director said, "Well it's obvious. If anyone has AIDS, they have a communicable disease and therefore cannot do personal care!"

I replied, "Another thing that is obvious is that we need an in-service so that you are aware of how HIV is spread. Plus, what happens if one of your children has HIV? The staff could request that they be isolated and refuse to support them."

"Oh I hadn't thought about that, Farren, good point."

We got our in-service training.

Then, I sat on a committee that developed, "respect in the work place." A few years later, we got same-sex benefits.

Two years ago, my partner of 14 years and I attended an award ceremony where they celebrated my 30th year with the organization. One of the founding members sat beside me. My partner was sitting across the table.

The founding member asked, "Who is that handsome man sitting over there?"

"My partner," I responded.

"Really? How long have you guys been together?"

"Almost fifteen years."

"That's amazing! Seems like you both did well! Congratulations!"

My motto continues to be: love it, leave it, or change it.

Taking LGBTQA2S+ Rights to the World Stage

An Interview with Ellen Woodsworth

CYNDIA COLE

Ellen Woodsworth has been actively working to expand women's and queer rights since 1964, over 50 years. In 2002, she became the first openly lesbian city councillor in Canada. While in office in the City of Vancouver, she founded Women Transforming Cities International Society (WTC). In 2005, she set up the City of Vancouver LGTBI Advisory Committee, another first in Canada. This interview focuses on her work to bring the Queer Declaration to UN Habitat 3, a conference sponsored by the United Nations.

CC: Please tell us how the Queer Declaration came about.

EW: In 2015, as Chairperson of Women Transforming Cities (WTC), I was asked and agreed to involve our organization through the Urban Thinkers Campuses in UN Habitat 3, which would take place in Quito, Ecuador, in October 2016. WTC had been working for five years to bring an intersectional gender lens to urban issues. We had held over 32 Café meetings in local neighbourhoods to listen to solutions from women and girls and bring them to the local government. We copartnered in creating *Advancing Equity and Inclusion a Guide for Municipalities*, which includes queer best practices. Over half the world population now lives in urban areas, and queers in particular migrate to cities looking for safety and community.

There were many smaller meetings and conferences leading up to Habitat 3 in Quito. At each of the advance regional meetings, we were working on the New Urban Agenda (NUA), the document of UN Habitat 3, which lays out the basis for global urbanism for the next 20 years. A broad coalition of international women's organizations worked very hard to get gendered wording in the document. I was asked to speak at the Regional Conference for EU/North America, held in Prague, in March 2016. I was very discouraged that every attempt I made to get LGBTQA2S+ into the New Urban Agenda was rebuffed, even by active lesbian feminists. Everyone said it would never get passed. It reminded me of the early days of the Women's Movement. Queers support women's concerns but often do not receive the same support in return.

CC: Did you give up at that point?

EW: No, in May, I was invited to speak to a related meeting in New York. This one was with Human Rights Experts convened by the Office of the High Commissioner of Human Rights and UN Habitat. I thought this might be a chance to get some support. Unfortunately, despite the wide range of global human rights activists involved, I was told publicly that Russia would never allow it. I said, "We have to challenge that," but even those who supported us remained silent. When the statement from the meeting came out there was no mention that we had even discussed the LGBTQA2S+ community. Once again, I came home to Vancouver very discouraged.

CC: What kept you going?

EW: At first, I couldn't see any other vehicle. Then, much to my surprise, I got an email from a Canadian friend in Nairobi who was working for the Youth Division of UN Habitat. He was also concerned there was no wording about either indigenous or LGBTQA2S+ people in the latest version of the New Urban Agenda (NUA). He suggested a Queer Consultation in Vancouver, and I offered to organize it even though we only had two weeks. I invited people who represented queer groups in the wider area. Forty of us met at Britannia Community Centre and decided to create a Queer Declaration. Small groups worked on key sections modelled on the Indigenous Declaration. Then a few of us took it home and began the hard task of bringing together a final document that everyone could agree to endorse. We sent it to national queer groups for their input, endorsement, and help to circulate it more widely. Then we posted it on the Change.org petition site. We got many more endorsements, including from international activists, all in our tight timeline. *Reuters* and *The Guardian* both wrote stories about our fight, as did the UN Habitat 3 newspaper *Citiscope*.

CC: Could the Queer Declaration be included in the New Urban Agenda?

EW: No, by this time all member states had agreed to a final version of the NUA, which had no reference to the LGBTQA2S+ community. The Canadian government negotiators had fought for inclusion of queers up until the final hours of the New York negotiations in September and generated support from the European Union, Uruguay, Mexico, and the United States. Although they had not succeeded, I sent them a thank you letter, so they learned about our work. The Canadian government was very excited to launch an event around LGTBQA2S+

issues and the Queer Declaration together with us in Quito. I received an email from Reuters who did a great article on our work.

CC: How could the Queer Declaration have an impact at Habitat 3 in Quito?

EW: The implementation of the New Urban Agenda is more important than the document itself. Three of us representing the Queer Consultation group went to the UN Habitat 3 Conference in Quito. Representing the Queer Consultation group, I personally gave the Queer Declaration to Dr. Joan Clos, the Executive Director of UN Habitat and asked for his support to ensure inclusion of LGBTQA2S+ issues in the implementation of NUA. He was supportive but said all member states would have to implement it. We set up a panel regarding including LGTBA2S+ issues in the implementation of the NUA hosted by the head of the Canadian delegation Minister Duclos, Secretary Julian Castro from the United States, a Mexican government representative, the Mayor of Oakland California, and two LGTBI activists, one representing *International Lesbian, Gay, Bisexual, Trans* and Intersex Association for Latin America and the Caribbean* (ILGA-LAC). They called upon fellow Member Countries to join in committing to ensure LGBTQA2S+ persons are included in domestic implementation of NUA. There they said "The LGBTQA2S+ community has unique vulnerabilities including disproportionate and extreme violence, discrimination and, in most of the world, lack of human rights protection. Cities are often where LGBTQA2S+ people go to find community but instead often find discrimination and violence. Despite many countries efforts to have them included in the Call for Action of the New Urban Agenda, unfortunately, LGBTQA2S+ persons have been left out. It is time to end violence and discrimination in our communities that target individuals based on their sexual orientation and gender identity." The LGTBI activists announced our Queer Declaration and encouraged the packed room to go to Change.org and sign the Declaration. The panel ended with two drag queens, "Pacha Queen," waltzing in, who were greeted by loud applause. *The Guardian* newspaper then interviewed us for an article. On the last day of the conference, the Canadian government had a debriefing for the entire Canadian delegation, and I again stood up and asked that they show their support for LGTBI2S+ issues by funding LGTBI2S projects. They said they would continue to support our issues.

CC: How will your struggles in UN Habitat 3 affect the lives of individual lesbian, gay, bisexual, two spirit, transgender, and intersex people around the globe?

EW: It will save lives. We know that saying our names, speaking out, and making visible who we are saves lives. We affirm our right to be here, our right to live, and our right to the city.

On October 16, 2016, the United Nations, referring to the extreme violence, murders, imprisonment, and lack of basic human rights to housing, jobs, and safety for the LGBT community, called for laws criminalizing same-sex sexual activity to be repealed around the world.

SECTION SIX

What Does It Mean to Be an Ally?

"Allies," by Nancy Strider.

What Does It Mean to Be an Ally?

VAL INNES

What does it mean to be an ally for queer (lesbian, gay, transgendered, questioning, intersex, two-spirited) folk? The details of that depend on who you are, where you are, and what your relationship to the queer person is, but, basically, an ally is someone who accepts the queer person and provides support and assistance. An ally can be anyone, of any sexual orientation or gender. Anyone who really cares about your right to be who are and is willing to support you come what may is an ally. Allies can support by listening nonjudgmentally, accepting and supporting. Ideally, they should avoid telling the person who's queer that it's not a big deal—because it *is* a big deal. They also should avoid "outing" the person to others without that person's consent. Behaving as if they are sorry for the person is another thing to avoid; a queer life is also a rich life. An ally may be a family member, a friend, a teacher, counsellor, or any other professional.

Family and friends can help by accepting and supporting their queer family members and friends and including them unconditionally in family and friend activities. They can help by respecting the person's choices, by using the pronoun that the person chooses and by accepting the changes in that person's life as she or he becomes more involved in his or her new life as a queer. Family and friend allies can be an enormous support, and so can other people.

A teacher, for example, can create a safe and positive space in the classroom, deal with homophobic bullying and talk positively about lesbians, gays, and transgender people and make queer life normal. School counsellors can help by accepting and counselling, obviously, but they can also educate the school by going into classes and talking about queers in a positive way, challenging homophobia and helping teachers create lessons that include LGBTQA2S+ people.

People with power can use it to be powerful allies. A principal can create a positive space in the whole school. A corporate president or the owner of a small business can set policy in his or her workplace that creates a comfortable, accepting space for queers. A union can do the same, educating members and forcing equality to happen in unwilling institutions. Institutional support makes a huge difference for queers, especially young ones, who are not getting support at home or in their communities. Doctors, nurses, and counsellors who are accepting and supportive can make a real difference in their queer clients' lives, especially in elder homes, hospitals, social programs, and prisons where often the person's lifestyle is, at best, ignored if not judged.

People who are able to be advocates, who have a willingness to be visible, to speak up, and to understand the issues involved will be especially strong and useful allies. Even better is an ally who recognizes that queers have much to offer: we are different than the mainstream culture and have something unique to contribute in terms of self-acceptance, strength, self-realization, and social and political analysis; we will change the culture for the better—politically astute allies welcome and embrace that.

One of the best ways to be an ally, if you're queer, is to be out yourself, leading by example and challenging homophobia when encountered. Queer allies can create a sense of confidence and safety for the questioning or coming out person, and without forcing the issue, help the person feel accepted and welcomed. Being an ally is an opportunity to develop and evolve as a person, to help another, and to face down stereotypes. However, it does bring with it the need to attend to your safety and boundaries, particularly in places where being queer is not safe.

As of 2016, 73 countries and five entities criminalize LGBTQA2S+ people, with 10 countries having the death penalty. In contrast, 76 countries and 85 entities provide protection for LGBTQA2S+ people with antidiscrimination and anti-hate laws (http://ilga.org/what-we-do/lesbian-gay-rights-maps/). Even in those countries, rural areas are often less safe than urban areas for queers, and it is often necessary to think out what you can or can't do as an ally and to know what resources are available. That's also true when helping young queers, particularly those living on the street in urban centres. Queer allies, particularly, need to consider how to offer support and help safely, both for the person they want to help and for themselves in their position or in their geographical area. Having said that, though, queer allies, anywhere, are in more of a position to help questioning people than many others are because of their own experience living as queer. Ultimately, however, the most important thing an ally, straight or queer, can do, is accept and be present as the queer person works through whatever she or he needs to in becoming a fully functioning, secure individual.

Allies can play a key role in the lives of LGBTQA2S+ people in a variety of ways. The writing that follows addresses the impact of allies through the lens of our writers' personal experiences. We begin this section with a chorus of youth responses to the question "Why are allies important?" We then move to Cyndia Cole's *An Ally in Queer Spaces*, which uses the form of timeline to trace a series of allies over an extended period of time. *Boy Do People Ever Piss Me Off* details the challenges of being an ally, which can include uncomfortable or even dangerous encounters. Gayle Roberts' *Dear Parent of a Gender-Variant Child* and Val Innes's *A Letter to School Teachers* address the family and educators of LGBTQA2S+ children and advocate for the significance of adult allies in children's lives. *Ham Sandwiches for No One* by Judy Fletcher, *Cousin Maurice* by Farren Gillaspie, *Jean, the Boy-Girl 1976* by Marsha Ablowitz, and *Gay Pride in San Francisco* by Val Innes all offer personal entry points into experiences with allies and allied communities.

The Importance of Allies

From a Youth Perspective

When I first went to the transgender Britannia Group in March 2004, I finally felt I was where I was supposed to be. I felt comfortable in knowing others who were in my situation and got my first binder; I was able to go camping with fellow transfolk and have a weekend of pure soul searching. It was then I chose to take hormones as soon as I was able to: February 2, 2015 was my day came true. A year later, I am slowly seeing my hard work show through. That group changed me. I started becoming me and I gained confidence. (Anon)

My first queer friend brought me to a queer youth group. I was a very shy person, but everyone there was "out loud," extroverted, and comfortable around each other. I had to get used to knowing it was okay for me to have a voice about myself being queer. I observed everyone and felt so excited to see so many people like me, so happy, and hearing that many of them struggled but were there for me and anyone else in the group. The best part was I could make eye contact and smile at the person I was attracted to and know people wouldn't be disgusted with me. I felt safe to openly be queer for the first time. (Shawnee Gaffney)

One of my favourite places I ever lived when I was homeless was called the House of Faith (or HOF). It was called that because if we had faith in the house we wouldn't lose it. People were constantly in and out, staying from anywhere between one night and quite a few nights. But one of the grandest moments is from when

I first lived there. The mass majority of the population at the HOF were dykes, which is when I found out that it was "okay to be gay."

Me: "What?! It's okay to be gay?!?!"

HOF Residents: "Yes, it is in fact OKAY to be gay."

'Twas a wondrous moment in my young life because for once everything clicked. I felt doors open, trumpets blaring, and dykes screaming "you're one of us." These lesbians at HOF accepted me as one of their own and taught me everything they know about being gay, which looking back on it wasn't much. They taught me what to say to girls, what not to say to girls, and how to tell homophobic gays to shove it. 'Twas a grand start to life of total gaydom, and now here I stand years later, to teach young potential queers that it is in fact "okay to be gay," and that there is no demon inside them telling them to sleep with the same sex. (Syd Oremek)

An Ally in Queer Space

CYNDIA COLE

1962—In seventh grade boys wear oxford shirts with a pleat at the back yoke, topped with a loop of fabric. These are called "fruit loops." Boys are called fruits if they don't cut these off. Fashionable girls wear "virgin pins." I think both are utter stupidity.

1964—My ninth-grade Art teacher is queer. Everyone knows, but no one names it. I like his designs for our spring dance. His "April in Paris" is a world away from our flat Wichita, Kansas.

1967—I visit Greenwich Village with my friend, Jeremy (a girl with a boy's name). Her father heads a poetry society and has a photograph in which he has his arm around Alan Ginsburg. He owns a signed copy of James Baldwin's book, *Giovanni's Room*. Baldwin has retitled this copy *Giovanni's Rum*, showing he's a close friend. I want to be avant-garde and bohemian like Jeremy and her dad, so I expect to seek out artistic and talented homosexual friends.

1968—I am interested in sociology. I buy a book called *The Gay World*. I know it is about the deviant subculture of homosexuals in distant cities. I never read it.

1968—At a party in a college dorm room, a stoned classmate clings to me and asks me to save him from the advances of a man across the room. I feel sad that he fears being gay but glad that he treats me as a safe confidant.

1968—In front of an entire Encounter Group at college, a young man accuses me of coming on to him and then rebuffing him. Then he dissolves into tears, confessing that his father is gay, and he fears he will turn out gay himself. I perceive the others as judging me for being a tease and for failing to save this poor fellow from his shame and fear of inheriting homosexuality. Though enraged, I stay silent lest I be condemned further. I swear off Encounter Groups.

1969—I am involved with anti-Vietnam War, civil rights, and student rights actions. I read pamphlets on Women's Liberation. I also hear about Gay Liberation and a bar called Stonewall in far off New York City.

1969—My friend Steve is called up before the draft board and definitely does not want to fight in Vietnam. He hopes to be rejected as "4F" by telling them he is a homosexual. He thinks his long hair and flamboyant hippie clothes will help convince them. "Of course, I'm not really gay," Steve tells me.

1970—In a tiny college theatre, I watch a movie called *The Boys in the Band* about a group of gay men friends gathered for a birthday party. It's the only gay movie I've ever seen. I think these men don't like each other or themselves very much and treat each other pretty badly. It's not a party I'd want to attend.

1971—My husband and I have left for Canada because we oppose the war. We volunteer to billet seven women from Seattle who are in Vancouver to attend the Indochinese Women's Conference. They bring sleeping bags and lay them out on every available foot of our apartment floor. One of them gives me a pamphlet called *The Woman-Identified Woman*, which makes lesbians sound pretty cool. She tells me she is a lesbian. She's the first I've ever met and not what I expected. She wears an A-line skirt and turtleneck and looks like a secretary. The straight, leftist women all wear boots, jeans, and t-shirts.

1972—I'm a student at university again. I get a phone call from a woman talking in a weird voice. "I've been watching you," she says lewdly. I ask her who she is but she won't tell me. So, I end the call. I feel sorry for her that she has to be anonymous and wrongly assumes I am interested. I think self-loathing is tragic.

1974—I'm in Montreal for the summer team teaching women's studies. One of the older students oddly refers to her lover as "they." My close friend, who is a lesbian, explains the student does it to avoid saying "my lover, she." We all go out one night to a club called "Madam Arthurs." My friend walks out in disgust as soon as we enter saying, "It's all men." I don't really get it—it was supposed to be a lesbian bar.

1975—I spend the summer at Sagaris, which bills itself as "the first independent institute for the study of radical feminist thought" on a university campus in Lyndenville, Vermont. There are 200 women and all but a few of us are out lesbians. It's a real education. I am too embarrassed to tell the woman who comes on to me that I am not a lesbian. When she figures it out she's more embarrassed than I am.

1976—I am no longer married. Despite swearing off Encounter Groups, I decide to attend "Woman Emerging" because it's led by my friend, a feminist therapist. She tells us to remember our dreams to work on the next day. That night

I have three dreams. I dream about kissing Michelle. Then I dream that my father expels me from the family in a rage. Then I dream I am in an earthquake but survive unharmed. It's very peaceful and beautifully brand new after the shaking stops. I don't share these dreams in the group. But that night in the dark, on my couch, I tell Michelle.

Boy Do People Ever Piss Me Off

REBA BROADHURST

I am at a Pride night event at The Met tonight, and while I went outside for a quick breather, I was approached by a man who looked to be late 20s. He began by hitting on me, and I said I was not interested. Then, he asked me what I was doing here. I explained that I was with Youth for A Change, and we were raising awareness of what we do in our community. We are also fundraising. He then became extremely rude and started yelling at me, asking why we are pushing for equality when we are already equals?! I started explaining that LGBTQA2S+ people are actually oppressed and not accepted. He got angry and started screaming that they are equals, we are all equals, and us pushing for gender neutral bathrooms is bullshit. I simply said I'll agree to disagree with you and walked back inside. He approached me again inside and started arguing with me again, to the point of me asking him to leave and walk away from me.

An ally is someone who will side with or support someone or something, whether it be a specific community of human beings or whether it be the events or fights for basic human rights. Being an ally can be challenging sometimes; people don't tend to see the oppression that still exists. Homophobic people assume that an ally of LGTBQ2SA+ people is a member of that community, rather than a straight person who believes in the equality of all human beings despite their identity or sexual interests, but as "one of the horrible gays that lives and breathes on this planet." A lot of people do not understand allies and why they have the urge to push their beliefs on equality, but to me it seems quite simple. We push on the equality of everyone standing on this Earth because we believe that we are no different, nor are we superior to those who are being themselves just like we are. As an ally it is hard to wrap my head around why people still have yet to accept all human beings as they are. I have yet to be affected personally by someone who is in a same-sex couple. And I have yet to see anyone be personally affected by a same-sex couple, a transgender woman/man, an intersex *human being*.

Dear Parent of a Gender-Variant Child

GAYLE ROBERTS

A little while ago your eight-year-old boy dropped a bombshell in your lap. He said he is really a girl. Or, perhaps, your rather tomboyish 12-year-old daughter has told you that she wants to get a boy's haircut and dress more boyish than she already does. You look at her long brunette hair and think to yourself how nice it looks.

"Why do you want to do that?" you ask.

"I've always wanted to be a boy," she replies.

Or perhaps it's your five-year-old, who says little and seems very withdrawn. Worried that he's depressed, you've talked to him to find out what's going on in his head, and he tells you that he saw a television program recently about a boy whose parents are letting him dress as a girl at home. "I'm like that," he says. "I want to be a girl just like he is going to be."

You were scared. You were upset, and you wondered whether you're a good parent or not. You told your partner what your child had said that day. Now you're both worried and wondering what you should do. You don't know anyone else who's gone through this. Relax. You are not alone. Society and the medical profession have come a long way in the last few years. There is support available for you and your child.

Unconditional love is the most important thing you can give your child. Demonstrate this with hugs and kisses and reassuring words. Encourage them to talk to you about their feelings. Listen to what they are telling you. Consult with them. Don't be judgmental. Don't tell them that they are silly. Let them know that you are there to support them not to judge them or, worse, to punish them. Tell them that they are fine, that they are not alone, and that there are many other children just like them. Ask them to tell you what would make them happier and what you can do to make that happen. Reassure them that they are safe.

Now that you have taken care of your child's immediate needs, look after your own, and look after your relationship with your partner. Don't blame yourself or your partner for your child's gender variance; upbringing cannot prevent it or cause it. Consider consulting your family doctor or a children's hospital and asking for a referral to a clinician who has specialized in the management of childhood gender variance. Learn as much as you can. There are many excellent websites that you can visit. Gender variance is no longer considered to be a mental disorder, and it is now considered unethical to attempt to change a child's gender identity. Remember that your child has not chosen to be gender variant; it is part of humanity's rich diversity, just like eye and skin colour and other collective cultural differences, all of which we embrace, not reject.

As you learn more about childhood gender variance, consider joining an organization that supports children and parents just like you. Peer support helps you and your child to learn what works and what doesn't. Such meetings can be safe places where gender-variant children can begin to learn what it is to be the "other" sex in a safe and supportive environment. Consider having your child use hormone blockers if your child, you, and a clinician who is qualified to assess gender-variant children and adolescents decide that transitioning is best; your child will thank you later in life for that decision. Consider educating and seeking the support of your extended family and friends. If necessary, stand up for your child in our still mainly binary gendered world. Sometimes people can be cruel. Be prepared to advocate for your child. Contact your child's school to discuss how they can best support him or her if he or she decides to socially transition. And, finally, take to heart the advice of a Toronto parent with a socially transitioning child: "Look for the hidden blessings. The bad stuff is going to be easy to see. It's going to be right in your face. But there are blessings too. Amazing chances to love and to be loved. To see your child blossom. To find out about your own issues and find freedom from the dark places inside that you didn't even know were there. Look for those things."

Ham Sandwiches for No One

JUDY FLETCHER

I am gay, and I also call myself a Christian. Is that an oxymoron to you? Does it offend you? Do I violate your interpretation of the Scriptures?

The Hebrew texts contain 613 laws. Why does Leviticus 18:22 have such priority for you? ("Thou shalt not lie with mankind, as with womankind: it is an abomination.") The dietary restrictions of the ancient Israelites go on for pages and pages. I hope you don't eat shellfish. Other abominations include cutting your hair at the temples and trimming your beard. Don't forget that you can't plant more than one kind of seed in your field and never wear a garment of two different materials. God knows you would never covet your neighbour's BMW. Because it's such an important statute, I will assume that you sacrificed a year-old lamb when your child was born. We all hope that you don't know anyone who has committed adultery, because if you do you will need to get in a supply of stones.

Picking and choosing which laws you will obey and which laws can be safely overlooked cannot just be a matter of convenience, can it? Is it really about sex? I understand sharing power with women is also an issue. So, is it about sex and power? Or is there just something about living in the 21st century that makes you uncomfortable? The subject that Jesus preached about most frequently was not sex or diet or good grooming practice either. It was money. The New Testament message is about not wasting our "talents" and using all we have to help those in need. Oh yes, and to love one another.

I am happy to be part of an inclusive Christian community, a growing, thriving, dynamic, and thoughtful Anglican congregation. Scriptural Orthodoxy, Core

Doctrines, Constitution and Canons, and Covenant versus Communion are all important stuff, but are they more important than loving one another as God created us? It appears that they are important enough to dissolve the 400-year-old Church of England. So, if it is schism that you want, it is schism that you shall have. The door is open. The door has always been open. If you are ready, be on your way, but don't pack any ham sandwiches for the journey.

Cousin Maurice

FARREN GILLASPIE

Maurice lived in the city; I lived on the farm. Our moms were sisters. He was 10 years my senior, so I never spent much time with him. I remember visiting one time in 1955. The adults were drinking and chatting. I was five years old, and I was bored. I went to find Maurice and saw him lying fully clothed on his bed, embracing his friend Bob. They bolted up. "Don't tell your Auntie or your Mom! Promise!" I shrugged and walked out. Why would Auntie and Mom care that they were hugging?

When I was 13, Maurice visited our farm with his mom and his friend Bob. I played outside. When they left, I overheard Dad say to Mom he didn't feel right about Bob and Maurice together. Maurice was mom's favourite nephew, and she launched into a tirade at Dad. "They are just as married as you and I. Maybe if you cared as much for me as they do for each other." She went on for quite some time. I couldn't understand why it mattered. Maurice just was.

In 1968 Maurice died. He was 26. His mom said it was a heart attack. My mom's youngest sister had died of heart complications when she was 17, so we were devastated, but not shocked. We knew heart problems ran in the family. A few years after Maurice's death, I went to visit my aunt. She had moved to Toronto to live with Bob.

One night, after she fell asleep, I sat up talking with Bob who told me about my cousin. After Maurice's father had been elected as mayor of Cornwall, his father and his mother's brothers had become increasingly ashamed of Maurice. Eventually, they told him he had to leave their city. Cornwall was a small city of about 40,000 people. They rented an apartment for him in Montreal, paid the first few months' rent, and told him not to come back. Bob said they actually threatened him with physical violence. It broke Maurice's heart but he went, and Bob went with him. I had no idea.

When Maurice's father was re-elected to a second term as mayor, they had a fancy dress party with all the mayoral people, wives, and sponsors. Halfway through the party, a beautiful woman in a designer gown, fantastic heels and flawless make-up swept into the ballroom. She floated around the room flirting with all the older men, accepting drinks and offers to dance. Everyone wanted to know who this delightful creature was. She was very coy, and of course that intrigued everyone even more. Then, like Cinderella, she disappeared at the stroke of midnight, never to be seen in Cornwall again. No one except Maurice's father knew the identity of the mysterious beauty.

Maurice's father died before his second term as mayor was up. He was drunk at one of his political parties, fell down a flight of stairs, and broke his neck. Maurice and Bob moved to Toronto as Bob pursued a career in retail. Although he had gotten some retribution, the damage was done. Maurice struggled with rejection and depression. A few years later, he felt he couldn't handle it any longer. He committed suicide.

After all that happened, the family still kept quiet about the reason for his death.

Jean, the Boy-Girl 1976

MARSHA ABLOWITZ

I was chatting with staff at the Kitsilano Mental Health team when I first noticed Jean hanging out in our waiting room. Embarrassed, I looked away. "Why does she have to wear a man's shirt? How come she's got a boy's haircut?" Then Judy, our team Occupational Therapist approached me:

"Marsha, can Jean join your hiking group?"

"Well it's pretty full ... but yah, I guess so."

"She's really sweet ... and Marsha, it might be really good for her to talk with you."

My stomach clenched. Fuck, had Judy told this patient I was gay? Well it was my own damn fault for being out at work. But I was out to my staff, not to my clients.

Jean was a dark slim teenager from the interior, some hick god-forsaken town like Castlegar. Her parents and probably the whole town had kicked her out. She ended up in Vancouver, in hospital and was discharged to Mental Health with a vague diagnosis of manic depression and some sort of sexual identity disorder. She seemed pretty sane to me.

Driving to the hike, I avoided Jean, stuck her in the back seat with Garry, the self-destructive First Nations artist, and Siegfried, the German guy who wore a suit every day and always walked half in the gutter. Jean bounced in the back seat laughing and joking around with the guys. When we parked in the UBC forest I hiked on ahead. She ran to catch up with me as we descended the path.

"Marsha, I heard that gays are legal in Holland."

"Um, yes I've heard that they are legal there."
"Do you think it will ever be legal in Canada?'
"Um ... I don't know."
"And I heard that gays are even allowed to get married in Holland."
"Yes, they are."
"Do you think it might happen here?"
"Maybe, some day. Maybe you could go to Holland."
I sure wasn't all that helpful.

Judy, the Occupational Therapist, asked me how Jean did on the hike I said "Fine." Actually, I was starting to really like Jean. She was smart, lively with dark eyes, and a quick smile. When I'd see her around the Mental Health team I'd always say "Hi." Then one morning at the staff meeting Judy was frantic.

"Jean missed her appointment. She never misses her appointments. She's never even late."

"Maybe she's left town."

"I went to her rooming house. Her landlady was worried. She's just disappeared. Everything in her room is totally neat. All her stuff is still there."

A few days later, a police officer called Judy. Jean's body had been found in the bushes under the south end of the Burrard Bridge. Judy's business card was in Jean's pocket. After meeting with the cops, Judy was crying.

"Marsha, the police say Jean jumped off the bridge. How can they just decide that? Jean wasn't depressed or suicidal. She didn't leave a note. She was so happy when I talked with her last session. She'd just met a nice girl."

"What do you think happened?'

"She used to walk home from that gay club downtown. She couldn't afford bus fare so she'd walk down Burrard and across the bridge. I told her it wasn't safe. Guys had been hanging out on the street outside the club at closing time. They had been stalking her and threatening her. The police don't even want to investigate."

"Um ... okay, Judy. I'll talk to the police."

The police officer agreed that he would find time to come over to our office. He was a gigantic guy standing very straight in his crisp blue uniform, looming over me. He had all the accessories: silvery badge, wide belt, shiny leather holster, and gun.

"Why aren't you going to investigate her death?" I asked.

"No need to waste our time. We know what happened."

"How can you know without investigating?"

"We're experienced. We know what we are doing."

"But officer she wasn't depressed. Men were following her. She might have been attacked."

"No, we know she jumped. She had a reason. We have evidence."

He smirked down at me. My throat was dry. I looked down. Finally I said:

"What reason, what evidence?"

"They do it, those people."

"What?"

I couldn't speak.

He shifted, hummed and hawed, sort of chuckled and cleared his throat. "Well she was … you know … she was one of those … homos … You know, she was a girl-boy."

A Letter to School Teachers

VAL INNES

As you may be aware, there are queer kids in most school classrooms. Some of them find adults who support them—teachers, parents, or guidance counsellors. They may be members of Gay-Straight Alliances or have friends who support them. Sadly, however, many do not have any support. In worst-case scenarios, they are teased, bullied, and even assaulted. At best, they have to listen to unchecked homophobic comments and slurs. Coming out can be a complex and gradual process, not just an overnight thing, as teens go through a process of questioning and "trying on" different identities. Most don't become gay and self-accepting overnight. As they are caught up in this "in between" stage, they can be uncertain, confused, and thus particularly sensitive to the homophobia and transphobia that surrounds them. Young people have an urgent need to belong, and of course, the classroom is an important space of belonging.

Change can be, and usually is, a slow process, and in the meantime Lesbian, Gay, Bisexual, Transgender, Queer (LGBTQA2S+ and questioning) adolescents must survive, and form their identity, many of them in an often hostile environment that, at best, silences and marginalizes them and, at worst, victimizes them. As a result, they have higher rates of emotional and behavioural difficulty, depression, and suicide, and they experience more hostility and bullying than their straight peers. The statistics are clear about that, as a 2009 EGALE/University of Winnipeg study points out:

- Three-quarters of LGBTQA+Q students feel unsafe in at least one place at school, such as changing rooms, washrooms, and hallways.

- Transgender students are especially likely to see these places as unsafe (87 percent).
- Three-quarters of all participating students reported hearing expressions such as "that's so gay" every day in school.
- Half [of the students] heard remarks like *faggot, queer, lezbo,* and *dyke* daily. Over half of LGBTQA2S+Q students, compared to a third of non-LGBTQA2S+Q, reported hearing such remarks on a daily basis.
- Six out of ten LGBTQA2S+Q students reported being verbally harassed about their sexual orientation.
- Nine out of 10 transgender students, six out of 10 LGB students, and three out of 10 straight students were verbally harassed because of their expression of gender.
- One in four LGB students had been physically harassed about their sexual orientation.
- Almost two in five transgender students and one in five LGB reported being physically harassed due to their expression of gender.
- On a good note though: current students were significantly less likely than past students to report that school staff never intervened. (http://egale.ca/wp-content/uploads/2011/05/EgaleFinalReport-web.pdf)

Your classroom is a good place to make these students feel they are in a safe place where they can learn to make meaning out of their lives. Your LGBTQA2S+ kids probably don't have parents who are their role models, and the violence they experience may come from their families as well as their peers, so making school safe and inclusive for them is even more important. It's easy to think that because Canada has gay and lesbian civil rights and same-sex marriage, all is well, but you have only to look around you in the typical school or university to note that LGBTQA2S+ presence is notable more by its absence than anything else—in curricula, events and what's up on the walls. And in or out of school, homophobic violence still exists. As Janoff comments in *Pink Blood: Homophobic Violence in Canada*, over "40 percent of the queer-bashing incidents I analysed involved teenage assailants. Can there be any better reason to support anti-homophobic education in schools" (p. 245)? Making your classroom inclusive and dealing with homophobia in school not only protects LGBTQA2S+ youth but also educates and changes potential teenage violent offenders.

If LGBTQA2S+ kids are approximately 10–11% of our student population, as statistics would suggest, they need to be represented at that level in the readings you use, the books you choose, the questions you form and the examples you use. Do you have lesbians, gays, bisexuals, and transgender people in these materials as well as straight people? Do you know who was or is LGBTQA2S+ in your field? Do you need to become more educated about that? (Check out Wikipedia for a list of 700+ famous LGBTQA2S+ folks in different fields). If LGBTQA2S+ folk remain unmentioned in your classroom, if homophobic statements pass by without comment, if all your students see or hear about in your classroom is heterosexual, you're missing out on an opportunity to educate the homophobic kids who might become bullies and to include those queer kids who need a place to belong, to explore, and to find themselves safely.

If you create inclusion, you're not alone; a lot of work has been done. Depending on where you are, there should be resources available to you through gay and lesbian groups and Gay-Straight Alliances in your area. If you are not in an area which has these resources, you should be able to contact gay, lesbian, and trans groups in the nearest major city who can help. For example, in British Columbia, Canada, groups such as Gay and Lesbian Educators of BC (GALE BC), Gay-Straight Alliances, Pride Education Network of BC, McCreary Centre Society, and the BC curriculum itself have LGBTQA2S+ teaching resources. You can reduce homophobia and transphobia by having positive LGBTQA2S+ visibility in your curriculum, by encouraging your school to have Gay-Straight Alliances, Pride events, and LGBTQA2S+ space, and you can deal firmly and immediately with homophobic remarks or actions in your classroom and in the school. You can create a classroom and institutional attitude of respect and inclusion.

As the saying goes, if you're not part of the solution, you're part of the problem—and the solution is clear. One of the reasons I'm writing this letter to you is a memory I have as a teacher that I have never been able to forget. It's a memory of an older teenage boy in our school who hanged himself in his apartment because his lover and he split up. He wasn't found for 10 days, so lonely and isolated was his life. Had we provided a safe, inclusive place for him to talk, perhaps this would never have happened. It changed the school, granted, but not in time for him.

Thank you for taking the time to read this letter. I hope your school is inclusive and safe for LGBTQA2S+ youth, but if it is not, I hope my writing this to you will make a difference in it in time for the next suicidal queer kid.

Yours sincerely,
Val Innes, B.A. (Hons), M.A., B.Ed., M.Ed.

Gay Pride in San Francisco

VAL INNES

One thousand dykes on bikes fill the streets
from Harleys' women in leather butch and solid
to minibikes and cute femmes
and everything in between
they fill streets

cordoned off
closed down
streets and streets of us
a whole city celebrating
us

a day long parade

gay boys strutting naked and plumed just a thong
beads and feathers dancing down the street
to cheers and laughter

bare breasted women leather dykes strong women
beautiful women thousands of women
float after float
colour beauty fun

friends of queers
hundreds cool and there

crowds thirty deep beyond counting
cheering yelling dancing laughing
crackling energy

and us monitors chanting, dancing
gleeful holding hands and filled with pride
with us with who we are—

gay pride

SECTION SEVEN

Born or Made

"Born or Made," by Cyndia Cole.

"Born AND Made," by Gayle Roberts.

"If It Ain't Broke …"

GWYNETH BOWEN AND NANCY STRIDER

When the question is raised as to whether queers are born or made, we're finding that most of us consider the question largely irrelevant as we echo Popeye and declare "I yam what I yam" without needing any longer to justify, explore or explain how we got to where we are. That said, for many struggling with questions about orientation and/or gender ID, and life changes depending on these questions, or for their parents, friends, or allies, the questions might well be important. Others become curious when a family turns up multiple queer members and when they begin to trace a pattern back to earlier generations as they support or celebrate a newly out child.

Until quite recently, queers were judged as broken and needing to be repaired. They were seen, in some religious traditions and cultures, first as "sinners" who intentionally broke the rules and then as "sick" people, incapable of following them. In Europe and North America at least, these attitudes have shifted, as people realize that since being queer does not mean that one is broken, no "fixing" is required (or desired). This is a big change. Before we talk about it further, however, let's go back and look at the history of more homophobic perspectives. It's important to know where modern homophobia comes from. Internet sites such as Wikipedia.com and ProCon.org, and news sites like CBC.ca are compilations of points of view that connect to a range of information. These resources were useful for the following synopsis of the search for a "cure" to being queer.

Many traditional religions (though not all) have historically regarded queer behaviour as sinful, and have applied a punitive, harsh, morality-based, judgment.

Queers were assumed to have control over how they experienced sexual attraction and gender. "Unrepentant" queers were seen as intentionally dishonouring themselves and others by breaking the rules of God and undermining marriage bonds. Some texts from early Judeo-Christian times, for example, some letters attributed to St. Paul, and some from the Old Testament, have been interpreted as condemning queers. Paul's Epistle to the Romans 1:26–27, around 55–57 AD, is still being used as the scriptural basis for ongoing condemnation. It appears that Jesus himself never directly condemned same-sex love, or at least, the Bible doesn't tell us so.

In the mid-19th century, a secular medical model began to emerge where queers were seen as "sick" rather than "bad," even while their behaviour continued to be condemned. In 1857, Tardieu argued that "inveterate sodomites" suffered from a form of insanity. This was regarded as a more compassionate approach than that taken by many religious people, since, if the impulse to the activity was not under the individual's control, then it was not their fault. However, it was still generally assumed that the queer behaviour was "bad" and needed to be stopped, and that the individual needed to be fixed, so that they no longer felt or responded to the impulses that had resulted in those actions.

There were two streams of thought about the causes of the "illness" of being queer that resulted in difficulty relating "normally" to the opposite sex:

"Born"—That there was an inborn physical or mental problem

"Made"—That the person had become queer as a result of life experiences

The "born that way" stream of thought began in the 1860s with the first use of the term "homosexual" in 1868 by Kertbeny, who called it a natural behaviour, and in booklets published by Ulrichs between 1864 and 1879, which said that homosexuality was a "third sex" and should be decriminalized. In 1896, Hirschfeld proposed that all people were bisexual at one stage in the embryonic state, but homosexuals fail to have this recede. Influential concepts followed that were less compassionate. In 1897, it was proposed by Ellis that homosexuality was the result of "an inborn perversion of the sexual instinct, rendering the individual organically abnormal." During the first couple of decades in the 20th century, Steinach's experiments with transplantation of testes and ovaries in lab animals led to the theory that these secretions were responsible for "sexualization" of the brain. In 1917, he claimed that a transplanted testicle from a heterosexual man had "cured" a homosexual one.

The "made that way" theories began in the early 20th century. Between 1900 and 1923, Karsch-Haack wrote about homosexuality as a social construction and not a medical problem, and suggested that there were other reasons for same-sex behaviour besides an innate drive. But the concept that homosexuality was an acquired problem gained ascendency in the West after the Second World War. In 1952, the American Psychiatric Association officially classified homosexuality in the *Diagnostic and Statistical Manual of Mental Disorders* as a mental illness. In 1973, the state of being homosexual was declassified, but it took until 1987 before a related "disorder" was also removed. There were a number of theories as to how parental or social influences could turn a child who had been born "normal" into a queer, most of them based upon Rado's theory, proposed in 1940, that homosexuality is a pathological phobic avoidance of the other sex due to parental prohibitions against childhood sexuality. For example, in 1962, Beiber attributed homosexuality to a detached father and domineering mother.

In 1905, Freud proposed a theory that combined "born" and "made." He visualized an inborn universal bisexuality, with individuals having varying mixes of tendencies toward the masculine and the feminine, with life experience also shaping the emergence of a sexual identity. In this framework, it was proposed that homosexuality could be a normal developmental outcome for some people. He did not see it, by itself, as a problem that needed a cure.

Whether the cause was seen as occurring before birth or after, for the most part, the underlying premise remained that the queer behaviour was "bad"—unnatural and harmful to both the person doing the activity and their partners—and should be stopped. For example, in 1920, the US Military criminalized sodomy, and in 1942, the US Military used a medical rationale to set up procedures for rejecting gay draftees. But in 1957, a "revolutionary study" by Hooker "challenged the widespread belief that homosexuality is a pathology … and provided evidence that normal homosexuals existed." In 1991, she received an award from the American Psychological Association for her work.

For the most part, however, the cultural response during the middle part of the 20th century had largely been to seek a way to make the queer person change, or at least to stop acting on their desires. Most treatment approaches were not as compassionate (or as realistic) as Freud's. They varied, depending on whether the "cause" of persistent queer behaviour was seen as something wrong in the body or brain, or whether it was seen as being due to an experience. An extreme example of using the physical medicine model with adjustment of hormone levels as a primary tool was the 1944 implantations of slow-release drug capsules into homosexual prisoners in a Nazi concentration camp. In 1976, Dorner suggested testing and correction of amniotic fluid in pregnant women. As recently as 2007, Reverend Mohler, President of the Southern Baptist Seminary, suggested prenatal treatment, if it was proven that homosexuality has a biological basis, as an "appropriate means to avoid sexual temptation and the inevitable effects of sin …"

In 1936, Moll used the "made that way" illness model to develop the concept of association therapy, which would convert the homosexual to heterosexuality by reversing the queering effects of environmental influences. Others followed Moll's lead. For example, McIntosh (1968) described homosexuality as a social label, and Gagnon and Simon (1973) saw it as socially scripted behaviour.

The "conversion" approach (also called "reversion" or "reparative") is another extension of Moll's theories. Both Masters and Johnson (1979) and Spitzer (2003) were influential in promoting this kind of treatment, although the research in each was disputed. In 2012, Spitzer apologized to the gay community. In North America, most current conversion therapy is belief-based mediation sponsored by religiously oriented groups, such as "ex-gay" organizations that cite research such as the 2011 study by Jones and Yarhouse (also disputed) as justification. Organizations such as the Catholic Church now advocate the approach of hating the sin, but loving the sinner, but, as Pope Benedict said in 1986, homosexuality is still considered "an objective disorder." The church still expects queer Catholics to remain celibate.

Recently, scientific research has provided support for a "born that way" model that is a nonjudgmental alternative. As we saw, as early as 1864, the "third sex" framework had proposed that queers had just been born with a different set of needs than "normal" men and women. In the early 1980s, the influential Kinsey Institute used frequency statistics and survey data to suggest that queer behaviour be normalized as a "fundamental predisposition." This could be seen as a precursor of the current trend where "born that way" is seen as interesting information which does not imply that there is anything that needs to be fixed. Indeed, Lady Gaga's iconic song has elevated this slogan to epic proportions in the queer community!

Published in 2011, *Gay, Straight, and the Reason Why: the Science of Sexual Orientation* was written by Simon LeVay, a gay British/American doctor. It gives us a detailed look at some of the research that approaches the topic from many angles, from the earliest theories and assumptions to the newest and most reliable studies. The research he looks at is compiled from studies of animal and human physiology and behaviour, and it supports his theory that individual genes influence prenatal hormone levels (mainly testosterone), which influence the sexual differentiation of the prenatal brain, leading to certain gender traits, including sexual orientation. These are also, LeVay believes, affected by environmental factors and random variability. LeVay's book concludes this way:

> The biological perspective on sexual orientation stands in marked contrast to traditional beliefs, which have remained largely silent on the origin of heterosexuality while ascribing homosexuality to family dynamics, learning, early sexual experiences, or free choice. There is no actual evidence to support any of these ideas, although we cannot completely rule out that they play some role. In my view, differences of opinion on this score often result from differences in what we mean by sexual orientation. Biological factors give us a sexual orientation in the sense of a disposition or capacity to experience sexual attraction to one sex or the other, or to both. Other factors influence what we do with those feelings.

What's missing from the book's careful conclusions, though, is any exploration of the "other factors" mentioned in the quote above. All human beings, and maybe especially we queers, have the absolute right to define ourselves in any way that seems like a fit. Each of us gets to live in any (nondestructive) way we decide to, and to state our belief about how we arrived at that way of being. Our choices may be influenced by, or based on, social factors, our life stories, or our political convictions and goals, but then so are everyone's—straight and queer alike.

As we said earlier, neither the "born" nor "made" models necessarily imply that queers need fixing. As early as 1935, Sigmund Freud famously advised a mother that a cure was not only unlikely, but also unnecessary. He said "homosexuality is assuredly no advantage, but it is nothing to be ashamed of, no vice, no degradation; it cannot be classified as an illness; we consider it to be a variation of the sexual function, produced by a certain arrest of sexual development."

Increasingly, there has been a cultural shift away from searching for a cause of homosexuality in order to cure it. Since the mid-20th century, research studies such as Green's (1978) about parenting styles, and Isay (1989) about the effect of dominant mothers, began to refute that people became queer due to poor parenting. The American Psychiatric Association stopped classifying homosexuality as mental illness in 1987, as we saw before, but it has also issued a position statement opposing reparative or conversion treatment (1998). In 2012, the Mayor of London forced the removal of bus ads claiming a cure. CBC news reported, during the 2015 Canadian Federal election, that the Conservative Party dumped a candidate who had written an editorial entitled *Is it Wrong for a Homosexual to Become a Normal Person?*

These days, queers are pushing back and refusing to be labelled as outsiders because of who they find sexually attractive, or how they experience their gender. We are moving away from the restricting cultural frameworks that had labelled queers as both the "breakers" and the "broken." This century marks a positive shift away from seeing queerness as a problem and towards acceptance.

In 2013, Pope Francis said, "If a person is gay and seeks God and has good will, who am I to judge?" The same year, Exodus International, an influential American "ex-gay" religious ministry that had claimed success with conversion therapy, closed its doors and apologized. Another positive development is the increasing respect for the capacity of youth to claim a queer identity. The last five years have seen a growing North American political momentum to ban conversion therapy for minors. California (2012), New Jersey (2013), and Ontario (2015) have passed such laws, and, in 2015 US President Obama called for a nationwide ban.

Also, there has been a re-emergence of the proposition that queer behaviour can be, at least for some, an active political choice, rather than the passive consequences of biology or postbirth experiences. The question "Why are you queer?" is increasingly an academic one—a moot point of most interest to scientists. None of the three possible sources of queer behaviour—"born this way," "made by experience," or "chosen preference"—have been proven or disproven by researchers. It is being proposed that the determinants of queerness are likely to be a mixture of all three: an inborn physiological "possibility"—a mix of genetic and embryonic influences—that results in an infant who self-selects into an orientation through a mixture of experience and choices. The only thing we do know for sure is that the queer individual can not only come to terms with who they've been, who they are, and who they want to become, but that they can claim, love, and celebrate themselves as perfect.

We begin the creative work in this section with two comic strips (above) that set out to disrupt and complicate notions of gender determination. The first rejects the idea that "born" and "made" are mutually exclusive possibilities, as it suggests that gender identification is perhaps a combination of both. The next cartoon flips the question that queers are often asked (Why are you queer?) as it points out that the question is rarely asked as those who identify as heterosexual. We follow this with a story written by Gayle Roberts, a transgender woman, who writes about her early dawning, and unshakeable, sense that she has been assigned the wrong sex. We conclude with three pieces from the youth. The first, by Aleisha Ross, *Do I Have the Right to Write?* complicates the question considerably as it voices the confusion that is generated by the very existence of labels. The second, by Skylar Cogswell-Shears, also resists the male/female binary as it suggests that gender is a spectrum. The final two pieces—a prose poem and a graphic poem by Candy Fine—end the section with a fitting representation of how restrictive our social conventions around gender can feel to those who can't or don't choose to, fit them.

The Girl in the Pond

GAYLE ROBERTS

"Remember, Michael, don't let go of my hand," my mother cautioned me as the crowd surged forward towards the edge of the platform. The train belched black smoke and white steam as it entered the station, and I felt her hand tightening as she pulled me towards the opening coach doors. Soldiers, sailors, and airmen flooded out of the coaches, dropped their kitbags and swept their wives and children into their arms.

As my mother pulled me around one of the celebrating families who blocked our path, my attention changed from the coaches to the man. He was wearing an army uniform and could easily have been my father. He was big even though he was kneeling down with his arms wrapped around his daughter. He kissed her tenderly on the cheek, supported her in the crook of his arm, and then stood up. With his other arm, he pulled his wife towards him and the three of them embraced. The soldier's daughter was about my age and, like me, had probably just started school as she was wearing a gray pleated skirt with matching knee-high socks and a green jacket with a crest on the breast pocket. Her shoes were black and, unlike my lace-up shoes, had narrow straps that went over her arches and buckled to the sides. But, it was her hair I noticed in particular. It was the same colour as my own, but, unlike my short back and sides, hers was long, loosely curled, and cascaded over her shoulders to swirl around her face as she moved. And then she was gone as my mother relentlessly pulled me towards the waiting coaches.

As we got closer, I noticed other families. A few of the women held their arms outstretched while holding their loved one's hands. I could see one woman staring into the eyes of her serviceman husband. She stood transfixed by the immensity of the parting, and then, in one smooth motion, he swept his kitbag onto his shoulder, followed us into the waiting coach, closed the door, lowered the window and waved. He waved until his wife could no longer be seen.

"Would you and your boy like this seat?" one of the soldiers asked my mother as he picked up his kitbag and swung it into the overhead rack.

My mother nodded. "I was worried about getting a seat. It takes a while to get to Oxford."

"Are you visiting friends?" the soldier asked politely.

"I'm going to see my husband for the first time since he was shot. He's a paratrooper … perhaps I should say he *was* a paratrooper. He was shot in the leg on a drop in Italy." My mother then turned to me and asked, "Would you like your colouring book?"

I shook my head, pulled up my knee-high socks, and stuffed my green cap with its gold braid into the back pocket of my new-for-the-trip gray short trousers. I turned away from the soldier and stared out at the passing bombed-out buildings. I used my jacket sleeve in an attempt to clean cigarette smoke from the inside of the window but gave up when I realized that most of the grime was on the outside. Then, my attention changed to the train. Ever since I had seen it enter the station, it seemed like a huge beast held captive by unknown people who forced it against its will to do their bidding. It puffed and wheezed in protest as its masters coaxed it into motion; its wheels had complained loudly as they alternatively slipped and grabbed the rails. But, as it gained speed, I sensed its anger at being forced to drag the coaches and the people within them subsiding. It became free. Now there was only effortless motion and the soothing clack of wheels on rails.

Then my mother and I were walking through the park-like grounds of the hospital. As we walked through a grove of tall and stately trees, we discovered a pond. The path split and my mother and I separated as I chose the one that led to the water's edge. I felt at peace. It was the only place I had ever seen that didn't show the ravages of war. For a few minutes, war-torn England did not exist. As my mother walked on, I stopped and stared into the pond and looked at my reflection. I stared at long, loosely curled hair that cascaded over my shoulders and swirled around my face when I moved. And then, through misted eyes, I saw my shoes were black and had narrow straps, which went over my arches and buckled to the sides.

"Come on Michael," my mother said, as she waited where the two paths rejoined. "Stop daydreaming. Don't you want to see your father?"

The girl in the pond stared back at me for a moment longer, and then we parted. My mother and I walked across a lawn to the hospital. Once, it had been a stately home but, at the beginning of the war, it had been commandeered as a rehabilitation hospital for wounded servicemen. My father's bed was in a large room that opened onto a garden. His leg was wrapped in white bandages, held up at an angle by pulleys attached to the ceiling, and his upper body was encased in plaster which, when I tapped on it, sounded like a drum. Strangely, I felt reassured; the solidity of the plaster confirmed that he was alive.

"Do you want to play cowboys and Indians?" my father asked, pulling me across the bed where I was sitting and onto his cast where I now found myself astride a horse. He bounced me up and down as best he could, and I broke into bouts of laughter as I slapped the sides of my horse with my hands and dug my spurs into the bed. We played horsy until my father could play no longer.

"Do you want to play in the garden?" my father asked.

"Can I play by the pond?"

"You won't be safe there," my mother said. "You can play anywhere you like in the garden as long as you're not out of sight."

As I climbed one of the many trees in the garden, I could see my mother and father talking while she held his hand in both of hers. Then, it was time to go home. My mother hugged my father as best she could and kissed him. I climbed once more onto his cast and tapped it several times. Despite my protests, my father rubbed his stubbled chin across my face and deposited a wet kiss on my cheek. Then we left.

We didn't walk through the grove of trees, but the girl in the pond was with me. I couldn't see her clearly in the train's smoke-stained window. But she was with me.

Do I Have the Right to Write?

ALEISHA ROSS

At the forefront of my brain is the question of whether I have the right to even contribute or write a piece representing someone else who is "actually" queer.

What gives me, someone who has yet to confidently "come out" as a 21st-century lesbian, the right to comment? Do I identify as a lesbian? No. Do I identify as heterosexual? No, not exactly. And do I ever intend on having a "coming out story" published somewhere or being whispered about between family and friends? No, absolutely not. Then when asked, "Are you gay or straight? (which happens often) how should I respond? Is there a politically correct response?

If I call a woman my girlfriend, if I tell her I love her and can see myself marrying her and raising children with two moms stead of one, does that make me a lesbian? (That may be jumping the gun a little, but you get my point.) I fell in love with her soul. I did not fall in love with her genitals. Her genitals are what originally drew me to her, that and her long black hair, but the reason why I stayed, the reason why I continue to stay is because of all the things I can't see.

Introducing her to friends is easy; the friends are the family you choose for yourself. Telling the family is the tough part and continues to be the most difficult. No "Mom," (insert serious look), "Dad" (insert double serious look), "I have something to tell you, I'm gay." It will read something along the lines of "Mom, Dad, Donna—the girl that's been around lately, she's my girlfriend." The end. No crying. No, "I will never have grandchildren." No, "How will we tell our friends?" If their being embarrassed or ashamed about their daughter's happiness is an issue, then we have much bigger problems to address.

I'm convinced my mother thinks I'm going through a phase. But I've got other things to worry about.

If people are born gay, do I have the right to claim that identity as my own? Never would I have thought I could have such an intense argument with myself and lose every time. So with that being said, here are the things I do know: I have never been happier with a partner, male or female, nor have I ever been more attracted to anyone in my life. I feel like those two points alone must count for something, I'll have to remain in the middle, with Switzerland. I do not identify as gay, nor do I identify as straight. I exist somewhere in the middle. I'm sure hundreds of thousands of lost souls do as well (I hope).

So kind stranger, if you exist and if you are reading my words, I say to you find a partner that brings you so much joy and love so that for whatever time you two have together it gives you the life to do all the wonderful things you want to accomplish.

An Inner Yearning Yet to be Named

FARREN GILLASPIE

This particular morning I was feeling bliss as my bicycle tires crunched on the gravel road unwinding behind me. When I reached the Baker place, Mr. Baker was herding his cows into the milking parlour while his wife clanged around in the milk house setting up the strainers. I skirted around the fresh cow droppings and waved as I went by. The word "escape" seemed to whisper in the cool morning breeze blowing through my hair. I wanted to shout out, "Not me!" I had a job now. I would get away. No matter where I was on our farm, I would be fantasizing about the day I would be someplace else.

This was my second week at the peat bog. Next week, I would actually get my first pay cheque. Not that it mattered. I had already spent it. I had ordered a steel blue Brother typewriter from the Simpson Sears catalogue. My mother was furious that I had squandered my money. What could I want with a typewriter? Earlier she had said that I would end up lazy if I read too much, so I hid under my blanket at night reading with the light of a banged up old flashlight. It was then that I not only fantasized about the characters, but I also dreamed about someday writing about adventures that some young boy like myself would read.

The bog was an interesting place to work. I had been hired very quickly. Country boys got preference over city boys since they already knew how to use most of the machinery. The city boys were always getting their tractors stuck or running their fork lifts through the tin walls of the storage sheds. Sometimes they would show up for work in sneakers, and the foreman would send them home until they came back with safety boots. Light tan coloured Kodiak boots were the accepted norm for farm boys. We wore caps from the local machinery dealers with logos like Massey Ferguson, New Holland, or John Deere stencilled on them.

The peat company supplemented their small full time crew of older men by hiring students like myself in the summer months. On dry days, peat particles floated through the air finding their way into our hair, ears, eyes, nostrils and even inside our clothes. On wet days, the air was filled with the dense rich smell of long dead ancient seabeds. Occasionally the bog would catch fire, usually from a careless smoker but sometimes from the exhaust stacks of the diesel tractors. When that happened, the bog would smolder for days and a foggy haze would envelop the area. The smell would drift for miles. My grandfather said it reminded him of his boyhood when they burned peat in their ancestral home in Ireland.

The two groups of men, old and young, did not mix very well. The older men seemed to relieve their boredom by constantly teasing and tormenting the younger men. They would staple their shirttails or their caps to the peat bags, hide their lunch kits or for the ultimate reaction, fill condoms with liquid soap and put them in the lunch kits. The more the young guys reacted the more they were picked on. One area that both intrigued and repulsed me was the lunch shack. The building was actually a repair shop that served double duty as a lunchroom. It was a long narrow building with a window at one end and the door at the other. Workbenches lined both sides with stools positioned in front of vices every few feet along. Lunches were stored at the far end on shelves on either side of the window. The lunch pails were pretty much all the same, black metal containers that were reminiscent of the covered wagons on Death Valley Days. The only differentiating details were decals that had been stuck on, missing handles or dents. On the walls were many calendars, most expired but retained for their artistic contributions. They usually had buxom women leaning over classic old cars or sometimes holding a large tool. The Snap On calendars usually had scantily clad women with their own tool chests. A lot of the calendars came from the farm machinery dealerships, but they sure didn't look like any that my Dad or Grandfather were given.

The older men always seemed to get to the lunchroom first for breaks and at lunchtime. They would perch on the stools in front of the vices. When the young men came in to get their lunch kits, it was like running a gauntlet. The older men would grab our asses or our crotches as we tried to quickly walk by. They would offer insightful comments like, "I wonder if his cock is long and skinny like his legs," or with that skinny ass he won't do the girls no harm, no ballast, no weight behind the ram!"

I quickly learned to skip snacks and just hang outside by the pop machine. That is where I got to know John MacKenzie, as we sipped frosty Fanta pop. He never hung out with the other older men and quickly became my oasis of safety and comfort. We didn't talk about much other than the weather or the job. I was content just to find myself drawn into his sparkling blue eyes. His tanned face was always framed by two or three days' growth of beard. He wore a blue and white striped railroad cap with matching bib coveralls and a tattered t-shirt underneath. As the day became hotter, the t-shirt would come off and there would be John MacKenzie with just his coveralls and his Kodiaks. He would often swab his forehead with a wrinkled old red and white handkerchief while sweat ran down his hairy chest and the back of his neck, disappearing underneath the coveralls. I would often fantasize about whether he was wearing underwear or not and if so, what kind? Then I would quickly catch myself and wonder if I had to confess this thought to Father LaPierre. I had never had that kind of intense eye contact with anyone before especially a virile handsome man like John. He always seemed genuinely interested in me, always smiling and engaging. I always found myself resenting the call back to work after our break. One time one of the older guys poured half of a cold pop into John's gaping coverall pocket while he was deeply engaged in conversation with me. I didn't realize what was happening until he slapped his pocket and jumped. Pop squished out of his pocket while the rest seeped through the dense cotton fabric. Anybody else would have cursed and chased the perpetrator. John just laughed, looked at me and said, "That should keep things cool down there for a while." If he was insinuating anything, it went right over my naïve young head. Anyway, it was soon to come to an end.

    The next week while riding home from the bog on an old bicycle refurbished by my father, I popped a wheelie going down the hill near our farm. The front wheel fell off and as the forks dug into the gravel I was flung over the handlebars landing on my shoulder. The result was a greenstick fracture on my collarbone. For the rest of the summer, I wore an over-sized t-shirt and looked like a football player I would never be.

    My Dad drove me down to get my pay cheque the following week. I was hoping to see John but he was out in the bog, so I never got a chance to say good-bye. Memories of John MacKenzie faded into the background, but he had awakened an inner yearning within me that had yet to be named.

Gender Is a Spectrum

SKYLAR COGSWELL-SHEARS

Gender is a spectrum. There isn't only biological male or biological female; there's transgender female to male (FTM), male to female (MTF). But that's not all; there's so much more. There's gender-fluid, gender queer, hell there's even bi-gender, pan-gender, a-gender, gender-flux, and a whole lot more than that. I know of at least 33 different gender identities. Did you know intersex people don't choose to be intersex? They're actually born that way. So there are actually three biological genders, male, female, and intersex. Intersex people can choose to live as a male or as a female; they can choose to do surgeries to "fix" themselves, or they can choose not to and live the way they were born. Now with anyone else under the transgender umbrella, FTM or MTF, they were also born this way. They were just born into the wrong bodies and didn't get the natural amount of testosterone or oestrogen that they were supposed to have. You know, everyone thinks we're different and that we're the freaks, and they laugh at us for being different. Well guess what? We laugh at all of you for being the exact same normal and boring. Now, as for the other identities I listed out, they can be whoever they want to be; they don't have to be strictly male or strictly female; they can be both or none at all. They can be one or the other or just whoever they want to be. They don't need hormones or surgeries, but that doesn't mean they can't go on hormones or do the surgeries. They can if they really feel the need to do that, but if they do the surgeries and do hormones, that still doesn't mean they are female or male. If they don't want to be that they can still be whoever they want and whatever gender they want.

John Doe Android Instruction Manual

GAYLE ROBERTS

AMBROSIA ANDROIDS

Ambrosia Androids is a supplier of superior androids worldwide. We stock Home Androids and Professional Androids for homeowners and small businesses. Ambrosia Androids is the world's largest supplier of military grade androids. All our androids are fitted with genuine Ambrosia Androids parts. Accept no substitutes when replacing parts or upgrading your Ambrosia Android.

Congratulations on the purchase of your Ambrosia John Doe Android.

Opening Your John Doe Container

- Your John Doe container contains one (1) complete, human, male patterned, fully functional android.
- If you ordered the Deluxe Model android, it will be wearing clothes. Our Regular Model is naked. Provincial and Federal laws require all androids to be dressed culturally appropriately when in public.
- Open the container cautiously if you are using sharp instruments. Clothing and delicate parts of your fully functioning android may be cut, damaged, or severed.

Switching on Your John Doe Android

Your John Doe android is placed face down in the container so that you may easily activate the ON/OFF switch located just underneath the hairline at the back of the neck. To activate your android, move the switch from the OFF position to the ON position.

Jane Doe Androids

If you chose our Super Deluxe android, your container includes a Jane Doe sex change kit along with culturally suitable clothing.

- WARNING! Use extreme care when interchanging male and female sex parts on your android.
- The positronic brain of your android is extremely sensitive. Under NO circumstances should you interchange male and female sex parts on your android without first switching it OFF. Your 12-month warranty on parts and labour is void if your android is damaged by mixed male and female parts.
- Male sex parts are in the BLUE BOX labelled MALE PARTS and female sex parts are in the PINK BOX labelled FEMALE PARTS.

Gender-Variant Androids

Other than for research purposes, all our androids are engineered to express stereotypical male or female behaviours. In the unlikely event that your android exhibits mixed male and female gender identities and expressions, we recommend the following:

- Switch the android OFF and then determine if it has mixed male and female sex parts. If it does, make sure the android is OFF and then replace sex parts as necessary so that your android is entirely male or entirely female. Switch your android back ON and monitor its gender identity and gender expressions.
- If the problem continues, REBOOT your android by switching the power switch to the OFF position, wait five seconds, and then switch it back to the ON position. This will usually resolve your android's gender variance.
- If mixed gender identities and expressions continue, we recommend ONE of the following:
  - Contact a factory android technician and arrange for the installation of a replacement positronic brain at no charge should the fault occur within the 12-month warranty period on parts and labour.

- OR, alternatively, consider keeping your gender-variant android. Many android owners tell us that they are fortunate to own a mixed gender android, as the condition is rare. We advise that before choosing this option, you ask your android if it is comfortable with its gender variance. If it is, simply enjoy the added diversity your android brings to your home. If your android, with your approval, prefers a permanent sex change, switch it OFF and install the appropriate sex parts as discussed above. Our android owners report a marked improvement in their android's demeanour and its efficiency after the sex change. If you choose this option, we will refund you the difference in cost between the Super Deluxe and Deluxe models. Please note that if the unsuitable cross-sex clothes have not been worn, you may return them to our factory for a full refund (less the Industry Standard Restocking Fee of 15%).

Ambrosia
The Food of the Gods
Ambrosia Androids
A Lifetime of Quality

As the Spotlight Shimmers

CANDY FINE

As the spotlight shimmers down across my sequin dress I feel whole. As if it was telling me that in this moment, I am who I was meant to be, and in that split moment of every second or every hour of every day is frozen. I am no longer stuck thinking that I can't be who I really want to be. I feel free. As the spotlight shines down on me in my sequin dress, I am now who I am supposed to be.

Looking in the mirror, crying. Wondering, why I was born the way I am. Why me? Why can't I have been born the sex I was supposed to be? Sitting, seeing a male in the mirror were there should be a female. I ponder, is life always going to this cruel to me? Every day walking down the street people call me Sir or say "he's a nice guy." I try so hard for people to see me as a female, as she. I go home every night and before bed I look in the mirror. I look to see if I had magically changed and every time I am sadden to see HIM. Looking back as if he was mocking her, mocking me

Candy Fine

"Looking in the Mirror," by Candy Fine.

SECTION EIGHT

Youth and Elders

About Youth and Elders

MARSHA ABLOWITZ AND FARREN GILLASPIE

Youth and elders have much to offer each other. Elders can take comfort in knowing that they have supported and even nurtured the dreams and goals of the youth. Youth can take pride and satisfaction in knowing that an elder has respected and admired their contributions and that they have value. Formerly, only the straight population has had the full support of religion, their family, and their culture. In the queer community, that has been almost nonexistent until lately. Now, some churches, synagogues, Buddhist groups, and others are becoming more gay positive, encouraging support groups, such as gay-straight alliances, antibullying awareness, same-sex unions, and so forth. Adoption is now possible by same-sex couples. The corporate culture is recognizing same-sex benefits such as pension plans. There are television shows now with not only gay characters, but gay roles in leading positions. Ellen DeGeneres has been voted most popular in a talk series. In BC, Canada, people like Sven Robinson, Libby Davies, and Ellen Woodsworth are familiar names, respected as out and contributing members of our community. International celebrities like David Bowie, Elton John, kd lang, and others have been proving that their queerness has not only not hindered their success but, in many cases, has accentuated their success.

However, there are some challenges along the way. The basis of any healthy relationship is trust and safety. For a lot of us, our journey has been based on the opposite, distrust, and fear. Both camps will often wonder why does this person want my friendship, what do they want from me? When our male culture has been hidden behind closed doors and often based on anonymous sex, and lesbians and transgendered folks are often hidden, it is difficult to be open and trusting. There is often the fear of perception from others. For the elder, it's the stereotype of the "chicken hawk," a paedophile, or someone who is, "recruiting." For the youth, it might be the perception that they are using their bodies to seduce and gain financial security or material comfort, the perception that they really don't have anything to offer other than their bodies. This can be an actual truth for youth who have been forced from their family homes. They have had little alternative than to turn to sex for survival.

There are divisions between elders and youth around the world. In many places, youth have no choice but to obey their elders. In the Western world, youth have more freedom; however, divisions exist between elders and youth based on differences such as power, wealth, lifestyles, mental and physical abilities, and generational values. Sometimes these differences make it somewhat difficult for youth and adults to find close connections with each other outside of family or school. In the LGBTQA2S+ community, due to the lack of intergenerational LGBTQA2S+ community events or LGBTQA2S+ family celebrations, often youth and elders don't even meet and talk with each other. When we do get together, if we wish in-depth rather than purely superficial contact, the elders need to look past the wild youthful energy, the clothes styles, and hair, and tattoos. Elders can learn from the youth culture. Youth need to look past the slower pace, wrinkles, and old fashion style and see what the elders have to offer. If one considers long-term relationships between generations, we mostly have successful families as our models, and young LGBTQA2S+ people may adopt more supportive elders if their own families are not too helpful. However, if we consider long-term intimate or loving relationships, one enters a minefield. Though an elder man in our society may court and marry a much younger woman, LGBTQA2S+ elders may fear accusations of child abuse if they even offer a youth a ride to the bus stop. There are some examples of very successful elder-youth relationships in the LGBTQA2S+ community, but youth are at real risk of abuse from predators, so how are they to know whom to trust?

Many elders value connections with the younger generation above everything else. However, since many LGBTQA2S+ elders never had the opportunity to marry and have a family they have no children nor grandchildren. Some LGBTQA2S+ elders wish friendship with youth in order to feel connected with future generations, play with children, and to pass on stories, history, and culture to the next generations. Also, elders remember well the problems of growing up in homophobic schools and families. Many LGBTQA2S+ elders have spent much of their lives fighting homophobia, racism, fundamentalism, and class prejudice. They have witnessed and experienced police harassment as well as oppression and prejudice in schools, in churches, and on sports teams. The elders have often also had very helpful mentors and friends along the way. These elders with their knowledge and experience wish to help LGBTQA2S+ youth have a better life. Both elders and youth in the LGBTQA2S+ community, like all oppressed people of the world, must face and overcome difficult challenges such as harassment, lack of access to health services, poverty, homelessness, and isolation. Internalized prejudices can lead to poor self-images and to self-destructive feelings. Community support between the generations can help us overcome these problems and move beyond them.

We begin this section with a piece by Jake Marchbank that underlines the importance of intergenerational work, and a piece by Shawnee Gaffney that describes the reverse experience of familial rejection. We, then, move to two pieces *In the Shadows of the Moment* by Val Innes and *Widowhood* by Chris Morrissey, which confront the challenges of being older and LGBTQA2S+. Following this, a short piece by Candy Fine expresses the frustration of being a young person whose voice is not always heard. *My New Moccasins* by Stephen Hardy, *Psalm 69* by Gwyneth Bowen, and *Backflips* by Cyndia Cole all address the significance of intergenerational relationships between youth and elders. We close this section with a witty and contemplative poem, *Shards and Scree*, about aging and friendship by Maggie Shore.

What We Queer Youth Have Got from Working with Our Queer Elders

JAKE MARCHBANK

I'm lucky. I'm not one of those youth that have no connection with their elders. I actually have three queer parents so my perspective is one of queer privilege. Having said that, I know that not everyone has the opportunity to interact with queers older than themselves. Working with Quirk-e these past few years on all the different projects has given me the chance to interact with seniors whose attitudes differ greatly from my own grandparents on issues of identity and sexuality—nice to know that not all people over 60 think the same way—but I do see how they had to live lives affected by homophobia and transphobia. Maybe it was those negative experiences that made the seniors very careful about how they could be with us. We know they were warned not to offer us rides—which might have been useful at times—but never mind, because then we just queered the SkyTrain!

You know we youth don't have much access to queer histories. We have to really search out in libraries and online. A lot of what we find is from the United States. In my house what's mostly available is from the United Kingdom. Meeting with the Quirk-es gave us youth an opportunity to learn what it was like to be a gay boy in rural Eastern Canada; to work in social work in the 1960s; to learn about the Vancouver bar scene and those mystical things known as lesbian bars which now no longer seem to exist!

A few years ago, we queer youth were being told, "It just gets better"; meeting the Quirk-es shows us that a queer life is difficult but that you can accomplish so much. Thank you Quirk-es.

Queer and in Care

SHAWNEE GAFFNEY

Home was not safe—not a place you wanted to be. It wasn't calming, nor exciting. Not even boring. I knew that I wanted to leave, but I was waiting for the right moment—that moment when the cops can no longer pick you up as a runaway and take you back to the house. That moment is your 16th birthday. I started planning how I would leave, long before my birthday. I grew more scared and excited the closer it got to that day. I had finally come up with what I thought was a genius plan—get kicked out! In order to get on a youth agreement, you cannot have a place to go.

Though home was not safe, my family wouldn't kick me out. My girlfriend was 14 years old and was already out of her home. So her house was not an option—she's had troubles with it for many years.

I had fun getting kicked out. I did what every teenager wants to do—party every night, skip school when I wanted, stay up for as long as I wished, and be with my girlfriend every day. Getting on a youth agreement is not as easy as I thought. When I called the first time to apply, I learned where the system begins with its flaws. When you apply, the office calls your house and asks if you are welcome back. Of course, many parents say "yes" because they don't want social services to get involved with whatever is going on in your home. I was no exception.

Refusing to go back home, I began my journey of homelessness with my girlfriend, who had so many experiences with this already. We stayed in many houses together. It was hard to couch surf with two people, but, as she pointed out, it's safer. We grew close; we had seen each other in our angriest and happiest moods.

We relied on each other, trusted, and loved one another. We accepted each other for what we were. Prior to this relationship, I had never experienced anything of the sort.

One day, I did a speech for local community workers about homophobia in schools. This is where I met the person who changed my life. She was a youth worker with Options Community Services. At the end of my speech, she confronted me, which led to me getting a youth agreement. I got into a semi-independent youth house. I was relieved and thought I could get my partner on a youth agreement as well. The house was nice, but so new to me. It was scary because I didn't know what the other youth in the house thought about gay people. My housing worker had even outed me to someone before I had gotten to meet them, which could have ended badly. Despite all my efforts, I couldn't get my partner on a youth agreement. In this new world of living with strangers in government care and rules, I soon learned that I could not have my girlfriend stay with me.

I was no longer used to this. My values had changed over the period of being homeless. I was no longer fighting for only my safety, but my partner's too. I couldn't leave her to sleep in a stranger's house while I was in a warm bed with food. I tried to talk to the supervisors, but they couldn't do anything about it, as it is not in their power. My girlfriend and I grew frustrated. I would stay out throughout the night with her on the nights I felt too scared to sneak her in.

After all, I could get kicked off the youth agreement I had tried so hard to get on.

In the Shadows of the Moment

VAL INNES

What lurks in the shadows of growing old? Fear. Loneliness, death, pain, diminishing capability, indignity, and dependence. Being stuck in a heterosexual old folks' home. Losing your partner. Take your pick. I'm afraid of having a heart attack and my dog being stuck in the house with me, perhaps for days, definitely for hours, before someone rescues her. I'm afraid of dying painfully.

If I had had a family, perhaps, I wouldn't fear all that. I know, though, from watching straight friends with their adult children, that having kids isn't any guarantee that they will be there for you when you're older. But they may be. In my family, we were there for both my parents. So here comes another fear. I watched my father disintegrate from the twin attacks of Parkinson's and dementia. From a brilliant, physically and mentally competent man, he became broken, unable to think or to move for a long time before he died. That's my major fear, gibbering in a tiny corner of my mind, and every time I walk into a room to fetch something which, by the time I get there, I have completely forgotten, I have to remind myself forcibly, that everyone else at my age also has this fear.

And what to do about all this?

Nothing. Everything. Walk through the fear; make faces at it; it's the only thing you can do.

Widowhood

CHRIS MORRISSEY

I don't know whether to scream or burst into tears.

My name is Chris, and I'm a widow. Not that I think of myself in those terms. Single is the word that comes to mind. Anyway, according to some, even to myself, how can I be a widow? After all, I was in a common-law relationship and a same-sex one at that. So, does that explain the experiences that are giving rise to my extreme feelings?

It all began … well who knows where it really began. With my partner Bridget's dementia diagnosis? With her death? I suppose her death is what gave the most immediate rise to the events that followed.

There's so much paperwork that has to be done when someone dies. Paperwork is the last thing on the survivor's mind. In fact, there is very little on my mind. Mostly, it's what's in my heart. I guess the experts would say that it's all in the mind. The heart has little to do with it all except keep the blood pumping and oxygen moving …

But I digress. Back to the paperwork. Many years before Bridget died, we had agreed that cremation would be the way our bodies would return to the earth. The company that I engaged to carry out that final task made an appointment to come and do the necessary paperwork. See, I am getting to the point!

So, there I was sitting at the dining room table with the employee tasked with doing the paperwork and getting my signature giving the company permission to cremate Bridget's body. The employee had arrived at the front door, kicked off her high heels, and come through to the dining room. I think she must have introduced herself but if she did, I can't remember. She pulled a folder and envelope out of her bag and spread out in front of her a couple of forms that clearly were for me to provide information and signatures.

With the mechanics done, they only took a few seconds. She raised her eyes from the table and said,

"So is it your husband who died?"

My eyes focused on her fingernails. Must be a new style. Stones encrusted, artificial diamonds,

"*She* was my common law partner."

I decided to let a couple of days pass. Well, decided isn't the right word. Sadness left me paralyzed. It would take a few days for the anger to kick in. Anyway a couple of days later, I made the call.

"Hello. This is Chris Morrissey. I'm calling about the person who came to my house for me to sign papers for Bridget Coll's cremation. I'm calling because when your employee arrived she asked me if the person who had died was my husband."

"Just a minute while I get the file."

She must have been sitting next to the filing cabinet because she quickly said. "Well it says on the file that you are her partner."

"I don't care what it says on the file. I'm telling you what happened."

What happened next was unbelievable. Well, it was to me! One more time. I heard, "Well it's in the file."

That's when I lost it.

"Listen. I'm calling to complain. I don't care what the fuck it says on the file. My partner just died, and it shouldn't be my job to educate your employees. I don't want her coming back. Don't want to see her ever again."

Click. I hung up.

Oh yes, I did eventually get an apology from the owner when he brought Bridget's ashes. Even then, I was the one to bring up the incident. It took him a while to come up with the words "sensitivity training." I was tempted to tell him I'd do it.

You'd think that things would go smoothly after that. Forget it. I'll spare you all the gory details of the next painful, insulting interaction. Access to money is critical when someone dies. Imagine my surprise when I used our credit card and it didn't work. Sometimes it's the machine, so I went to the second machine. What the heck! Didn't process my card either. Next on to the cashier. This was the pits.

"Your card's been declined."

Many phone calls later, and I'm standing in the credit union branch signing an application for a new card. The teller knows the background story. Well I thought he knew the back story. I'll just give you a synopsis. Bridget was the primary cardholder and me the secondary.

"Didn't they tell you that when your husband died the card was cancelled?"

It seemed pretty clear to me that we were both women, with names like Bridget and Christine. Sound like my husband?

"*She* was my common law partner."

They say bad things come in threes. So, I shouldn't have been surprised! Yup, you guessed it. Next I had to advise the investment group that managed our retirement fund.

Don't get excited. I didn't. We don't have that much in our fund. But since I'm Bridget's beneficiary, I had to tell them that she had died. Naturally that meant more paper work. And another person to tell the story to.

"The company wants to know what relationship you had with the deceased. For the forms. What shall I put down? Friend?"

We had been clients of this company for around 20 years! And there was a file.

"*She* was my common law partner. Put that," I said.

What's the mystery? I just don't get it. We live in a very enlightened part of the world and one of the best cities for this kind of thing! Or so I thought. So, what is it? People can't or don't read these days? Are they incompetent or very sloppy workers? Perhaps.

I don't, I can't believe that all these people are homophobic. Heteronormative? What? My spell check doesn't recognize the word. No spelling suggestions appear. One click: LEARN!

Wish I could hit a button and change the world! And if *you* don't know what the word means, go look it up!

Youth

CANDY FINE

When you're young you hear people saying that the youth are the future, and yet we ignore them. We tell them that they don't know what they're talking about because they are young. And as you get older, you tend to think that youth don't know what needs to be changed because they have not experienced life yet. But if they are our future, we need to listen to them because they will have to live in the world that we leave for them.

My New Moccasins

STEPHEN HARDY

"Here they are Stevie. Grandmère made them for you."
I looked at the light brown leather moccasins, at the rawhide laces around the tops. I inhaled the smoky leather smell. But what overwhelmed my eyes was the beads, the coloured flowers on the top of each foot, each flower carefully sewn with brightly coloured beads. They sparkled in the low winter sun, blue, red, some green. I noticed the circles of beads, not full circles, only arcs, with smaller ones inside, forming layers of coloured arcs, like the petals of a flower.
"Here, let's try them on," said my mother.
Timidly, I placed my left foot in the one moccasin.
It fit!
My foot felt cuddly and warm inside, as the soft leather enveloped my toes, up to my ankles.
"Let's lace them up!"
She tied the rawhide laces around my calves. Now my whole foot and lower leg felt warm and snug.
"Now the other one."
With the second one on and laced up, my feet felt light and free, as if I could run and run through the snow!
Stepping outside the back porch into the snow, I looked up at the kitchen window. There was my Grandmère, her round dusky face and soft kind eyes looking down at me.
She smiled. I smiled back as I ran into the snow!

With the laces done up, my feet and calves felt warm and snug. I really liked that feeling. It was safe. I didn't have that feeling very often. When I did have it, it wasn't safe. When my mother cuddled me, she was always drunk, and I couldn't trust her. I never knew what she would do. Would she smother me, like she did with my baby sister? Would she pass out with her arms locked around me, so I would be trapped, unable to escape?

But with the moccasins laced up, I felt warm and snug, but safe and free! I could run as fast as I wanted. No heavy boots, just light moccasins, snugly laced up around my feet and calves. Safe and free!

Safe but also free! That conjunction of feelings was to become my goal in my life, governing my choice of friends, my choice of career, my choice of partners. Safe, but free! Warm and cuddly moccasins, but free to run, run away, run from the ties of my baby crib, the ties of my baby high chair. Tied, never free.

"Li Gens Libres"—the free people, yes! That's who I was! Free! Freedom to go where I wanted, when I wanted. Free to run away, run far away from the drunken craziness, freedom to run in the snow, free to disappear into the woods, free to find my two spirits! Free to explore who I would become.

Psalm 69 (and All the Other Numbers)

GWYNETH BOWEN

O ye parents, ye elders, ye wise teachers, hear now my plea:
    for there is no time to be lost.
May the young ones revel in the Spring: it is their own true season.
Smile ye as they come nubile together; yay, bless them from afar as they frolic
    in the sun and in the moonlight.
For their smooth, strong limbs burn to run and play: their blood glows
    and verily merrily must obey the electric pull of flesh to flesh
    that then they may find bliss in sleep. long and untroubled.
The unloving ones, the desiccated, miserable, predatory or hidebound ones
    shall be made to lay off, and shall be corralled away from the lustful young
    things
        that they may be insouciant and juicy
        may jubilantly kiss whomever and wherever they wish
        and be curious as to the possibilities of protuberances and orifices.
Enquire not about the details of their playful or urgent exploring, for the stories
will be theirs alone
    to whisper lickingly in each others' ears, or anon to fuel moaning solo
    action replays.
Yo, I thus entreat thee: for now is the time of the engorged peak of their desirous
discoveries:
    and their memories, unsullied, will be their enduring pleasure;
    yay, even unto death.

Backflips

CYNDIA COLE

Jake is six. His cherubic face is round and flushed. He is popping up and down, bursting with excitement. He wants his Auntie Bess and me to be his audience. There is nothing more important than for us to listen while he sings "Rudolph the Red Nose Reindeer." He has choreographed moves and a solo part at the Grade One Christmas Concert. This makes school worth bearing.

He rehearses in his grandma's living room. For each run through, Jake calls out my name and beams, "Watch this!" Despite the triteness of his material, I am drawn in and held by his unbounded enthusiasm (although by the tenth rendition, my attention starts to wander).

Bess' entire family is theatrical or what she calls "artsy fartsy." His grandparents have only recently retired from their tours on the stages of the world. I love the glossy promo photos plastering their study. Their colleagues were these flamboyant vaudeville and variety show artists from the 1930s all the way through the 1980s. Bess and her three brothers all have day jobs but perform their passions on the side. Her nephew's antics seem entirely ordinary to me in this long line of performers. So, I am jarred when I overhear Jake's mum confessing to another relative off in the kitchen that she hates her son cutting out women's costumes when he plays with scissors.

When Jake asks Bess and me, "How many bedrooms do you have?" his mum just about loses her lunch. When he asks, "Can I come over to your place for a sleepover?" the frost his mum sends out is Arctic. "Too bad he can't," I think, but keep to myself. Jake waits until she is safely out of earshot to ask in a whisper, "Can two boys ever get married?"

We just say "Sure," and let it rest there.

Twenty years later, I find out where all this leads. After Bess and I split up and I disappeared from the family gatherings, Bess says Jake blamed her with unremitting resentment.

Today, I am so stunned to see him again, doing backflips while singing into the mike at the Stonewall Festival. He is a featured performer. I buy his CD and once he is off stage, we exchange a sweaty hug.

"What acrobatic dancing!" I say with admiration.

"Thanks, I've won a lot of gymnastic competitions, he says with a shrug. "You look just the same."

I am touched, and don't mention that I can barely recognize him. He's no longer pudgy and cherubic. But he's still popping up and down, craving applause, just like I remember him.

Shards and Scree

MAGGIE SHORE

Ellie and Doris smile at each other
across the cafe table, sipping chamomile tea
between tidbits of news,
their white hair two halos of light.
Ellie suddenly brightens over an important
insight about their trip to Reno.
She is preparing to speak,
her mouth poised, savouring the taste
of the first words.

A long pause hangs between them.

"Dammit Doris, I had this great idea
I was going to tell you, something about …
and it just went 'poof', disappeared
as if the words had leaped off a cliff
and fallen into darkness."

Doris replies nonchalantly:
"If you don't use it, you lose it."

Ellie sniffs into her yellow hanky
and dabs her eyes,

wonders aloud:
"God, Doris, where does that stuff go?
Those unsaid things that just disappear
a whole sentence formed in your mouth—gone.
It happens to me a lot these days."

"Oh dear," Doris offers. "Don't you worry so."

Ellie continues:
"All those words and ideas -
gone in a flash, dropped into oblivion,
wherever that is. Maybe those lost fragments are just
lying about at the base of the cliff,
piles of dark shards and scree of lost memories."

"Well dear," said Doris, "Maybe they're recycled, who knows?
So let's head back now. You know they don't like it
when we're late for supper."

SECTION NINE

Tips and Tricks for Living Queer

"Untitled," by Gwyneth Bowen.

"Hetero Lessons," by Bill Morrow and Cyndia Cole. Believe it or not, this is a true story!

On Giving Advice

CLAIRE ROBSON

We've tried to steer away from giving advice in this book, for a couple of reasons—first, one size does not fit all. The Rainbow Umbrella covers a huge range of people in terms of age, race, ethnicity, location, wealth and class, so what might make sense to a young white lesbian in Vancouver might not make sense to a middle-aged gay man in Idaho, or a young black queer in Copenhagen. Also, as most young people know, "advice" is often offered by those who "know" to those who do not—often the old to the young and the powerful to the less powerful. And it can come with all kinds of baggage and hidden messages, like "We know best" or "Do as you're told."

That said, the authors of this book, both young and old, have survived coming out, homophobia, transphobia, parents and families who were opposed to their life choices, time on the streets, in the closet, being fiercely queer and/or pretending to be straight. We think we've learned a thing or two, and we wanted to pass along some tips and tricks for living queer. We know that you'll ignore them if they don't sound right.

We begin this section with two pieces which take a proactive approach to life: Farren Gillaspie's up-beat *Start with Smile*, and Stephen Hardy's *Keep Healthy*, which provides a practical approach for maintaining one's wellness as an LGBTQA2S+ person. We follow these pieces with Nancy Strider's *Tips and Tricks for Asexuals (and others travelling alone)*, which homes in on the day-to-day opportunities of moving through the world as a single person. Following this, Anna R. Westhaver's tongue-in-cheek *A Practical Guide to Lesbian Identification* provides a humorous approach to "spotting" lesbians in the 21st century. We conclude with two lists, one from the youth, the other from the elders, filled with nuggets of friendly wisdom.

Start With a Smile

FARREN GILLASPIE

A smile says I am friendly, I might like to know you or at the very least, it says I see you, I acknowledge you.

Know there will always be people with more scruples and people with less scruples. Trust your gut. Older people may have more experiences, but not all of us have learned from them. Your job is to sort the chaff from the grain, keep what serves you, and pass on the rest. Every human being has something to share even if they aren't aware that they do.

Remember, that you are an awesome lens through which older people can be reminded of the possibilities that surround us.

Take caution in never thinking you know it all. You never will because, just when you think you do, you will be humbled by more doors of understanding and awareness opening. Never stop learning.

Harvey Fierstein once reminded older men who would prey on much younger men to remind themselves that each of these boys is somebody's child. I would add that we are all somebody's child. We all hurt, we all feel, and I believe we all want to be valued. There is a lovely First Nations saying, "If you want corn, plant corn." In other words, give what you want. If you want respect and understanding, offer respect and understanding.

Keep Healthy

STEPHEN HARDY

Keeping healthy is the basis for having a rich and rewarding life, and for having fun too.

Most large urban areas with a large queer community have agencies that will help you maintain your physical, sexual, social, and mental health. It's a good idea to get to know the people at these agencies and to connect with some of their ongoing programs. It's pretty easy to find these. You can start by looking in the phone book, which usually has a section called Government Agencies or Health Agencies, often in the white pages. The Web is a good source too—just use the words "health agencies" to get to your local providers, then narrow your search to find what you're looking for (use key words like "queer," "AIDS," "youth," and "support").

GET TESTED

Whether you're male, female, straight, queer, trans, young or old, you need to get tested for diseases like syphilis, HIV, and others, and for other illnesses like diabetes and cancer. If you're highly sexually active, you should probably get tested every three months. All test results are kept confidential if you say so.

HIV is still a danger, for men with multiple male partners and for lesbians with multiple female partners (some of whom may have had sex with men, even if they don't say so). If you think you might be at risk (say the condom broke, or you find out a lover may have been exposed), you can go (within 72 hours) to your local gay health clinic and request postexposure prophylaxis (PEP). You take PEP for a month and it eliminates the HIV virus from your body, in most cases. If you have a lot of unprotected sex, or sex with multiple partners, or if you are a sex trade worker, you might also find out about pre-exposure prophylaxis (PrEP). PrEP is a pill you take regularly, and it stops you from getting infected with HIV. But, you have to take it every day. And you have to be negative for HIV before you start it. And finally, if you have been diagnosed with HIV, then you need to be under the care of a doctor or queer-friendly health clinic, and take your medicines regularly, to keep the virus suppressed so you won't get sick.

Just because lesbians/gay men don't have sex with men/women doesn't mean that they're not at risk for illnesses that affect everyone—gay or straight. We all need to get routine tests recommended for our genders, like pap smears, prostate exams, and mammograms. Trans people need such tests as much as anyone else—something that caregivers may not always understand. It seems a no-brainer, but not everyone gets it that someone who identifies as and looks male still needs regular pap smears. You may have to be your own advocate, or go with a friend or mentor.

LOOK AFTER YOUR SOCIAL AND EMOTIONAL HEALTH

In many parts of the Western world, there are social groups for maintaining your mental, physical, and social health. If you're lucky, a town or city may have an LGBTQA2S+ organization (Vancouver's is called QMUNITY), a local school might have a Gay-Straight Alliance, and a college or university will also have LGBTQA2S+ groups. These are great places to start looking for friends and activities you can share with others. These range from Fruit Camps, Same-Sex Dancing, Book Clubs, Gay Sports Clubs, Yoga for HIM, writing groups, or just good old social get-togethers. You can find good information at some places on the street too, like queer/women's/alternative bookstores, restaurants, and cafes. Check out their bulletin boards and posters. It's important to be a little bit persistent. The first event you go to might not be dazzling, and you might not even like the people who are there, but hang in for a while—the point is to start somewhere and find information. If you're patient, you'll eventually find people with similar interests.

Websites and apps like Meetup, TG Personals, Gaydar, Gay.com, Silver Daddies, Squirt, and Grindr are the places to hang out to find hook-up partners or maybe just social friends. Apps like Grinder have an added feature of geo-location, so you can focus only on people that are close by, maybe even in the same bar! Check them out! Lesbian Connection is an amazing site—available in online and print versions. It has contact information for lesbians all over the world.

A word of caution here to younger readers particularly (though several of the older authors have also experienced scams and worse)—not everyone is well intentioned. Always meet new people in a safe public location. Maybe take a friend along, always have your cell handy, let someone know where you're going, and arrange a phone call so they can check you're okay.

Explore what's available in your community. It'll be an adventure with lots of positive experiences!

COUNSELLING

You can get free and confidential counselling in most local settings. Again, use the Internet or the phone directory. If all else fails, most places have a suicide hot line and even if you're not suicidal, they have all the local services at their fingertips. No one needs to know that you called.

For both old and young people, isolation and depression can be really hard to combat. For queer people, additional challenges such as rejection, low self-esteem, and difficulties finding friends and allies can make us feel like no one will ever understand. But help is there. You can reach out.

QUEER TRAVEL

Queer people love travelling! The adventure of a new city, a new gay community! If you are visiting another large urban centre, there will almost certainly be lots of information online about gay centres, organizations, websites, and apps. There are queer bed and breakfasts (purpleroofs.com is a worldwide resource), queer cruises (like Olivia) and even queer enclaves (like Provincetown in Massachusetts), queer festivals (like the Queer Film Festival in Vancouver). If you define as a lesbian, Lesbian Connection has a number of these listings in every edition.

Tips and Tricks for Asexuals (and Others Travelling Alone)

NANCY STRIDER

Being asexual means embracing and utilizing the state of being alone without falling into the trap of isolation. Asexuality is about an absence of sexual desire, but this does not necessarily mean that every asexual person has a preference for solitude. Those of us who are comfortable in our skin know many ways to enjoy being with other people beyond a sexual relationship. But by definition, a single lifestyle without a sexual partner means that there is no other half of a couple close at hand to share activities. It helps to have strategies that keep you out there, and that often means going out of the door by yourself.

FIND YOUR TRIBE WITH GROUP ACTIVITIES

Queer wisdom is that we need to look for our queer tribe. That is true for asexuals as well. That said, it also helps to widen the scope of "tribe" beyond sexual preference, and invest time with groups of like-minded people with common interests, doing things such as meditation, sport, social justice activism (or even bird watching). People often come solo to these activities, even if they have a sexual partner.

GO ANYWAY: MAKE YOUR OWN ADVENTURE

Using the framework of a project, such as an educational experience or conference, can give you a base from which to explore a new setting. Youth hostels are designed for solo travellers of any age and often have reasonably priced single rooms, dorms, common rooms, and cooking facilities. Most importantly, they are places where you can strike up conversations with strangers without it being misinterpreted as a sexual advance. The management of many hostels often provides bulletin boards and creates opportunities for outings that support the formation of ad-hoc groups of people that can see the sights or go to the pub together.

Solo travellers who do not have to negotiate a plan with a companion often have more freedom to take a whimsical approach to tourism called "Experimental Travel," which utilizes serendipity, humour, and structuring your plans using games. Another method of mixing it up is an online global game called "Geocaching." Players around the world are hiding small caches, posting clues, and GPS coordinates, seeking caches hidden by others, and reporting their finds.

When you are alone, it helps to have strategies to share the intense experiences—both the highs and the lows—and to have creative approaches for preventing the "medium" time from producing feelings of boredom and isolation. An upside of travelling solo is more control about plans. Also, solo travellers are much more likely to meet the locals and other folk from different cultures. Indeed, some people choose to leave partners at home, to decrease the temptation to focus on a comfortable companion rather than leave their comfort zone.

A Practical Guide to Lesbian Identification in the 21st Century

ANNA R. WESTHAVER

These days, with such trends as shorthaired soccer moms and flannel-clad hipsters, the line between queer women and our heterosexual counterparts has become increasingly blurred. Although this is indicative of a perhaps more accepting community, it only creates a great deal of confusion and heartbreak for the modern lesbian who, in courting these pseudoqueers, is met with sneers and repulsion. Where plaid used to stand as a proud flag of our fine people, it is now an integral part of the "edgy" straight girl's wardrobe. Where referring to another woman as your "girlfriend" used to mean that the woman you are in love with, it is now a colloquial term for friend (and the bane of the author's existence). Today I will attempt to give you a practical guide to the identification of modern lesbians in this strange and confusing century.

(i) Grooming
- If she has coloured hair and/or piercings (especially if it is a piercing of the septum) she is probably queer.
- All queer women have short hair. This was an integral part of the initiation ceremony employed by modern lesbian covens when freeing a new recruit from her heterosexual past. Sadly this has been appropriated by the modern female heterosexual; see the following point.
- Avoid all those with "soccer mom" hairstyles (asymmetrical with blonde highlights, you know the kind) this is a common decoy employed by the heterosexual woman to confuse and distract the general public.

- Tattoos are always a promising hint as to the queerness of your potential lesbian. This is especially true if aforementioned tattoo is queer-related in any way. Protip for my baby-dyke readers: get the name of your favourite character from *The L Word* tattooed somewhere on your body, this will make the identification and dating process (the latter of the two is inevitable once one lesbian has identified another as is dictated by the International Lesbian Law 80.08) much easier.

(ii) Manner
- Pay attention to how the potential lesbian walks. Does she do so in a way that is akin to the stroll of a lumberjack? Or does she sway her hips as she walks? Does she walk in steel-toed boots or in designer heels? If the former of both options is true she is most certainly queer. If the latter option in both cases is true, she is straight as lesbians do not wear high heels due to their incompatibility with carpentry and hiking, the two mandatory activities that each lesbian must take part in.
- If, when walking to your potential lesbian, you notice that in her eyes there lies the fiery glow of predatory lust that is characteristic of every lesbian, she is queer.
- Listen to her voice. Is it husky or cheerful? Does she smirk while she talks, or does she upturn her sentences at the end as if questioning her every statement? If the former of both statements is true, she is queer.

(iii) Conversation Content
- Now that you have begun speaking to your potential lesbian, carefully analyse each statement that she makes for possible notes of gayness.
- If the following things are mentioned throughout the course of your conversation, she is probably gay:
    - Tegan and Sara
    - The L Word
    - Feminism
    - Body Hair (as dictated by International Lesbian Law 204.57, every lesbian must refrain from shaving her body hair)
- If the following things are mentioned throughout the course of your conversation, you must flee mid-conversation (she is straight):
    - Strawberry Daiquiris
    - Eat, Pray, Love
    - Her BOYFRIEND (run screaming)
    - Pink Uggs (in favour of)

CONCLUSION

These are trying times for lesbians. After reading this expert guide, hopefully you will come away with the skills needed in order to successfully distinguish the real lesbian from those vicious heterosexual impostors. Thank you for taking time to read this guide.

Queer 101

What Everyone Needs to Know, From the Youth

- Queer people don't just have queer problems.
- Many queers experiment with the opposite sex, that doesn't mean they're straight. Many queers are told "They can't possible know they're gay. How can they know they don't like something if they don't try it." Some queers start to believe this and try experimenting with people of the opposite sex.
- Not just queer people can get HIV and AIDS.
- Just because someone is queer doesn't mean they are promiscuous.
- Butch women are more of a target of "corrective rape" than other lesbians.
- There are so many identities that it is almost impossible to know about all of them. Just have an open mind when someone tells you about the pronouns they prefer—"they, them, their"—use them out of respect, just as you want people to use the pronouns you prefer.
- Don't scream or point it out when someone walks into the washroom, and you don't think they identify with the sign outside the door. Relax! It's a toilet. It makes the object of the pointing feel awkward and unsafe. Often times they are already using the washroom they feel most safe in.
- Tell straight people that there isn't a "straight pride" because you didn't have to fight for your rights.
- If someone is gay, and you are the opposite sex, no matter how hard you try, if they aren't interested nothing is going to happen. There is no such thing as "converting" someone's sexuality.

- Not everyone is comfortable talking about their sexuality or gender—for many reasons, from the setting to just not wanting to talk to you.
- Queer isn't a sickness. Some queer people have a mental illness because of past abuse, accidents or they just happen to be born with it. Being queer doesn't lead to a mental illness.
- There is still abuse in same-sex relationships.
- You don't need to know what is in someone's pants unless you are planning to have sex with them.

Queer 101

What Everyone Needs to Know, From the Elders

- If someone asks you, "Are you a lesbian, gay, queer, bi, trans?" and you don't want to come out to them, reply by saying "Why do you ask?" Listen to their answer, whatever it is, pause and then say, "How interesting." Then walk away, change the subject, or say nothing more.
- When you feel like it, look people straight in the eyes and say "Yes, and I'm proud of it."
- Speak out when someone is discriminated against, when hateful words are said about someone in reference to their identity. This helps make you proud of being queer.
- Send announcements out to friends about queer events.
- Dress as you want. Forget about age. Flaunt what you've got.
- Make friends, not just lovers. You'll need friends and may keep them longer.
- If you are naturally queer, you don't have to become queer by looking or acting like others. To be yourself can be scary and challenging, but nothing is more attractive than authenticity. Keep it real.
- When someone breaks your heart, just accept that you will feel devastated. Take care of yourself, pull your friends around, grieve, and move forward.
  - Don't decide this pain will go away if you try being heterosexual. (Straight people don't "go queer" to solve their heartbreak!)
  - Don't try to turn all your mutual friends against this person you so recently loved. You may lose both your love and your friends this way.

- o Don't go ballistic and become violent, criminal, or self-abusive. You will heal and love again.
- Pursue what you love with abandon. The love of your life will be pursuing one of those things too.
- If you expect to meet "the one" at drinking and drugging events they will likely be someone with a drinking/drugging problem. Is that really what you are looking for?
- Above all else, remember that though homophobia and transphobia can make our lives difficult and even dangerous, we have much to celebrate about our bold queer identities and selves. We've survived and more than survived. In fact, we've changed the world for everyone. Though queer folk can feel isolated at times, there's a huge community of us out here, having fun, learning about our long history, making art, and supporting each other when it's needed.
- I am gay and old, not dead or confused.
- Just because I am nice to you or smile at you doesn't mean I want you.
- If you are nice to me, don't assume I will hit on you.
- Respect given is respect received.
- I will try not to assume you are gay just because you are well groomed and accessorized.
- My sexuality is not my total definition.
- I am gay and old, not desperate.
- Age difference is not necessarily a block to a good sexual relationship.
- Hook-up websites are not the only way to meet new people.
- Old(er) lesbians/dykes want to hold onto their identity; they fought hard for the word "lesbian" in a time when gay was all about men. Allow that without question.
- Older lesbians and gays may, or may not, use the word queer, or LGBTQA-2S+Q, depending on their comfort level, or awareness of issues. Is that ok with you?
- Asking and answering questions is a means of educating about queer issues. Are you ok about talking about your gender, orientation?
- Don't assume that just because someone tells you they are transsexual that you have the right to ask them if they have had surgery. Everyone's medical history is private.

Final Thoughts

There can be no easy conclusion to this book, just as there can be no lockstep guide to queer life, no single definition that will contain the unruly and creative performances of LGBTQA2S+ people, and no end to our queer inventions.

We have shared information, history, and analysis. We have also offered you stories, graphics, and poetry that have complicated this more "rational" or "left brained" work, because we know that human life can't be fully captured by reason. You will most certainly have drawn your own conclusions as you have responded to our words in ways we can only imagine, taking away all kinds of different messages and interpretations. Our best hope for this book is that it may help you to start conversations with your partners, family, friends, and others—even if it's someone you just met at the bus stop. Conversations like these ripple through our culture, and we think that they are an effective way to create social change. Social media networking is a wonderful thing, but face-to-face encounters are still a great method of influencing people's hearts and minds. For many straight people, actually getting to know someone queer is key to their tolerance, acceptance, and eventual celebration of life choices they may initially have not understood.

Sigmund Freud once said that all people were "polymorphous perverse," and we would agree, but we'd add that queer people are particularly good at perversity and kicking over the traces. Perhaps the greatest contribution that LGBTQA2S+ people have made to contemporary culture is our resistance to rigid and unexamined norms and rules—around gender, dress, behaviour, appearance, and what might be considered "acceptable." As old and older people, we don't have time to waste, and as young people, we are looking at the vast expanse of the lives that lie ahead of us. This sharply focused relationship with time makes us agree on one thing—life is just too short (and at the same time too long) to waste even a second of it in being straight and narrow.

As queer folk, we are used to living outside certain social norms and thus more able than many to see them for what they are—just cultural conventions, and not maxims written in stone. Rather than slavishly conforming to social structures just because they're there, we insist on our right to examine them critically and to ask if they support the values we believe in—equality of access and opportunity to what the world has to offer, freedom of person and speech, love, tolerance, and respect for everyone, regardless of race, ethnicity, religion, ability, class, sexuality, or gender. These things we *are* passionate about, and we believe that they are inalienable.

We want to end by adding a word or two about the notion that our culture is, or should, be becoming "post gay." What people generally mean when they use this term is that it's time for all of us marginalized people (women, queers, blacks, Jews, Muslims) to let go of the labels and "just be human beings," since we've all achieved equal rights, so sexual, gender identity, and all the other identities just mentioned are not an issue any more. Some people also point out that the labels can serve to define us too rigidly, and it's more natural just to be whoever we feel like being at any given point—maybe bisexual one day and gay the next. There's some merit in these arguments for sure. Many of the elder authors value the more fluid and complicated identifications of some of the youth. But the reverse is true, as many of the youth respect and honour the historic struggles of queer elders and feel grateful that we planted our rainbow flags in contexts where it was illegal or unsafe or uncomfortable to do so. And all authors agree that these identity flags are still a necessary way to stake claims to equal justice.

There are definitely increased signs of popular acceptance of LGBTQA2S+ individuals. In Western culture, we see more images of ourselves in the popular media, more politicians and celebrities are out, and there is greater general acceptance of our life choices. As queer enclaves (like Provincetown in the United States, or Vancouver's West End) become more gentrified and diverse, more inclusive policies and laws are enacted, and same-sex marriage is legalized in many countries, there's an underlying suggestion that we are making a fuss about a battle that has already been fought and won.

Our first response is to say that we can give up the struggle for LGBTQA2S+ rights when they have been won across the world and for everyone. This is clearly not the case, as trans people are oppressed, killed, and mistreated in all countries across the globe, and queers of all descriptions face death and imprisonment in many countries. Even in "liberal" countries, hate speech and stigmatization is still all too common. Most high school students will tell you how often casual slurs and slights occur, unchecked, and on a daily basis. No one just gave queers the rights we now have; they were fought for, often bitterly, and as the political climate in the United States at the time of writing is heated up by populist, anti-immigrant, misogynist, and homophobic discourses, we are all too well aware that we need to stay vigilant. We simply cannot assume that everything is and will always be okay.

Our second response is to say that it is not just acceptance and tolerance that we are looking for, but *celebration* of our differences. The authors of this book don't want to be "just like everyone else." Some in the LGBTQA2S+ community do prefer to fit in with the mainstream, and we respect that choice as we respect all individual choices. At the same time, we believe that it will always be important for queer folk to be visible, outspoken, and countercultural. It matters to the younger queers next-to-be-born because they need to see themselves represented and to know that they are not the only ones. It also matters to the rest of the world, queer and straight, as we push and explore the boundaries of gender, sexuality, and relationship. We believe that our queer inventions, in language and community, in activism and thought, in art and science, have been an essential part of human progress, and that they will continue to be so. We don't just want the world to "accept" us, but to embrace the diversity we offer, in the understanding that it is, and has always been, essential to human evolution.

Though the word "queer" is our umbrella, it shelters all colours of the rainbow, and they are all beautiful. We hope that our stories, poetry, and images have helped you see that rainbow shine and rediscover your place there.

About the Authors

Editors' note: These bios reflect the authors' ages at the time of publication and do not necessarily reflect when they wrote the work included in this anthology.

Marsha Ablowitz is a 72-year-old "nice Jewish lesbian." Her story *Max Dexall* tells about her uncle's colourful lifestyle. *Jean* tells a tragic story from her 40-year social work career. *All the Women* is from her naive idealistic days in the 1960s.

Kelsey Blair, 32, is a PhD student, an applied theatre artist, and the author of three novels. She was the co-lead artist for Quirk-e for five years, and she has worked on several community-based intergenerational projects.

Gwyneth Bowen, 67, has lived straight and lesbian lives and worked at her passion, counselling women who have survived trauma. She met her partner Val in Quirk-e. She has two daughters (one with a wife) and two granddaughters. She sings, is a show-off in male or female drag, and loves to babysit.

Reba Broadhurst is 20, an activist because she believes that the world could be a better place with more acceptance. She likes to push people to think outside of the box. She is a member/peer leader of Youth for A Change and an ally.

Jasmine Broeder is a spoken word poet with a wild imagination for short stories and various other creativities. She is 18 but has been writing since her young years. She plans on going into the policing field and has spent many years of her life being a youth advocate for the LGBTQA2S+ community.

ABOUT THE AUTHORS

Skylar Cogswell-Shears is 17, a transman and an activist because he wants to make a difference even if it's the smallest things like having a safe place for LGBTQA2S+ youth or doing an art bomb and having many people admire it. He likes doing art and to write because when writing he can say things he's too scared to say out loud. He believes that people hear him better through writing than by spoken words.

Cyndia Cole is 66. She moved from the United States to Vancouver in 1970 and came out as a lesbian at 26 in 1976. She worked with others to found/develop Women's Studies at Simon Fraser University, Vancouver East Housing Co-op, Humanistic Home Support, and SGI Vancouver Buddhist Pride Group. She loves Spud Palace, the big purple home she shares with her queer family. She treasures all her relations.

Bridget Coll, born in Ireland, was a wonderful caring, loving partner, sister, and gramma. True to her Irish heritage, she was a great storyteller. She was an out proud lesbian including the years she lived in residential care. She died peacefully at 82, having lived for several years with dementia.

Caroline Doerksen, 21, is a queer femme, feminist, and LGBTQA+ activist. She is a gender, sexuality, and women's studies major and labour studies minor at Simon Fraser University. She has been a member of Youth for A Change since 2013. She is the 2015 recipient of Vancouver Pride's Youth Pride Legacy Award.

Candy Fine is a two-spirited preop transgender woman and a founding member of Youth for A Change. Candy loves to draw and do drag performances. Candy is a title-winning drag queen with the Empire of the Peace Arch Monarchist Association, a member of the international Imperial Court System.

Judy Fletcher is 71. Her mother often described her ersatz curly headed youngest as "a queer duck." Judy was not offended because she knew that she was different. Rural Ontario didn't provide any gay, lesbian, or trans role models either on television or out in the community. Judy grew into the "queer" label but didn't understand why she was a duck. She doesn't even like the water.

Shawnee Gaffney, now 22, is a former street youth and a former youth in care who used to sneak out to a queer youth group where they found a passion being involved with advocacy. Having known firsthand the flaws in the system, they are now well on their way in the Youth Justice diploma program to work with other youth that are facing similar issues.

Farren Gillaspie is 65 and lives in Vancouver with his partner of 15 years. He came from very humble beginnings on an Ontario farm and escaped when he was 17. His stories reflect his queer journey, from youthful awakening through family tragedy and celebration.

ABOUT THE AUTHORS

Stephen Hardy is Métis, one of the three aboriginal groups recognized in Canada's Constitution. His great grandfather fought with Louis Riel during the 1885 Northwest Resistance and signed Riel's Declaration of War against the Government of Canada. Stephen worked as a professor of engineering science at Simon Fraser University and is now retired.

Pat Hogan, 77, loves being an activist and an organizer in the LGBTQA2S+ community and has been so since the mid-1970s. She supports the plethora of identifying words used in the queer community while proudly holding on to her lesbian roots. Dance, travel, family, and friends enrich her life.

Greta Hurst is 80. *Love in Montreal* tells the story of her first relationship with a woman—people's reactions were frightening. *The Cost of Coming Out* describes the trauma of leaving her husband and children. Now she has a 20-year plan to do everything that interests her, whether she's successful or not. A lot of life happened in between.

Val Innes, at 70, is recently retired from university teaching with more time to spend travelling, painting, and writing. She's a feminist who has worked at making the world a better, more equal place, both personally and professionally, teaching, volunteering, and protesting to help bring about positive change.

Jake Marchbank joined YfAC when he was 13; he's now 16. Jake is active on many issues, during elections and on youth mental health. He kinda does his masculinity a bit differently from the "norm" and is very proud of his beautiful long hair, which makes one of his Mums very jealous.

Jen Marchbank, 52, is cofounder and cofacilitator of Youth for A Change (with her wife Sylvia Traphan) and a professor in the Department of Gender, Sexuality, and Women's Studies at Simon Fraser University. She is also an LGBTQ2SA+ activist and seeks for her work to create positive social change.

Chris Morrissey is a 74-year-old White lesbian. Her partner of 40 years, Bridget, died after living with dementia for several years. Together, they worked with others to change Canada's immigration legislation to recognize same-sex relationships as family. Their family expanded when they were adopted as grammas, a role they loved.

Bill Morrow is an 84-year-old gay male who came out of the closet at the age of 54 when he moved from a fundamentalist area in the Fraser Valley to Vancouver. He could have been fired from his jobs for being gay. Because he was a nurse and worked in home care, he was able to care for people with AIDS without fear. He has been able to join in gay activities through Quirk-e, QMUNITY, and the SGI Buddhist Pride Group.

Shilpa Narayan is a 20-year-old gender, sexuality, and women's studies and psychology student at Simon Fraser University. She has been a member of Youth for A Change for two years and is a provincial advocate for mental health wellness. As a queer youth and person of colour, it has been an honour for her to be in this book. Activism changes lives.

Syd Oremek is a 21-year-old queer and homeless activist. Houseless for six years now, Syd travels and writes about these experiences through song lyrics and short stories.

Robin Rennie died at the age of 70 on January 4, 2015, from Alzheimer's disease. As a high school counsellor, she took huge risks to help girls who came out to her. Family Services hired her in 1978, and she began some of the first counselling and groups for gays and lesbians. She and her partner Christine founded Dragonstone Counselling.

Gayle Roberts is a 76-year-old retired high school teacher who transitioned from male to female on the job 20 years ago. Since her transition, Gayle has actively supported transitioning children, adolescents, and adults. She is a coauthor of the guidebook *Supporting Transgender and Transsexual Students in K–12 Schools*.

Claire Robson, 67, is cofacilitator of the queer imaging and riting kollective for elders (Quirk-e) and adjunct faculty at Simon Fraser University, specializing in arts-engaged community practices. Her most recent book, *Writing for Change*, shows how collective memoir writing can effect social change.

Aleisha Ross is 24 and has volunteered with Youth for A Change for over two years. She holds a masters degree in gender, sexuality, and women's studies. She is a youth worker and operates her own sexual health education service that provides inclusive, affirming sexuality information for all.

Paddy St Loe, who died at 75 in 2014, was a consummate storyteller with a real comic flair, a writer, traveller, mother, and friend who loved to make people laugh. Born in England, Paddy moved to Canada as an adult, becoming a Human Rights Commission worker, a feminist and activist working for women's rights and then, later on, a lesbian. She was well loved and lived a full life.

The safety and encouragement of Quirk-e supports **Nancy Strider's** articulation, at age 65, of an emerging asexual identity. For eight years, the group has provided a home for her creative work. After initially connecting as host artist for digital imaging, she committed to membership, gaining skills in writing and performing.

Paula Stromberg, 66, collaborates with activists to communicate efforts to address women's empowerment and human rights issues, including same-sex marriage. Exploring queer difference can challenge core structures in society including gender oppressions, international conversation about economic systems, and our approach to the ruling class of elites—ideas that could energize the next wave of queer activism.

Harris Taylor is a 57-year-old writer and documentary filmmaker who has contributed programming to Vision TV, CBC, and Northern Native Broadcasting, Yukon. Where mainstream media has often failed issues of social justice, Quirk-e has allowed Harris to tell stories that triumph over homophobia.

TJ is a 21-year-old trans man, part of Youth for A Change for three years. He's into videogames, comic books, movies, music, reading, artsy stuff, anything outdoors, and anything and everything nerdy. TJ is always down for a good pun; the more terrible it is, the better.

Seventy-six-year-old **Christine Waymark** met Robin Rennie when she was 40 and took her into her home when Robin left her own relationship. Robin never left. When the United Church tried to drop Christine as a candidate for ministry, she took on the challenge and was one of 12 authors of a report demanding ordination for gays and lesbians, losing her job in the process. She and Robin founded Dragonstone Counselling, an openly queer centre.

Anna Westhaver is a young, queer poet/activist from Vancouver BC. She has been involved in LGBTQA2S+ activism for nearly five years and has been directly involved in creative action initiatives (art-ivism). She is currently extending her scope of activism to issues of food security and urban agriculture.

Ellen Woodsworth is an international urban consultant on intersectional planning and was the first out lesbian city councillor in Canada. Chairperson of Women Transforming Cities (who partnered in authoring the *Advancing Equity and Inclusion Guide for Municipalities*), she hosted a queer consultation that created the Queer Declaration calling for inclusion in the New Urban Agenda of UN Habitat 3.

Recommended Reading

GENERAL

Bechdel, A. (2008). *The essential Dykes to Watch Out For.* New York: Houghton Mifflin Harcourt.
Blege, K. (2011). *Queer: The ultimate LGBT guide for teens.* San Francisco, CA: Zest Books.
Boylan, J. F. ((2008). *I'm looking through you.* New York, NY: Broadway Books.
Clinton, K. (2005) *What the L?* New York, NY: Carroll & Graf.
Coyote, I. (2016). *Tomboy survival guide.* Vancouver, Canada: Arsenal Pulp Press.
Garden, N. (1982) *Annie on my mind.* New York, NY: Farrar Straus Giroux.
Hugel, K. (2011). *GLBTQ: The survival guide for gay, lesbian, bisexual, transgender, and questioning teens* (2nd ed.). Minneapolis, MN: Free Spirit Publishing.
Lynch, L. (1986) *Home in your hand.* United States: Naiad Press.
Planned Parenthood of Toronto. (2005). *Hear me out: True stories of teens educating and confronting homophobia.* Toronto, Canada: Second Story Press.
Pohlen, J. (2015). *Gay and lesbian history for kids: The century-long struggle for LGBT rights, with 21 activities.* Chicago, IL: Chicago Review Press.
Quirk-e. (2014). *The bridge generation: A queer elders' chronicle from no rights to civil rights.* Vancouver, Canada: Simon Fraser University.
Singer, B. L. (Ed.). (1994). *Growing up gay/Growing up lesbian: A literary anthology.* New York, NY: The New Press.
Savage, D. (2011). *It gets better: Coming out, overcoming bullying, and creating a life worth living.* New York, NY: Dutton.
Thompson, M. (1995). *Gay soul.* San Francisco, CA: Harper Collins.
Woodrow, T. (Ed.). (1989). *Lesbian bedtime stories.* Willits, CA: Tough Dove Books.

REPRESENTATION IN GAMING AND TECH

Coming Out Simulator https://ncase.itch.io/coming-out-simulator-2014
Dys4ia—transgender experience http://www.newgrounds.com/portal/view/591565
Gone Home—a murder mystery game with a wide variety of characters, not just LGBTQ http://www.metacritic.com/game/playstation-4/gone-home-console-edition
The Last of Us Left Behind http://ca.ign.com/games/the-last-of-us-left-behind/ps3-20008511

TWO-SPIRIT

Gilley, B. (2006). *Becoming Two-Spirit: Gay identity and social acceptance in Indian country*. Lincoln: University of Nebraska Press.

Williams, W. (1992). *The spirit and the flesh: Sexual diversity in American Indian culture*. Boston, MA: Beacon Press. Retrieved from http://www.beacon.org/The-Spirit-and-The-Flesh-Revised-P350.aspx

ASEXUAL

Carnes, P., & Moriarty, J. M. (1997). *Sexual anorexia: Overcoming sexual self-hatred*. Minnesota: Hazeldon Press.

TRANS

Print Resources

Bornstein, K., & Bergman, B. (2010). *Gender outlaws: The next generation*. Berkeley, CA: Seal Press.

Brill, S., & Pepper, R. (2008). *The transgender child: A handbook for families and professionals*. San Francisco, CA: Cleiss Press.

Central Toronto Youth Services. (2008). *Families in transition: A resource guide for parents of trans youth*. Retrieved from http://www.ctys.org/wp-content/uploads/2013/06/familiesintransition.pdf

Ehrensaft, D. (2011). *Gender born, gender made: Raising healthy gender-nonconforming children*. New York, NY: The Experiment.

Griffin, P., & Carroll, H. (2010). *On the team: Equal opportunity for transgender student athletes*. San Francisco, CA: National Center for Lesbian Rights. Retrieved from http://www.nclrights.org/wp-content/uploads/2013/07/TransgenderStudentAthleteReport.pdf

Kirkey, S. (2016, November 17). "I feel like a boy, Mom": Doctors seeing an increase in preschoolers convinced they are in the wrong body. *National Post*. Retrieved from http://news.nationalpost.com/health/1117-transgender

Parents and Friends of Lesbians and Gays (PFLAG). (2009). *Our trans children: A publication of the PFLAG Transgender Network* (6th ed.). Retrieved from http://www.transfaithonline.org/fileadmin/TFteaching/PFLAG_Our_Trans_Children_V_6_Web.pdf

Pride Education Network. 2011. *The gender spectrum: What educators need to know.* Vancouver, Canada: Author. Retrieved from www.pridenet.ca

Russo, F. (2016, January/February). Transgender kids. *Scientific American Mind*, pp. 26–35.

Simon Fraser University Gerontology Research Centre. (2016). *Elder abuse in the LGBT Community.* Retrieved from www.sfu.ca/lgbteol/lgbt-elder-abuse-2.html

Transgender Archives, University of Victoria. (n.d.). http://transgenderarchives.uvic.ca/

Wells, K., Roberts, G., & Allan, C. (2012). *Supporting transgender and transsexual students in K-12 schools: A guide for educators.* Ottawa, Canada: Canadian Teachers' Federation. Retrieved from http://www.ismss.ualberta.ca/sites/www.ismss.ualberta.ca/files/Supporting_(Wells, Allan, Roberts, 2012).pdf

World Professional Association for Transgender Health (WPATH). (2011). *Standards of care for the health of transsexual, transgender, and gender-nonconforming people, Version 7.* Retrieved from http://www.wpath.org/site_page.cfm?pk_association_webpage_menu=1351&pk_association_webpage=3926

Video Resources

de Guerre, Marc. (2015). *Transforming Gender.* https://vimeo.com/124200023

From This Day Forward https://www.youtube.com/watch?v=gl7721H84wI

"Growing Up Trans." (2015, June 30). *Frontline.* http://www.pbs.org/wgbh/pages/frontline/growing-up-trans/

Human Rights Campaign. *Debunking the myths: Transgender health and well-being.* http://www.hrc.org/resources/entry/debunking-the-myths-transgender-health-and-well-being

Laverne Cox Presents: "The T Word" https://www.youtube.com/watch?v=mDy0DhfuxfI

The Transgender Project. (2015). http://www.thetransgenderproject.com/

Walk With Me https://www.youtube.com/watch?v=qtwBgm8HEpM

Index

abortion, 55
activism. *See* antidiscrimination laws; feminism; LEGIT; Quirk-e; refugees; same-sex benefits; same-sex unions; Stonewall protests; UN Habitat 3; Youth for A Change
adoption, 90, 92, 209
African Americans, 44
allies, 10,–11, 13, *160*, 180, 159–83
    queer, 162, 164–65, 177–79
    teachers, 161–62, 180–81
    See also queer-positive spaces, impact of
androgyny, 102
antidiscrimination laws, 41, 43–45, 135–39, 153, 158, 162
    Canadian Charter of Rights and Freedoms, 43, 136
asexual people, 10, 12, 18, 35–37, 67, 73–76, 235–36
assisted living. *See* care homes

BC Council to Reduce Elder Abuse, 3
benefits, same-sex, 43–44, 136, 138, 209
bereavement, 91, 131, 216–18
bicurious, definition of, 18
Bill C-16, 44, 138

biological arguments about gender and sexuality. *See* medicalization
birth certificates, 137
bisexuality, 12, 18, 27, 30–31, 99, 138, 188
bullying, 13, 66, 161, 180–81
butch and femme, 56, 183, 240

Call & Response project, 3
Canadian Charter of Rights and Freedoms, 43, 136
Canadian Criminal Code, 43–44, 138
Canadian Human Rights Act, 44, 136
care homes, 146, 215. *See also* dementia
Catholic Church, 32, 61, 190–191
children, 46–47, 55, 57, 115–18, 171–72, 223–24. *See also* family; youth
cisgender, 12, 14
class, 33, 53, 65, 210, 229
closet, definition of, 12
coming out, 26, 45, 52, 55, 58, 98, 99–101, 162, 180, 196
    choosing not to come out, 89, 127–29, 242
    definition of, 12
    responses to, 56–57, 99, 112, 135
Commercial Drive, Vancouver, 21, 28, 71

conversion therapy, 43, 189–191
criminalization of same-sex sexual activity, 41–43, 50, 66, *134*, 138–39, 158, 189
    death penalty, 41, 162
    See also police
cross-dresser, 12, 99
Cvetkovich, Ann, 16

decriminalization of homosexuality, 43, 138, 188
dementia, 91, 119–21, 216
demisexual, definition of, 18
depression, 3, 92, 176, 177–79, 180, 234
desire, 35–37, *51*, 54, 168, 199–200, 222
Diagnostic and Statistical Manual of Mental Disorders (DSM) (American Psychiatric Association), 43, 188–89, 191
drag queens, xiii, 43, 46–47, 68, 110, 158
    definition of drag, 12

Egan, Jack, 136
elder abuse, 3–4
elders, xiv, 215, 210, 226, 241–42. *See also* care homes; dementia; intergenerational work
employment, discrimination and, 66, 135–36

family
    chosen, 95–98
    coming out/not coming out to, 127–29, *160*
    queer, 90–91, 122–26, 212
    rejection by, 89, 110, 112, 175–77, 210
    See also children; parenting
feminism, xv, 32, 44–45, 54–55
    and lesbians, 55–58
Freud, Sigmund, 189, 191, 245
FTM/F2M, 12, 26, 201

gay, definition of, 18
gay movement, and lesbian feminists, 56, 58
gay-straight student alliances, 12, 180, 182
gender, definition of, 19, 201
gender and sexual minority. *See* queer
gender dysphoria, 12, 16
gender expression, 12, 19, 202–4
gender identity, 13–15, 172, 243
    in human rights legislation, 43–44, 137–39, 158
gender queer, definition of, 13, 19
gender reassignment surgery (GRS). *See* sex reassignment surgery
gender-variant/gender nonconformity, 13, 171–72, 202–4. *See also* nonbinary; transgender

Haig v. *Canada*, 136
Hall, Radclyffe, 56
hate crimes, 41, 43–44, 139. *See also* language, abusive; violence
health and health care, 146, 211, 232
    mental health, 43, 177–79, 180, 233
    See also elder abuse; HIV/AIDS
heteronormativity, 9, 65, 78, 216–18. *See also* language, abusive
heterosexism, definition of, xv, 13
heterosexual, definition of, 13
HIV/AIDS, 44–45, 112, 117, 130–31, 154–54, 232–33
homelessness, 69–70, 164–65, 213–14
homophobia, xv, 13, 45, 49–52, 67, *134*
homosexual, definition of, 14
hormone blockers. *See* transition
hormones, 146, 201
House of Faith, 164–65
human rights protections. *See* antidiscrimination laws; criminalization of homosexuality; hate crimes

identity, 10, 11–17, 37, 180, 189, 191, 196–97, 242–44. *See also* gender identity
immigration and same-sex relationships, 136–37
    refugees, 138, 147–48, 152–52
income, xv, 45, 65, 136. *See also* class
Indigenous peoples, 44; two-spirit, 10, 16, 19, 220–21
intergenerational work, xiv, 3–4, 209–13, 231
internalized transphobia. *See* transphobia
International Lesbian, Gay, Bisexual, Trans and Intersex Association (ILGA), 41–42
International Tribunal of Crimes Against Women (1976), 55

intersex people, 137, 201; definition of, 14, 18
isolation, 3, 44, 215, 234

Jews, 109–112

Klippert, George, 138

language, 34–35, *34*
    abusive, 7–9, 16–17, *20*, 21–25, 28–29, 49, 71–72, 181
    queer, 10–16, 33
    reclaiming of derogatory terms, 32–33
    See also pronouns
legal rights, protection of. *See* antidiscrimination laws
LEGIT (Lesbian and Gay Immigration Task Force), 137
lesbians, 237–39
    coming out as lesbian, 32
    definition of, 18
    and feminism, 45, 56–57
    parents, 31
    separatism, 32
LeVay, Simon, 190
LGBTI advocacy, countries outlawing, 41
LGBTQ/GLBTQ, definition of, 14

makeup, xiii, 147
marriage
    heterosexual, 144–45
    same-sex, 146, 150–50
masculinity, *228*
medicalization, 50, 66, 81, *186*
    Diagnostic and Statistical Manual of Mental Disorders (DSM), 43, 188–89, 191
mental health. *See under* health and health care
Montreal, 53–54
Morrissey, Chris, 137
MTF or M2F, definition of, 14

natal sex, definition of, 12, 14–15
National Gay Women's Conference (Canada), 57–58
National Organization for Women (United States), 55

Nesbit, Jim, 136
New Westminster, British Columbia, 3
nonbinary, 19, 26

Other Woman (newspaper), 57

pan gender, definition of, 14
pansexual, definition of, 19
parenting, 31, 46–47, 212. *See also* family
passports, gender markers on, 138
police, xv, 44, 50, 143, 178–79
Pride parades, 2, 83, 113, 141, 183–84
pronouns, 10–11, 27, 92–93, 161, 240

queer, 10–11, 14, *20*, 45, 65–86
queer agenda, idea of, 135, 140–41
Queer Declaration. *See* UN Habitat 3
queer movement, xv; history of, 41–45. *See also* antidiscrimination laws; feminism; LEGIT; refugees; same-sex benefits; same-sex unions; Stonewall protests; UN Habitat 3
Queer Imaging & Riting Kollective for Elders (Quirk-e), xvii, xviii, 2–3, 135
queer-positive spaces, impacts of, 67, 83–85, 100–101
questioning, 14, 118, 162, 180. *See also* identity; coming out

racism, experience of, xv, 45, 210
Rainbow Refugee, 149
rape, 55, 240
reclaiming of derogatory terms. *See under* language
refugees, 138, 147–48, 152–52
relationships, 54–55, *64*, 100, *228*. *See also* desire; family
religion, 32, 43, 45, 47–48, 49, 81, 110–111, 142, 173–74, 187–88, 190–191, 209
rights. *See* antidiscrimination laws; feminism; refugees; same-sex benefits; same-sex unions
rural queers, xv, 44, 89, 162

safety, 9, 81, 98, 158, 178, 199, 234
    cities and, 44, 69–70, 156, 162
    families and, 172, 213–14, 221
    safe spaces, 57, 101, 161, 164, 172

schools and, 161–62, 180–82
washrooms and, 78, 240
same-sex benefits. *See* benefits, same-sex
same-sex unions, legal recognition of, 41, 43–44, 89, *134*, 137, 146–147, 150, 181, 209, 244
Sappho, 56
school, 3, 32, 60, 103–5, 161–62, 180–82, 210, 244
    gay-straight student alliances, 13, 180, 182
scoliosexual, definition of, 18
sex, definition of, 19
sex reassignment surgery (SRS), definition of, 14
sexual anorexia, theory of, 35, 37
sexual minority, definition of, 15
sexual orientation, definition of, 15
sexual trauma, 35, 37
social transition. *See* transition
sports, 25, 152
stereotypes
    of elders and youth, 3
    of gender and sexuality, 67, 77, 79–80
Stonewall protests, 43, 46
students, 13, 44, 56, 142, 149, 167, 180–82, 244
substance abuse, youth risks of, xv
suicide, youth risk of, xv, 3, 180, 182
surgery, 13–16, 46, 201, 243
Surrey, British Columbia, 2–3

target sex, definition of, 15
teachers, 161–62, 180–81
tomboys, xiii, 57, 106, 171
tranny/trannie, definition of, 15
transgender/trans-identified/trans/trans*, definition of, 15, 18
trans people, 193–95, 201, 205
    family response to, 92–93
    legal rights of, xv, 43–44, 137–38, 139, 158
    violence toward, 44ie
transboy/transgirl/transman/transwoman, definition of, 16
transition, 15–16
transphobia, 16
transsexual, definition of, 16, 18
transvestite. *See* cross-dresser

trisexual, definition of, 18
Trudeau, Pierre, 43, 138
two-spirit people, 10, 16, 19, 220–21

UN Habitat 3 (United Nations Conference on Housing and Sustainable Urban Development), Queer Declaration to, 156–57
United Church of Canada, 44, 47–48, 144
United Nations Human Rights Council, 41
United Nations High Commissioner for Human Rights, 41–42, 139, 157
United Nations New Urban Agenda, 43, 156–57
Universal Declaration of Human Rights, 138–39

Vancouver, British Columbia, 3, 69–70
verbal abuse, 7, 8–9, 16–17, *20*, 21–25, 28–29, 49, 71–72, 181
violence against LGBTQA2S+ people, 44, 72, 142–43, 158, 181
Vriend, Delwin, 135

Wolfe, Della, 137
women of colour, 33
Women Transforming Cities International Society (WTC), 156
women's movement. *See* feminism
Women's Organization for Equality (Brussels), 54–55
women's rights. *See under* rights
Woodsworth, Ellen, 139, 156–57

youth, 222
    in care, 213–14
    and family rejection, 67
    hearing the stories of, xiv, 219
    perspectives on rights, 146–147
    risk for suicide and substance abuse, xv, 3, 44, 180, 182
    wisdom of, 240
    See also bullying; children; intergenerational work; schools
Youth for A Change, xviii, 2–3, 135

Studies in Criticality

General Editor
Shirley R. Steinberg

Counterpoints publishes the most compelling and imaginative books being written in education today. Grounded on the theoretical advances in criticalism, feminism, and postmodernism in the last two decades of the twentieth century, Counterpoints engages the meaning of these innovations in various forms of educational expression. Committed to the proposition that theoretical literature should be accessible to a variety of audiences, the series insists that its authors avoid esoteric and jargonistic languages that transform educational scholarship into an elite discourse for the initiated. Scholarly work matters only to the degree it affects consciousness and practice at multiple sites. Counterpoints' editorial policy is based on these principles and the ability of scholars to break new ground, to open new conversations, to go where educators have never gone before.

For additional information about this series or for the submission of manuscripts, please contact:

> Shirley R. Steinberg
> c/o Peter Lang Publishing, Inc.
> 29 Broadway, 18th floor
> New York, New York 10006

To order other books in this series, please contact our Customer Service Department:

> (800) 770-LANG (within the U.S.)
> (212) 647-7706 (outside the U.S.)
> (212) 647-7707 FAX

Or browse online by series:
> www.peterlang.com